Power, Profit and Prestige

POWER, PROFIT AND PRESTIGE

A History of American Imperial Expansion

Philip S. Golub

PlutoPress

www.plutobooks.com

First published 2010 by Pluto Press
345 Archway Road, London N6 5AA and
175 Fifth Avenue, New York, NY 10010

www.plutobooks.com

Distributed in the United States of America exclusively by
Palgrave Macmillan, a division of St. Martin's Press LLC,
175 Fifth Avenue, New York, NY 10010

British Library Cataloguing in Publication Data
A catalogue record for this book is available from the British Library

ISBN   978 0 7453 2872 0   Hardback
ISBN   978 0 7453 2871 3   Paperback

Library of Congress Cataloging in Publication Data applied for

This book is printed on paper suitable for recycling and made from fully managed
and sustained forest sources. Logging, pulping and manufacturing processes are
expected to conform to the environmental standards of the country of origin.

10   9   8   7   6   5   4   3   2   1

Designed and produced for Pluto Press by
Chase Publishing Services Ltd, 33 Livonia Road, Sidmouth, EX10 9JB, England
Typeset from disk by Stanford DTP Services, Northampton, England
Printed and bound in the European Union by
CPI Antony Rowe, Chippenham and Eastbourne

To Leon Golub and Nancy Spero

Contents

List of Tables

List of Figures

Acknowledgements

This book, the expression of a lifelong ethical and intellectual concern over the inequities of power, was made possible by the many friends and intellectual companions who were kind enough to support the project from the start. My debts are many and I would like to particularly thank Kees Van der Pijl, Ronen Palan, Jean-Christophe Graz, Jean-Paul Maréchal, Olivier Le Cour Grandmaison, Christopher Newfield and Richard Falk for having in various ways offered their encouragement as well as always useful critical comments. Thanks are also due to Wendy Kristianasen for her friendship and constant support, to Philippe Rekacewicz for his cartographic talents, Danielle Brunon for her generosity and to Thomas Stevens and Claude Albert for their help on the manuscript. The many interviewees who over the years offered me their time, knowledge and insights also deserve thanks. Above all, though it be 'too little payment for so great a debt', my thanks to Noelle Kyriazi Burgi, my life companion and intellectual accomplice, without whom none of this would have been possible.

Abbreviations

ABF	Asian Bond Fund
ABM	Anti-Ballistic Missile Treaty
ACU	Asian Currency Unit
AMF	Asian Monetary Fund
ASEAN	Association of South East Asian Nations
CBRC	China Banking Regulatory Commission
CFR	Council on Foreign Relations
CIA	Central Intelligence Agency
CRS	Congressional Research Service
DESTIN	Development Studies Institute (London School of Economics)
DOD	Department of Defense
DOL	Department of Labor
DPG	Defense Planning Guideline
EROA	Economic Recovery in Occupied Areas
ERP	European Recovery Program
FDI	Foreign Direct Investment
FIRE	Finance, Insurance, Real Estate
FRUS	Foreign Relations of the United States
GCC	Gulf Cooperation Council
HST	Hegemonic Stability Theory
IBSA	India, Brazil and South Africa
ILO	International Labour Organization
IMF	International Monetary Fund
JIC	Joint Intelligence Committee
JPY	Japanese yen
NACLA	North American Congress on Latin America
NATO	North Atlantic Treaty Organisation
NBER	National Bureau of Economic Research
NEC	National Economic Council
NIC	National Intelligence Council
NSA	National Security Archive
NSS	National Security Strategy
OECD	Organisation of Economic Cooperation and Development
OPEC	Organization of the Petroleum Exporting Countries

PNAC	Project for a New American Century
PPP	Purchasing Power Parity
QDR	Quadrennial Defense Review
SIPRI	Stockholm International Peace Research Institute
UN	United Nations
UNASUR	Union of South American Nations
UNCTAD	United Nations Conference on Trade and Development
UNSC	United Nations Security Council
WB	World Bank
WEF	World Economic Forum
WTO	World Trade Organization

1
Introduction

This historical sociological study of American expansionism was begun a few years ago to account for the puzzling monopoly-seeking behaviour of the United States in the early years of the twenty-first century. It was completed in the midst of the breakdown of the US financial system and the most severe global economic crisis since the 1930s. While national and international regulatory authorities have managed, at least for the moment, to avert a cataclysmic collapse thanks to counter-cyclical interventions of unprecedented scope, the crisis has brought about a sharp decline of world output, of international trade and of transnational capital flows. The most developed economies have experienced severe economic contractions, leading to a compression of global demand affecting 'emerging' countries, many of which rely on the export of a narrow range of commodities and/or industrial goods to sustain growth. Locked into dependency relations with dominant markets, many smaller emerging countries and many countries in transition are hovering on the edge of bankruptcy. Worldwide unemployment and underemployment have risen sharply, generating what the International Labour Organization (ILO) has called a 'global jobs crisis'. The situation is certainly not as dire as the early 1930s, at the economic, social or political levels. Nonetheless, in the absence of universally recognised sources of authority and empowered institutions of global governance, economic disintegration is accentuating fragmentation along national lines as rulers, sitting on top of simmering social volcanoes, respond to the increasingly urgent demands of society for protection from the destructive gales of the world market. It is too early to tell how far disintegration will go. What is quite clear, however, is that late twentieth-century American-centred globalisation, simply if summarily defined as the creation of a borderless, integrated and interdependent world capitalist economy, has begun to fray.

The crisis, which is universal in scope, marks a historical reversal of the process of economic internationalisation that occurred after the dissolution of the Soviet Union in 1991. It coterminously represents a major setback for the United States. Coming on top of the Bush administration's failed imperial wars and its methodical effort to deconstruct the international legal and political order established in 1944–1945, which eroded American political legitimacy, the worldwide disruption caused by the breakdown of the American financial system has deeply undermined the US' historical claim to world economic leadership. It is no longer in a position, as it was in the 1990s, to define the norms and frameworks of economic behaviour, much less to assert the coincidence of national and universal interests. These dimensions of the present world crisis are inextricably linked. While the power political aims of the state and the deterritorialised logic of capital are not always congruent, intertwining as David Harvey puts it 'in complex and sometimes contradictory ways',[1] late twentieth-century globalisation was driven by the coincidence of visions and interests of transnational firms, the multilateral institutions and the American state. This was evidenced in a common agenda to tear down the last remaining barriers to free capital flows (the now defunct 'Washington Consensus') and establish a hegemonic model of economic and social behaviour. Seeking universal reach, transnational capital required the power and authority of the American state to lift residual regulatory constraints and curb political resistances to world market expansion. The American financial industry, which stood to gain the most, was the leading component of the galaxy of international and transnational actors that gravitated around the American core, formed what Susan Strange called the natural 'constituency' of the informal American Empire and looked to the United States as a source of authority and as a guarantor of their interests.[2] For its part, the state reaped the political benefits of the 'inexorable trend towards market capitalism', in Alan Greenspan's rash 1998 forecast,[3] since global economic liberalisation and capital mobility enhanced the United States' ability to shape behaviours and obtain outcomes that were considered favourable to American economic and political interests. During the 1990s American leaders 'saw the unchecked power at their disposal as an opportunity to mold the international environment, to enhance the US position even more, and to reap even greater benefits in the future' by using a mixture of persuasion and coercion to get 'as many countries as possible to embrace their particular vision of a liberal-capitalist world order'.[4] Together with the multilateral institutions in which it has a dominant say and private transnational clubs such as the World Economic Forum

(WEF), the American state set the global agenda and played a decisive political role in advancing global liberalisation, setting the frameworks in which it occurred and enforcing its disciplines. The US thus found itself in the post-Cold War at the centre of a 'complex but coherent power constellation', in Robert Cox's words,[5] that was underpinned by American military power, the armour of coercion that secured the global environment for the expansion of capital and enforced American political authority.

Given differentials of power and sovereignty in the international system, global liberalisation had asymmetric impacts, which varied according to the nature of countries' insertion in the global division of labour and the relative political autonomy of their states. Following patterns of dependence and vulnerability analysed by students of the international political economy,[6] weaker peripheral states caught in the magnetic pull of the most developed economies and having a feeble capacity to resist were subject to the policy choices of a handful of dominant states. World market forces conditioned their economies and their national economic systems were called into question by decisions over which they had no control. Even the highly successful northeast Asian developmental states, whose exit from the 'Third World' during the Cold War had been favoured by the United States, came under serious and sustained challenge. In the late 1980s Susan Strange had pointed out that 'all the decisions about the regulation of market operators and intermediaries that used predominantly to be the prerogative of each national government are now shared unevenly between a few governments of the largest and richest countries, of which the US is by far the most important'.[7] A decade later, at the high tide of global liberalisation, before the 'Asian financial crisis', the US' singular prerogative power had become even more evident. At the turn of the millennium, Robert Wade accurately noted that capital mobility and liberalisation '[freed] the American government of constraints while putting everyone else under tighter constraints'.[8] There were in fact some important exceptions to this rule: a few politically autonomous 'emerging' state actors not enmeshed in webs of constraint and control such as China were able, due to a gradual and controlled process of internationalisation and capital controls, to harness capital flows to endogenous development purposes.[9] In most other cases however, global liberalisation gave the United States a lever to assert its preferences and to exercise a tight grip on the policy choices of other states.

EXPANSIONIST BEHAVIOUR

The global economic liberalisation agenda pursued by successive US administrations, notably the Clinton administration, and the power-political agenda pursued single-mindedly by the Bush regime, represent distinct forms of expansionist behaviour. The first involved the peaceful but nonetheless coercive pursuit of economic advantage. Wrapped in a discourse of interdependence and convergence that disguised its hegemonic purposes, global liberalisation required a modicum of international consent, at least at elite levels, as well as the preservation and/or construction of overlapping international and transnational public and private institutions to provide frameworks for and to sustain the effort. The second was a more obviously predatory and illiberal effort to exploit the extraordinary post-1991 military imbalance and establish a disciplinary world order under exclusive American control. These were dissimilar exercises of power, reflecting the choices of different elite components: on the one hand, internationalised segments that are stakeholders in the world market system ('liberal international-ists' to use traditional categories of political analysis) and, on the other, ultra-nationalist segments ('sovereignists') umbilically tied to the military industrial complex and the national security state. The naked monopoly-seeking of the military expansionists, which by way of contrast makes global liberalisation appear attractively cosmopolitan, required the '[destruction of] the main schemes of co-operation [established in 1945] aimed at introducing some order and moderation into the jungle of traditional international conflicts'.[10] Its aims could not be accomplished without tearing down cooperation and abandoning international law, which Condoleezza Rice dismissed during the 2000 election campaign as 'illusory norms of international behavior'.[11] In other words, the internationalist economic neo-liberal agenda maintained the fiction of equality and pluralism under conditions of great and growing power asymmetry, while the second overtly asserted American dominance, 'unashamedly laying down the rules of world order and being prepared to enforce them'.[12]

These are significant differences. Nevertheless, both forms of expansion were coercive and intrusive, affecting the autonomy of states and calling into question the social structures of societies on the receiving end. Both were 'imperial' in the strict sense of the term (definitions are given below), proceeding from the assumption that the United States had the power and the right to remake the world in its own image, to act as the pivot of the international system and assert or impose its preferences. Both the liberal internationalists and the ultra-nationalist expansionists who were successively at the helm after 1991 interpreted the end of the Cold War as a historic 'victory' of far-reaching significance, comparable to the United States' 'rise to globalism' during and after the Second World War. In different ways they imagined the post-Cold War configuration as an historic opportunity to lock in economic advantages or to expand the United States' considerable reach. To borrow E.H. Carr's apposite remark regarding the worldviews of American interna-tionalists and nationalists at the turn of the twentieth century, both harboured 'visions of world supremacy'.[13] Indeed, as I show in Chapter 6, by the end of the 1990s spokespersons for all the major strands of the power elite, joined by parts of the chattering class, routinely compared the United States to the 'greatest empires of the past' (Henry Kissinger) and influential forces began dreaming of a new 'American Century' and a renewed and much expanded 'American Peace'. This ideational trend was particularly marked on the right of the political spectrum and in the national security complex. However, notwithstanding their differences, expressed in varying prescriptions regarding the way to assert American authority, in particular the balance to be struck between coercion and persuasion as well as the role of international institutions, all the main strands of American elite opinion aimed to consolidate or extend the US' post-Cold War 'primacy'. In other words, the two forms of expansion were varying expressions of a common imperial ethos. Ironically enough, these efforts of expansion, operating through various channels, generated the present crisis of American power and authority.

Today, the US' grip has loosened and the coherence and authority of the 'power constellation' behind late twentieth-century globalisation has waned. War-making under George W. Bush generated a nearly global political backlash, the rest of the world rightly interpreting military expansion as an attempt to inhibit pluralism and establish a new world order under a single disciplinary world authority. At the same time, the abandonment and violation of international humanitarian law called into question the character of the United States as a liberal democratic state. In the early years of the new century, the US appeared to be morphing into an unpredictable and authoritarian military giant. Now, having through a different form of predatory behaviour caused the first systemic breakdown since the 1930s and wreaked global chaos, American-centred transnational finance has wrecked the foundations on which its power and autonomy rested. As a consequence, the breakdown has called into question one of the structural dimensions of American power, the ability to set the global agenda and define the frameworks of governance of the world economy. To be sure, the United States still retains the 'exorbitant privilege' of being able to finance its debt in its own currency, since the dollar remains the world's principal reserve currency, but it is more dependent than at any time in the past on the decisions of surplus countries, China in particular, to finance its mounting deficits. Even if it weathers the storm as well as, or better than, other states, the US is no longer in a position where it can decide unilaterally, as it did in the 1970s, to alter the conditions of world economy operation by transferring adjustment costs to the rest of the world via the dollar without paying prohibitive economic and political costs. Hence, coming on top of the disorder generated by military expansionism, the 'collapse of the western financial system' marks, in the words of the *Financial Times*, 'a humiliating end to the "unipolar moment"'.[14]

A HISTORICAL SOCIOLOGICAL APPROACH

The purpose of theory and social scientific enquiry is to try to make some sense of unexplained social phenomena, if possible by identifying underlying patterns amidst constant phenomenal flux. Peter Katzenstein has pointed out that the unexpected end of the Cold War revealed 'the inability of all theories of international relations, both mainstream and critical to help us explain fully... the dramatic changes in world politics since the mid-1980s'.[15] The same can be said of the subsequent and equally unexpected changes that have occurred since 1991, which have culminated in the current world crisis. All the dominant assumptions about the trajectory of world politics and the world economy in the post-Cold War have been found wanting. Various interpretations of US behaviour have been proposed, with greater or lesser explanatory power, none of which is entirely satisfactory. Leaving aside lazy accounts of current international history that simply dismiss monopoly-seeking behaviour as an 'aberration' or a 'mistake', three principal structural interpretations need to be mentioned briefly here.

The predominant explanation, advanced by neo-realist scholars, is that it was the inevitable expression of the power asymmetry that followed the dissolution of the Soviet Union, reflecting the power-maximising mechanics of international anarchy. Kenneth

Waltz has articulated this view most clearly, writing that the US' 'dictatorial aspiration' derived simply from the new imbalance of power. Power disparity, he writes, 'spawns despotic rule at home and abroad...the disappearance of balance unleashed the impulses of the remaining great power. Superiority fosters the desire to use it. The dictatorial aspiration, whether of ruler or country, is to perpetuate supremacy and to transcend the processes of history'.[16] As critics have underlined, this Newtonian model of unit interaction at the international level has nation states or their pre-modern functional equivalents moving around like automata in 'abstract systemic structures' and envisions them as 'programmed to meet only one objective'.[17] Since international history is considered a permanent recurrence of the same, American efforts establish to 'hegemony, primacy or empire' were the normal if unfortunate action of a 'normal state that has gained a position of dominance'.[18]

The second explanation, founded on the analysis of domestic social structures, is that it reflected the inherently expansionist character of a self-perpetuating military-industrial establishment that, in C. Wright Mills' words, feeds on 'war or a high state of war preparedness' and requires a state of 'emergency without foreseeable end'.[19] (Or, in Joseph Schumpeter's elegant earlier formulation, a military machine that was 'created by wars that required it' and which then creates 'the wars it requires'.[20]) Andrew Bacevich has been the most prominent exponent of this thesis in recent theoretical debates. In his influential reformulation of Mills, he interprets recent US expansionism as the expression of a 'new American militarism' which evolved out of dominant Cold War domestic social structures – the military industrial complex and the national security state – which 'reshaped every realm of American life' and ultimately led to the 'marriage of military metaphysics and eschatological ambition'. Bacevich thus argues that the Bush administration's 'Wilsonianism under arms' was an exacerbated but not aberrant expression of a bi-partisan militarism that has 'deep roots in the American past' and that a 'militaristic predisposition was already in place both in official circles and in Americans more generally'. This predisposition has been accentuated by domestic consumption patterns that rely on commanding a predominant share of world fossil fuel and other resources, and which have therefore led to constantly expanding global strategic commitments.[21]

The third structural framework, proposed by world systems theorists working in a macro-sociological and historical perspective, is that late twentieth-century US expansionism was the response of a declining hegemon to the long-range redistribution of world wealth and power in Europe's and east Asia's favour begun in the late 1960s, the pathological expression of a tired hegemonic power trying to re-establish control of a world system sliding inexorably out of its hands. Articulated in various ways by Immanuel Wallerstein and Giovanni Arrighi, this hypothesis is based on a historical reading of cyclical patterns of rise and decline of 'world hegemonic' states, the rhythm of which is given by recurrent general crises and restructurings of the capitalist world economy. It relies on two interrelated postulates. First, that 'the capitalist world-economy entered into a structural crisis as an historical system' in the late 1960s;[22] second, that that crisis marked the beginning of the end of the American hegemonic cycle, now thought to be reaching its climactic point. In Arrighi's reading, such moments of 'systemic chaos' create the conditions for hegemonic successions in which 'whichever state or group of states is in a position to satisfy the system-wide demand for order is presented with the opportunity of becoming world hegemonic'.[23] Much like Wallerstein, he argues that the US expansionism in the aftermath of the Cold War constitutes the latest of the several 'bubbles that [have punctuated] the terminal crisis of US hegemony' that began in the late 1960s.[24]

This quick brushstroke does not do justice to the complexity of the arguments or to the variety of viewpoints within each of these structural frameworks. Nonetheless, it suffices to distinguish the approach and argument of this book, which emphasises the role of imperial state formation and imperial identity construction over long periods. Through a historical sociological framework that puts contemporary change in long historic context, and assessing the degree of variation of the 'imperialist urge' of the late twentieth and early twenty-first century with historical patterns of imperial expansionism and coloniality,[25] it aims to shed new light on levels of causality and historical patterning and hence to make sense of the disorder of the present. In keeping with critical international relations and world sociological perspectives that pay detailed attention to the historical genesis of the social structures of the present,[26] the approach taken here assumes that while there are no seamless continuities in history, nor are there ever complete discontinuities since, as Fernand Braudel nicely puts it, the past inescapably 'contaminates' the present.[27] The starting assumption here is that if current history is never a mechanical outcome of a determining past, social phenomena that at first sight appear radical breaks often, on closer inspection, reveal their embeddedness in remote patterns and longstanding ways of thinking and being. The second basic assumption, shared with Gramscian theorists who have renewed and broadened the scope of critical international relations enquiry, is that worldviews and material interests are mutually constituting parts of a single social reality and cannot be disentangled into neat explanatory variables. This study accordingly emphasises the interaction of outlooks and interests in the shaping of American imperial worldviews and practices over long periods. It weaves together the ideational and material dimensions of the American expansionary experience and shows how post-Cold War expansionism, the proximate source of which was the structural imbalance ushered in by the end of bipolarity, can be traced back to a *causa remota*, empire-building and imperial identity construction over the course of the past two centuries.

The imperial outlooks that crystallised at the end of the twentieth century were certainly exceptional in their explicitness and intensity but they were hardly an aberration. Rather, this book argues that they were a radical manifestation of a pervasive culture of expansion and force,[28] rooted in deep currents of American and transatlantic imperial history. In the course of nearly continuous territorial and economic expansion during the nineteenth and twentieth centuries, which was an integral part of the process of global late-modern western imperial expansion, American leaders developed what I call an imperial cosmology, that is, a belief system about the ordering of the world that naturalises hierarchy and inequality by assuming the need for an authoritative and disciplinary world centre of gravity. Expansion, during the nineteenth and twentieth century cycles of territorial and economic expansion, nurtured and was nurtured by visions of international hierarchy and world order founded on notions of cultural and racial superiority that were common to all western imperial states. The comparison made in this book between the imperialist outlooks of the late nineteenth century, when the United States began its international expansion in earnest, and of the late twentieth century shows that the cosmological scheme persisted well after the end of the era of formal empires.

That persistence, in a country that never had extensive overseas colonial possessions and has always asserted its supposedly exceptional status among the western imperial states, requires an explanation. Historical structures, which Robert Cox aptly defines as a particular and relatively coherent 'combination of thought patterns, material conditions and human institutions',[29] do not remain constant. The post-1945 *Pax Americana*, which appears to be ending today, did not simply reproduce the hierarchical political and economic structures of the nineteenth-century European imperial system but supplanted them with a new non-territorial imperial system that underpinned a restored and renewed capitalist world economy.

The explanation given in this book is that collective mentalities were shaped by continuous expansion in the nineteenth and twentieth centuries, which ultimately led to the internationalisation of US strategic commitments and the globalisation of American economic interests. Expansion, as the 'Wisconsin school' of American historiography has demonstrated, has been at the very core of the American experience. Empire constitutes the *habitus* – the dispositions that generate perceptions, practices and policies – of US elites. Imperial outlooks permeated the US as much as they did the European imperial societies where empire is a past that has never really or entirely passed. The United States emerged as a nation state in a global political economy of empires. Its expansion was conditioned by the overall expansion of the Euro-Atlantic imperial system. Notwithstanding American exceptionalist mythologies, expansion was founded on concepts of racial and cultural difference that were common to all the nineteenth-century empires. Nourished by notions of 'manifest destiny', a concept invented by southern slave-state expansionists, an imagination of world-empire took form within US elites as the country's space and place grew in the inter-imperial system. As I emphasise in Chapter 3, the US was already actively involved in that system in the mid nineteenth century, participating in common inter-imperial ventures alongside the European colonial states and intruding recurrently in east Asia in particular to gain access to local markets. Having the world's leading economy by the end of the century, American leaders self-consciously sought out a world role that would place the US on a foot of equality with the major imperial states.

THEORISING AMERICAN EMPIRE

The 'logic of world power'[30] consistently pursued by American leaders after the Second World War was in continuity with this earlier experience. Like their late nineteenth-century predecessors, their historical imagination framed the US as a bigger and 'better British Empire', in William Appleman Williams' words,[31] indeed as the successor of a long line of historical empires. Founded on the debris of the European imperial system, *Pax Americana* was a world imperial system based on a pattern of unequal relationships in various parts of the post-war capitalist world economy. By system I mean the organised array of social structures, institutions, international relationships and commitments – for instance, the interlaced international economic and security structures of *Pax Americana* – that institutionalise interstate hierarchy. To be sure, this was not quite the same kind of imperial system as the European colonial order. Given its conditions of emergence in the midst of world war and colonial upheaval, the post-1945 American imperial system differed from the European in some important respects, notably its lack of territoriality. It is therefore important to define the American imperial object.

In recent years, the US has been variously described as an 'incoherent empire',[32] an 'empire lite',[33] a 'post-territorial empire',[34] an 'empire of consumption'[35] or, more classically, as a 'reluctant empire',[36] an 'accidental empire',[37] a 'benevolent empire'.[38] Some of these unhelpful qualifiers reflect the continuing sway of American mythologies or, to borrow a remark made by the classicist Moses Finley regarding the British Empire, the 'persistence of the still tenacious nonsense' that the US acquired its empire by 'invitation' or by historical accident.[39] But they also reflect a real difficulty in naming a worldwide system of power that, because of the mostly informal character of American expansion in the twentieth century, and the generally consensual character of the transatlantic relationship, ostensibly differs from earlier forms of imperial rule. The problem is made apparent by the ubiquitous use in the international relations literature of the term 'hegemony', a word whose etymology implies leadership and the consent of the ruled, to describe the system-wide structure of rule of the United States since 1945 and to contrast it with European colonial rule. The conceptual problem is overcome however if one fades, as one should, the distinction between formal and informal empire and between formal and informal modes of imperial expansion. As Stephen Howe argues, 'the contrast between a formal British or wider European colonialism and an informal American imperium should not be overstated'.[40] Indeed, as John Gallagher and Ronald Robinson suggested more than a half-century ago,[41] the sharp distinction operated between territorialised empire and non-territorial regimes of control veils the complex ways in which hierarchy and subordination are established and maintained by imperial states.

Arguing against the then dominant view of the mid-Victorian period as a liberal age that witnessed a contraction of Britain's direct territorial commitments and a concomitant spread of free trade, and hence against the periodisation of British imperial history into imperialist and anti-imperialist phases, they proposed that formal and informal empire should be seen as 'variable political functions of the extending pattern of overseas trade, investment, migration and culture' in a 'total framework of expansion'. During the mid-Victorian supposed 'age of indifference' to empire, formal and informal expansion often proceeded simultaneously in different areas of the imperial system:

> ...between 1841 and 1851, Great Britain occupied or annexed New Zealand, the Gold Coast, Labuan, Natal, Sind and Hong Kong. In the next twenty years, British control was asserted over Berar, Oudh, Lower Burma and Kowloon, over Lagos and the neighbourhood of Sierra Leone, over Basutoland, Griqualand and the Transvaal; and new colonies were established in Queensland and British Columbia. Unless this expansion can be explained by 'fits of absence of mind', we are faced with the paradox that it occurred despite the determination of the imperial authorities to avoid extending their rule.

At the same time, Britain widened its informal reach, transforming ever-wider parts of the non-colonised world into 'complementary satellite economies'. Variations in imperial practice, for instance the relaxation of metropolitan authority and the devolution of colonial responsibilities to local government or the determined pursuit of free trade, were not the sign of waning British expansionism or changing imperial purpose. Rather, they reflected the constant adaptation of the metropolitan centre to the ever-changing circumstances of international expansion and colonial rule. Late Victorian imperialism was thus not a 'sharp deviation' from the supposed 'innocent and static liberalism of the middle of the century': in the total framework of its worldwide expansion in the nineteenth century, Britain established informal empire when possible, formal empire when necessary.[42]

Said otherwise, empire is not bounded by territories incorporated in sovereign imperial space directly administered by metropolitan centres. It extends to all social spaces enmeshed in direct or indirect regimes of control and subject to the magnetic pull and the disciplines of imperial cores. Imperialism, then, can be understood as a spectrum of coercive expansionary and intrusive practices that institute hierarchy and produce and reproduce international inequality: the annexation of territory through the annihilation or subjugation and dispossession of indigenous populations; the use or the threat of the use of force against nominally sovereign states and societies to impose metropolitan preferences and sustain imperial order and hierarchy; the remote control of protectorates, satellites and *de facto* dependencies or, at the least perceptible edge of the spectrum, the institutionalisation of economic asymmetries caging weaker states and societies into dependency, conditioning or warping their development paths and restricting their autonomy. To be sure, this is a very large spectrum covering a wide array of coercive practices with different functions and significantly differing impacts on subordinate societies. Settler colonial expansion through the 'removal' and/or enslavement of indigenous populations is obviously not commensurate with coercive diplomacy, much less with unequal terms of trade and other inequalities induced by the workings of the 'invisible hand' of the world market. Differences of degree very much count. Still, variation occurs within a continuum of expansion and a constancy of imperial purpose – the accumulation of power, profit and prestige (not necessarily in that order) – changing domestic and international circumstances and configurations of power accounting for the relative importance of one or another form of expansion, intrusion and rule at any given place and time. This multi-dimensional approach to empire and imperialism, not perchance pioneered and refined by critical British scholars excavating the United Kingdom's imperial past while looking sideways at the American imperial present, overcomes the interpretive problem raised by the protean character of American expansion over the past few decades and indeed over the past two centuries. It offers analytical tools, exploited throughout this book, to assess variation and continuity in different historic contexts.

The post-1945 American imperial system, which itself was the outcome of a much longer historical cycle of formal and informal expansion in the nineteenth and early twentieth centuries, is neither formal in the sense classically ascribed to territorial empires nor entirely informal. The informal sphere operates, or rather operated, through international and transnational financial, commercial and technological linkages, public and private institutions of governance, as well as the more diffuse workings of culture and ideology (international acculturation to the norms and outlooks of a dominant society which acts as a diffuser of cultural signifiers producing and defining the contents of 'modernity' such as consumption patterns, lifestyles, branding and design, etc.). One can usefully compare the state-market configuration, briefly described at the outset, to the late nineteenth-century symbiosis between the City of London and the British imperial state. Until the First World War, 'London was the center of a financial empire, more international, more extensive in its variety, than even the political empire of which it was the capital' writes Herbert Feis, an early historian of global finance. Profit and power went hand in hand: 'In the small circles of power, financial power was united with political power and held mainly the same ideas...the main course of British foreign investment was in accord with the main national purposes'. Capital investment was made safe by British imperial power and successive governments saw it as their 'duty', in the words of Sir Edward Grey, the Secretary of State for Foreign Affairs, to 'give utmost support' to '*bona fide* British capital in any part of the world... and to endeavour to convince [concerned foreign governments] to give concessions' to British firms.[43] Smaller nominally sovereign debtor countries in the periphery that were enmeshed in London's financial web were obliged to defer to British preferences or, when they proved recalcitrant, were forced to do so under martial constraint. A more diffuse but structural form of control was exercised through the Gold Standard and the disciplines it imposed. As Karl Polanyi notes: 'The *Pax Britannica* held its sway sometimes by the ominous poise of heavy ship's cannon, but more frequently it prevailed by the timely pull of the international monetary network'.[44]

The visible and the invisible hands of Empire thus complemented each other in constructing and then institutionalising the hierarchical western-centred world political economy. In like manner, the vast informal sphere of American Empire has always rested on a planetary security structure established during the Second World War whose forward points, the archipelago of land-based and floating military platforms disseminated throughout the world, constitute the mobile frontiers of US sovereignty. These platforms can and should be understood as the territorialised nodes of empire. The potential and often actualised violence of the security structure secures the wider informal sphere and allows the US, in the words a former Pentagon official (Alberto Coll), to 'move the international order in a favourable direction'. One can go a step further in the comparison and argue, in line with Peter Cain's and Anthony Hopkins' remark regarding the British Empire,[45] that the American Empire has been economically predatory and developmental, and politically liberal and despotic in different times and different places. During the Cold War, the US exhibited all of these behaviours at the same time in different places, through a differential assertion of power and authority in northern Europe, northeast Asia and the rest of the post-colonial periphery. Like *Pax Britannica*, with its different jurisdictions in the Crown colonies, the dominions and the homeland, the *Pax Americana* has been based on multiple hierarchies. In northern Europe, the United States encouraged economic development, horizontal economic cooperation and liberal-democratic states. In northeast Asia, outside Japan, it helped to set up and to sustain semi-sovereign authoritarian developmental states that it controlled. In the post-colonial periphery, it acted as a classic imperial power even if it did not annex territory. Force was consistently used to curb revolutionary social transformation, nationalist or communist, and to contain challenges that would have led to greater post-colonial autonomy.

AN INDETERMINATE FUTURE

'The owl of Minerva spreads its wings only with the falling of the dusk.' The world historical meaning of the present crisis of the American imperial system and of the world economy is beyond what can be known in the present. In the midst of the less acute world economic crisis of the 1970s, Fernand Braudel, founding his judgment on the record of successive decentrings and recentrings in the European *économie monde* since the fourteenth century and the later recentring of the world capitalist economy from London to New York, speculated that if the American 'centre cracked', an idea that he rightly dismissed at the time, the world would have to 'find or invent a new centre'.[46] Following in Braudel's footsteps, Giovanni Arrighi has argued that prolonged moments of 'systemic chaos' of the capitalist world economy generate the opportunity for 'whichever state or group of states is in a position to satisfy the system-wide demand for order [to become] world hegemonic'.[47] For their part, founding their analysis on sparse evidence, American neo-realists argue that the decay of 'hegemonic' order and the rise of contenders for world hegemony inexorably leads to international conflict: 'hegemonic wars of succession'.[48]

Yet unless world leaders prove to be suicidal, a 'war of succession' is out of the question today since it would lead to mutually assured destruction and the probable end of life on earth. The Cold War nuclear equation still holds. Moreover, there is no successor to the US on the horizon. Put into sharp relief by the world economic crisis, diverging national agendas and the lack of strong central political institutions capable of articulating common policy prevent the European Union (EU) from exercising world leadership (this is reflected in the monetary sphere by the euro's still marginal role as a world reserve currency). Aggravated by the recent waves of EU enlargement that led to a diffusion of authority, this is a structural problem not likely to be fixed any time soon. Nor, in spite of their rapidly growing economic and political weight, are the large 'emerging' states such as China, India or Brazil presently in a position to supplant the US and exercise hegemonic leadership. China's gradual and apparently irresistible re-emergence as *a* centre of the world economy undoubtedly constitutes one of the most important transformations in international history since the industrial revolution, marking a return to the polycentric systemic configuration that preceded Western predominance in the nineteenth century. Nonetheless, China will not supplant the United States, which remains the world's primary source of technological innovation and has a far more differentiated and complex economy, and become *the* centre of the world political economy, at least in the foreseeable future (speculation about long range futures is quite useless). The end of *Pax Americana*, in other words, does not mean that the world will find a new centre. Rather it probably means that the international system will be gradually restructured leading to a configuration with multiple semi-autonomous world regions.

The future is indeterminate. The waning of an historical structure opens structured options of change – structured in the sense that those pathways are not infinite but limited by the conditions of possibility given by the historical structures of the present – and new possibilities for agency. Crises, etymologically speaking, are moments of decision. They are also moments of opportunity. As Richard Falk writes, in the aftermath of the Cold War there was a 'historical moment of unprecedented opportunity' to demilitarise, reinforce international law and interstate cooperation, to create a fairer and more inclusive international order, and to 'promote humane global governance'.[49] Successive US leaders chose instead to expand the informal and formal frontiers of the American Empire. Today, under new and much more enlightened political leadership, the US appears ready to engage in more inclusive world order bargains, to de-escalate conflicts, to disengage from at least some of the US' worldwide strategic commitments and to accept the inescapable fact of interdependence and plurality. Of course, even if he so wished, Barack Obama cannot dismantle longstanding imperial social structures overnight, a problem addressed in the conclusion of this book. Though the conditions of possibility have been created for the realisation of the opportunity that was not seized in 1991, the long record of past predictive failures suggests that we should remain agnostic as to ultimate outcomes.

STRUCTURE OF THE BOOK

This book draws on the work and insights of historians, international relations and international political economy theorists and post-colonial scholars who have placed the question of empire at the centre of enquiry. The parts of the book dealing with the early phases of US expansion rely mainly on the work of world historians, economic historians, students of the British Empire, and the intellectual community of critical social scientists that since the 1960s has done so much to reinterpret American history. They also include some primary source materials: statements and writings of historical actors of the late nineteenth and twentieth century. The result is a detailed rendering of the imperial cosmologies that have shaped US international policy over long periods. The last three chapters of the book dealing with post-Cold War expansionism are based on my own years' long work and experience as a student of world politics in east Asia, Europe and the United States.

Chapter 2 situates American expansionism in its world-historical setting, framing it as an integral part of the global process of western expansion in the late-modern era. It argues that British and American expansion involved a symbiotic development dynamic and emphasises the role of violence in the constitution of imperial state space – the 'almost incessant series of open wars [that] accompanied the march of industrial civilisation'.[50] While Europe exported colonial despotism overseas, the US endogenised tyranny, expansion being founded on concepts of racial and cultural difference inherent to all settler colonial projects, in large parts of its constantly expanding domestic sovereign space.

Chapter 3 challenges the conventional periodisation of US expansion into continental and international phases and engages in a detailed examination of the sources and ideological contents of the late nineteenth-century 'imperialist urge' that led to the constitution of an overseas empire in the Caribbean, Asia and the Pacific. Continental expansion was accompanied by worldwide imperial interventions, the frequency and intensity of which grew in the latter part of the nineteenth century. By the 1890s, the US had become an 'active unit' in the international system, displacing

Britain as the world's leading manufacturer. Overseas imperialism was not an anomaly: it expressed the widening scope rather than a change of character of American ambitions. This moment of international expansion was a defining transitional moment between nineteenth-century expansion and the 'globalizing of America' in the twentieth century.

Chapter 4 engages in a discussion of *Pax Americana* and critically re-examines the notion of hegemony. Having supplanted Europe at the centre of the world capitalist economy and finding itself in possession of a planetary military structure, the United States reconfigured international relations. If hegemony indeed applied to Europe and Japan, it was not a system-wide norm. Global military containment during the Cold War 'became the rationale...not for a plural world but for an American Empire'[51] which, like the British Empire that 'supported despotism in Asia and democracy in Australia'[52] (once cleared of its indigenous peoples, of course), established different patterns of hierarchical relations in Europe, northeast Asia and the post-colonial periphery.

Chapter 5 stresses the decisive importance of the security structure in the US imperial system. It reviews the 'declinist' debate and describes the mechanisms that inhibited systemic transformation in the 1970s and 1980s. It highlights the interacting roles of the international security and monetary structures of the American Empire that, while functionally distinct, were/are interlaced parts of a system that constrains the autonomy of states enmeshed in the imperial or the hegemonic realms, as the case may be. Using an ideal-typical typology distinguishing different elite social groups and visions, I argue that three broad US policy options emerged in the aftermath of the Cold War, all of which were imperial in the strict sense of the term, but that had different implications as far as the exercise of power was concerned.

Chapter 6 engages in a detailed examination of the crystallisation of imperialist outlooks during the 1990s, the growing influence of nationalist-expansionist political forces in Congress, and the policy translation of these trends after 2000. It disconfirms September 11 as a causal factor of subsequent US state behaviour and argues that one cannot assign explanatory primacy to any of the particular motives that have been raised to account for the Iraq war (gaining access to and control of fossil fuels, securing Israel, making Iraq a cautionary example for other 'rogue states', etc.). The hierarchy of these particular motives is impossible to establish. Rather, based on the behaviour and statements of the administration, the chapter suggests that the September 11 events were seized as an opportunity to alter the basic configuration of world order or, as Condoleezza Rice put it, to 'capitalize on [the opportunities offered] by the shifting of the tectonic plates in international politics'.[53] September 11 simultaneously created the conditions for domestic authoritarian transformation and an extraordinary concentration of power in the hands of the executive.

Chapter 7 studies the global consequences of the US' drive for empire. Drawing on Karl Polanyi, I argue that it closed off the potential for a long period of cooperation and peace and I hypothesise that, by stimulating the re-nationalisation of world politics, it marked a turning point in late twentieth-century globalisation. At the interstate level, the US demand for unquestioned deference without counterpart proved unacceptable not only to world public opinion but to a great number of states which well understood that the underlying issue of the war in Iraq was 'whether the future world order [would be] unipolar or a multi-polar system in which others have an influence on the sole superpower'.[54] Monopoly seeking deeply undermined US authority and legitimacy, weakened the US position in the Gulf and Middle East and accentuated centrifugal economic trends. The eruption of the systemic financial crisis has added a new dimension to this, accelerating the shift of the international system toward polycentrism.

The conclusion summarises some of the main findings of the study and opens a discussion of the prospects for pluralist cooperation in the emerging polycentric world system.

2
The American Empire in its World Historical Setting

Expansion is everything...the world is nearly all parcelled out, and what there is left of it is being divided up, conquered, and colonized. To think of these stars that you see overhead at night, these vast worlds which we can never reach. I would annex the planets if I could.

Cecil Rhodes, Last Will and Testament, 1902

The American empire was not established in a 'fit of absence of mind' any more than were the Athenian, the Roman or the British empires. It emerged in the eighteenth and nineteenth centuries within and alongside other western empires and found its place and space in the hierarchical world order that resulted from the global movement of western expansion, of which it was an integral part. Indeed, the United States' 'rise to globalism' cannot be properly understood outside of the world historical context in which it occurred. I argue in this chapter that American territorial and economic expansion over the course of the nineteenth century was an integral and dynamic component of the general movement of western imperial expansion that created the historical structures and hierarchies that have shaped the modern world. To make that case I describe the polycentric world system that preceded the European industrial revolution and briefly review the transformations produced by the global expansion of the west in the nineteenth century. American economic and territorial expansion is then situated within that overall process. The periodisation chosen here draws a demarcation between the early-modern and late-modern phases of imperial expansion. Of course, western overseas imperialism began well before the nineteenth century, with the colonisation of the Americas and the commercial colonialism of the Dutch and British East Indian companies, which set the conditions for the 'rise' and subsequent globalisation of the west. It was only in the nineteenth century, however, and in particular the latter part of the century, that imperialism took on a world-encompassing scope, when expansion, in Hannah Arendt's words,[1] became the 'permanent and supreme aim of politics', leading to the establishment of social structures that entrenched international inequality. A vertical transatlantic world order supplanted the polycentric world economy that had lasted until the end of the eighteenth century. Hence, while there is no fundamental discontinuity in the process of western expansion, one must nonetheless distinguish between the circumscribed overseas expansion of early modern Europe and the later world-transforming effects of global western expansion during the age of empire, internationalised finance and industry.

A PLURAL AND POLYCENTRIC WORLD ECONOMY

These assertions require some elaboration. Recent world historical scholarship has given new weight to the argument that the 'great divergence' between the west and the rest of the world became marked only during the maturation of the industrial revolution and the spread of empire in the nineteenth century. There is a growing body of evidence that suggests that although Europe was expanding economically and territorially prior to the 1820s, it was far from being the dominant centre of world production, finance and trade that it later became. Rather, it was merely one among many centres – *économie-mondes* in Fernand Braudel's formulation – in a plural and polycentric world economy in which there were multiple and relatively autonomous polities (the Ottoman Empire, the Mughal Empire, Russia, China, etc.). The same evidence undermines the other, still commonly held, notion that long before global western expansion began in earnest, the non-western world was 'immobile', much less uniformly, or even partially, in decline. The world historical literature on this subject,[2] the salient points of which are briefly synthesised here, questions the Eurocentric meta-narrative of modernity and highlights the role of slave labour-based resource extraction from the Americas as a major explanatory factor in the creation of the late-modern Atlantic-centred world political economy.

The picture of the world prior to the industrial revolution and worldwide European expansion that has emerged thanks to these studies is not one of longstanding western advantage built on culture, rationality and supposedly superior scientific, technical and economic capabilities. Rather, following Kenneth Pomeranz, they depict a world of 'surprising similarities in agricultural or commercial development and proto-industrial activities'[3] between major world regions, with significant parts of the world population moving synchronously along parallel proto-industrial developmental pathways. In this new picture, the early modern societies of Asia and the Middle East are no longer represented as 'stationary' or 'immobile' economic and social systems fatefully locked in feudal pre-capitalist modes of production or religious systems of representations inhibiting modernity. Rather, they are shown to have been developing along similar rhythms as western Europe and engaged in their own 'industrious revolutions':[4] intensifying exchanges, growing markets, rising incomes and widening proto-industrial activities. Pomeranz's groundbreaking comparative study of the most developed regions of western Europe and China prior to 1800 shows that pathway divergence between the western and far eastern parts of Eurasia occurred much later than had been previously thought. Before 1800, writes Pomeranz, 'there is little to suggest that Western Europe enjoyed decisive advantages' in terms of physical capital, life expectancy, average incomes, market institutions, agricultural productivity or proto-industrial capacities. Nor did Europe have decisive technological and scientific advantages that would account for radically diverging trajectories:

> In many areas, various non-European societies remained ahead. Irrigation was perhaps the most obvious; and in many other agricultural technologies, too, Europe lagged behind China, India, Japan and parts of the Southeast Asia...In many areas of textile weaving and dyeing, western Europeans were still working on imitating Indian and Chinese processes; the same was true of manufacturing porcelain. As late as 1827 and 1842, two separate British observers claimed that Indian bar iron was as good or better than English iron...various parts of Africa also produced large amounts of iron and steel that were of a quality at least as good as anything available in early modern Europe...Medicine was probably not terribly effective anywhere in the world, but east (and probably southeast) Asian cities were far ahead in crucial matters of public health, such as sanitation and the provision of clean water...Overall, then, arguments that Europe in 1750 already enjoyed a unique level of technological sophistication need significant qualification.[5]

The late eighteenth-century Chinese economy, confirms Christopher Bayly, was characterised by 'buoyant trade, increasing inter-regional specialisation, and a positive engagement by peasants and gentry with the emerging market'. China, the world's largest economy at the time, most clearly shows the convergence of conditions of life, levels of knowledge and types of economic activity across continents late in the eighteenth century. But the 'industrious revolution' outside Europe also encompassed south Asia, the Ottoman Empire and other east Asian countries (Japan, Siam):

> Similar patterns were appearing in Japan over the course of the late seventeenth and eighteenth centuries...more surprising perhaps, in terms of the old historical literature, is the impression that parts of India and the Middle East also experienced broadly favourable economic conditions until at least to the middle of the eighteenth century...Prasannan Parthasarathi has estimated that the standard of living of weavers in contemporary South India was actually higher in real terms than that of British ones in the mid eighteenth century.[6]

The Indian Ocean had for a long time been the centre of an *économie monde*, the heart of 'an enormous trade network, a kind of world system [of which India was the centre], stretching from the Near East to the coast of Vietnam, and down to Indonesia, and into the China Seas towards the Philippines'.[7] In the Indian sub-continent, as in China, there were articulated markets with peasant communities that were tightly linked to the villages and the cities through merchant and banking institutions and a complex system of production and trade. Europe was neither a central actor in sub-continental trade nor a major factor in the region's proto-industrialisation, which flowed from the sub-continent's position in longstanding regional and domestic networks of trade and production. Andre Gunder Frank goes even further, arguing that Asia enjoyed absolute comparative advantages in leading proto-industrial manufacturing sectors, amounting to effective Asian world economic 'dominance' in a 'Sino-centric world economy':

> The two major regions that were most 'central' to the world economy were India and China. That centrality rested primarily on their outstanding absolute and relative productivity in manufactures. In India, these were primarily its cotton textiles that dominated the world market...The other, and even more 'central' economy was China [whose] centrality was based on its greater absolute and relative productivity in industry, agriculture, (water) transport, and trade.[8]

Whether Frank is right or not regarding absolute Asian manufacturing advantages, there seems little doubt that parts of China and the Indian sub-continent enjoyed levels of productivity generally comparable to Europe's in proto-industrial activities. Paul Bairoch's estimates of the global share of world proto-industrial or craft manufacturing of various countries and regions, and of their respective per capita Gross National Product (GNP), indicate that productivity differentials were indeed unremarkable until the early nineteenth century. With anywhere between 27 and 30 per cent of world population in 1750 (200–250 million people), China accounted for nearly 33 per cent of world proto-industrial output, whereas Europe, with a population of 163 million, accounted for 23.2 per cent. Given east and south Asia's demographic weight (see Table 2.1) these world regions were clearly the most important economies of the world and accounted for a predominant share of world proto-industrial output and GNP.

Table 2.1   World Population by Region, 1750–1900 (millions)

	1750	1800	1850	1900
World	791	978	1,262	1,650
Europe	163	203	276	408
Asia	502	635	809	947
Africa	106	107	111	133
Americas	16	24	38	74

Source: UN Department of Economic and Social Affairs, Population Division[9]

Table 2.2   Share of World Manufacturing, 1750–1900 (per cent)

	1750	1800	1830	1860	1880	1900
Europe	23.2	28.1	34.2	53.2	61.3	62.0
GB	1.9	4.3	9.5	19.9	22.9	18.5
USA	0.1	0.8	2.4	7.2	14.7	23.6
China	32.8	33.3	29.8	19.7	12.5	6.2
South Asia	24.5	19.7	17.6	8.6	2.8	1.7
Japan	3.8	3.5	2.8	2.4	2.4	2.4
Non-west	73.0	67.7	60.5	36.6	20.9	11.0

Source: Bairoch.[10] Asia here does not include the Ottoman Empire or Persia.

Bairoch's findings regarding per capita GNP disparities between the western and the non-western worlds show that average per capita GNP in extra-European regions was in fact higher than the

European average in 1750. Variations were as great or greater within world regions as between them: Great Britain was well ahead of most continental European countries with respect to per capita GNP, levels of industrialisation and other measures of standards of living such as energy use. In 1800, per capita GNP in France and Germany was four-fifths of that in Britain. Yet, as Pomeranz shows, in about 1750 living conditions in the Yangzi delta (31–37 million people in 1750) were similar to those in Britain: life expectancies, per capita calorific intake, market activities and market institutions were all comparable. Writing on the eve of the industrial revolution and Europe's global expansion, Adam Smith surmised that China, 'long one of the richest, most fertile, best cultivated, most industrious and most populous countries in the world', remained a relatively opulent country, though he thought it had become 'stationary'. He also remarked that 'China, though it may perhaps stand still, does not seem to go backwards'.[11] In fact, according to Bairoch's computations, China's share of world proto-industrial output actually rose slightly between 1750 and 1800, from 32.8 to 33.3 per cent.

Table 2.3 Per Capita GNP 1750–1995 (1960 dollars)

	MDC	ADC	ATW	World
1750	230	182	188	188
1800	242	195	188	190
1860	575	324	174	218
1913	1,350	662	192	360
1950	2,420	1,050	200	490
1995	5,230	3,320	480	1,100

Source: Bairoch.[12] MDC stands for Most Developed Country (GB then USA after 1890), ADC for Average Developed Countries (including settler colonies) and ATW for Average 'Third World'.

Nor, as we have seen, were Asia or the Middle East 'going backward' prior to European intrusion. Rather, if these world regions appeared 'immobile' or in decline to western observers by the mid nineteenth century it was because colonial expansion had provoked stagnation and, in many cases, regression. Living standard differentials between Europe and the European settler colonies on the one hand, and the rest of the world on the other, remained insignificant until the turn of the century (see Table 2.3). However, by mid-century, average per capita GNP in the newly constituted 'Third World' had declined in absolute terms, recovering to mid eighteenth-century levels only in the early years of the twentieth century. Between 1800 and 1900, the colonial world's share of global manufacturing output fell from 73 per cent to 11 per cent. China's share declined from 33.3 per cent to 6.2 per cent and south Asia's from 24.5 per cent to 1.7 per cent. Average per capita GNP in the 'Third World' was only marginally higher in 1950 than it had been in 1750, representing less than one-fifth of the western average (and a mere one-eighth of American per capita GNP).

Cultural factors clearly cannot account for the sudden shift, historically speaking, from the 'surprising similarities' of 1750–1800 to the acute core/periphery divergence that appeared less than half a century later. Pomeranz argues that even if there were some European 'differences that mattered', notably in emerging energy and textile production techniques, these would have had 'smaller, later and probably qualitatively different effects without both the fortunate geographic accidents essential to the energy revolution and Europe's privileged access to overseas resources [in the Americas]'. Until the late 1760s the British cotton industry was, in the words of another economic historian, 'backward, small and unable to compete with Indian calicoes or muslins in either quantity or price unless protected'.[13] Later advances in textile spinning machinery, that began to be widely used in Britain in the last two decades of the century, would not have had world-transforming outcomes had British traders not had easy access to abundant and cheap New World cotton resources worked by slaves, and had the imperial state not imposed manufacturing and trade restrictions on India and other Crown colonies. As discussed in greater detail below, 'the exploitation of the New World and of the Africans taken there to work…did more to differentiate Western Europe from other Old World cores than any of the supposed advantages over these other regions generated by the operation of markets, family systems, or other institutions within Europe'.[14]

THE DISTINCTIVENESS OF WESTERN GLOBAL EXPANSION

These findings underscore the impact of western global expansion in the nineteenth century, the distinctiveness of which resided in the novel conjunction of the worldwide expansionary dynamic of late modern capitalism and the nation state's concomitant drive to endlessly expand its scope and power. Wolfgang Mommsen emphasises that in the latter part of the century imperialism became an 'extraordinarily dynamic force'.[15] Formal and informal expansion, the visible and invisible hands of empire, enmeshed world regions that had previously enjoyed relative autonomy and prosperity in webs of political and economic dependency. This process proceeded at varying rhythms, involved differentiated forms of metropolitan rule and had varying impacts on subordinate societies. Nonetheless, by the end of the nineteenth century most of the societies outside the west had been coercively brought into the gravitational pull of the core economies and their polities subordinated to imperial state sovereignty. With the exception of the neo-European settler colonies and a handful of countries that escaped colonisation and dependency, the structural outcome of the economic and spatial globalisation of the west was, as we just saw, the fracture of the world into 'developed' and 'underdeveloped' areas and the establishment of durable hierarchies and deep international inequality – the construction of the 'Third World'.[16]

Webs of Political and Economic Dependency

Great Britain was the leading, though not the sole, agent of this world transformation. Eric Hobsbawm notes that at its economic apogee in the mid Victorian period, Great Britain accounted for 'two thirds of the world's coal, perhaps half its iron, five sevenths of its small supply of steel, about half of such cotton cloth as was produced on a commercial scale, and 40 per cent (in value) of its hardware'.[17] It stood at the apex of a new international division of labour which linked the 'various regions of the world economy to the British centre' in a web that 'widened and tightened' over the century[18] and in which British manufactures were exchanged for primary goods produced in the colonies of exploitation and the neo-European settler dominions and countries. As overseas extensions of the core, the latter established factor complementarities that served endogenous developmental purposes. They also became the primary recipients of British investment flows. The colonies of exploitation, in sharp contrast, were locked in coercive regimes of constraint and control. The two were nonetheless interconnected parts of a global system of production and exchange. In the course of the nineteenth century, Britain imported ever larger volumes of primary products from the New World and financed its rising Atlantic trade deficits through the surpluses generated by the production in India under 'highly coercive circumstances' (Pomeranz' term) of consumption goods sold in Europe (tea, indigo) or China (opium).[19] By the end of the nineteenth century, the formal British empire, by far the largest of the European colonial powers, encompassed one-quarter of the world population, far more if one includes China, which was under *de facto* if not *de jure* colonial rule. At the same time, by end of the century, London became the centre of a financial empire 'more international and more extensive in its variety than even the political empire of which it was the capital'.[20]

The colonial system was based on unilateral manufacturing and trade restrictions (the 'colonial pact'), which created and then reinforced development differentials, with lasting 'underdevelopment' effects that are still apparent in many world regions today. Rather than leading to convergence, late modern globalisation led to divergence, the destruction of the proto-industrial fabric of non-western societies. Paul Bairoch and Richard Kozul-Wright note that 'deindustrialization in developing countries predated the era of global integration':

> Both in absolute terms and as a share of world manufacturing output, the position of the developing world declined sharply between 1830 and 1860. But this process continued and, indeed, accelerated during much of the period of global integration. Between 1860 and 1913, the developing country share of world manufacturing production declined from over one-third to under a tenth. There seems little doubt that deindustrialization in the South was the result of a massive inflow of European manufacturing imports. This was particularly true of the textile and clothing industries, where free trade exposed the local artisanal and craft producers to the destructive competitive gale of more capital intensive, high productivity Northern producers.[21]

In the colonies of exploitation, unequal terms of exchange were imposed under martial constraint. In the latter part of the century, Japan was the only significant Asian exception in this broad pattern (becoming itself a coloniser in 1895). Though it was forced to 'open' its market to foreign trade under the threat of American armed intervention in 1853, the archipelago avoided colonisation and successfully launched endogenous industrial development under mercantilist state policies following the Meiji Restoration in 1868. Japan's experience as a late industrialiser provides the frame for a counterfactual narrative to the 'North–South' divergence of the nineteenth and twentieth centuries. The archipelago's modernisation, which had little to do with supposed singular cultural traits,[22] suggests that the industrial revolution could have diffused to the many then 'advanced' non-European regions under appropriate framework conditions – modern state institutions, developmental economic policies and, most crucially, political autonomy. A few independent countries in Latin America – Argentina, Chile and Uruguay – enjoyed far higher standards of living than the rest of the extra-European world. One can presume that in the absence of intrusion and formal or informal mechanisms of dependence and control the passage from industrious to industrial revolutions would have been far more widespread. There is no reason to believe that the industrial revolution would not have spread to China, the Indian sub-continent, or indeed the Ottoman Empire (Egypt, for instance, had a significant domestic textile industry prior to British colonisation in the 1880s).

GLOBALISATION AND WAR

At any rate, it is highly questionable to argue, as Niall Ferguson does in his 2004 apology of 'liberal imperialism', that 'on balance [British] liberal imperialism was a good thing'. From the 1850s until the 1930s, writes Ferguson, 'The British approach to governing their sprawling global imperium was fundamentally liberal both in theory and practice. Free trade, free capital movements and free migration were fostered. Colonial governments balanced their budgets, kept tariffs low and maintained stable currencies. The rule of law was institutionalized'.[23] Nor does the historic record bear out Robert Gilpin's Eurocentric claim, widely shared in mainstream scholarly accounts of globalisation, that the *Pax Britannica* 'ushered in a period of economic growth that spread from England *throughout* the system' (emphasis added), and that 'never before or since has the cosmopolitan interest been so well joined to the national interest of the dominant power'.[24] (Following Edward Said, one can argue that the conflation of the interests of dominant power elites within the core and the cosmopolitan interest is itself one of the instrumentalities of domination: imperial discursive formations are not external or epiphenomenal, but consubstantial to what Said calls the 'relationship of power, of domination…of complex hegemony' that the west has historically maintained with non-western societies.[25])

Colonial Tyranny

To be sure, the *Pax Britannica* and the 'long peace' in Europe that followed Waterloo created the conditions that ushered in late-modern globalisation: the unification of the world economy around a dominant western core. Yet the larger historical reality, elided in the mainstream literature on globalisation, is that peace within the European-cum-western core was synchronous with constant war outside the west. Hendrik L. Wesseling calculates that between 1871 and 1914, Great Britain, France and the Netherlands alone were 'involved in a total of at least one hundred [colonial] military operations', including a number of conflicts that he defines as major wars rather than 'small colonial' wars. The figure does not include the wars of conquest and the 'pacification' campaigns in the previous century, or the nineteenth-century wars of conquest and 'pacification' campaigns of other imperial powers such as Italy, Germany (84 important military 'operations' and two major colonial wars between 1888 and 1905), or the United States' innumerable 'operations' against Native Americans over the course of the nineteenth century, the war with Mexico in mid century, the colonial war in Cuba and the Philippines, 'operations' and punitive expeditions in Central and South America and joint US operations with the European imperial powers in Asia. In Africa, writes Wesseling, 'not one year passed without there being a war; not one month without violent incidents and repression'.[26] The same can be said of the US' continental and overseas military activity. In his important study of the breakdown of the nineteenth-century international order and the end of the 'long peace' in Europe, Karl Polanyi also remarks, somewhat offhandedly: 'An almost incessant series of open wars accompanied the march of industrial civilisation into the domains of outworn cultures and primitive peoples'.[27] Despite its Eurocentric bias, the remark lays bare an essential truth of the expansionary movement of the west: the *Pax Britannica* and western globalisation were coterminous with ever widening extra-European conquest, coercive systems of control and what should properly be called colonial tyranny.

The phrase is appropriate since the most prominent nineteenth-century theorists of political liberalism in Europe quite explicitly advocated despotic rule in the colonies. Differentiating the range of freedoms that should apply in the homeland, the settler colonies and the colonies of exploitation, John Stuart Mill notoriously affirmed that 'despotism' was a 'legitimate mode of government' for 'barbarians' living in societies that, he claimed, stood outside history. Arguing against intervention between 'civilised' states and in favour of intervention elsewhere, Mill wrote: it would be 'a very grave error to suppose that...the same rules of international morality can obtain between one civilised nation and another, and between civilised nations and barbarians'. It is immaterial that Mill imagined this despotism to be benevolent. In fact, he suggested, making a comparison with Rome, that the 'sacred duty' to eventually bring 'backward' peoples to civilisation required brute force: the task simply could not be accomplished with 'clean hands'.[28] Alexis de Tocqueville, likewise, though with less moral compunction, advocated despotic rule and unrestrained violence to subdue colonial subalterns.[29] In a typical comment, Tocqueville enthused about European expansion in the following terms: 'Something more vast, more extraordinary than the establishment of the Roman Empire is growing out of our times, without anyone noticing it; it is the enslavement of four parts of the world by the fifth'.[30] In that sense, the construction of the modern liberal state was co-extensive with the exportation of violence and tyranny. Present international politics would seem to suggest that we are still living with this central contradiction of liberalism.

The Violence of Expansion

The intensification of world trade and financial flows that brought about global integration at the end of the nineteenth century occurred under conditions of constraint and inequality. The visible and the invisible hands of empire operated as the twin faces of a single process of expansion, leading to the unequal or perverse economic specialisation of the newly constituted peripheries. Widening productivity differentials between the newly industrialised countries and the pre-industrial economies produced deep asymmetries that were locked in by colonial rule, leading to a divergence of conditions that persisted and amplified in the twentieth century. While the average per capita gross national product of the industrial countries increased by a factor of 3.6 from 1750 to 1913, it stagnated throughout the newly constituted 'Third World'. The extraordinary breadth of the European expansionary movement is immediately apparent in the increase during the nineteenth and early twentieth centuries of the territories and peoples under colonial administration or control: the total subaltern populations in the European colonial 'domain' rose from 27 million in 1760 (less than 4 per cent of the estimated world population of 791 million), to 205 million in 1830 (around 20 per cent of the estimated world population), to 554 million in 1913 (300 million in Britain's territorial empire alone). If one includes virtual colonies such as China (430 million people) the total population under the direct or indirect rule of the west nears one billion, or 62 per cent of the world population in 1913.[31] The peak was reached in 1938, with 1.2 billion people out of a world population of 2.3 billion under western imperial authority.

As I noted in the introduction, there were significant variations in the types of rule and the methods used to subordinate and suppress indigenous populations. These variations do not, however, correlate with the domestic character of imperial states: all the colonial powers, including those with liberal-democratic domestic political institutions, had recourse to exemplary massacres, mass deportations, scorched-earth tactics, torture and mass executions to establish and then consolidate their rule. Autocratic regimes – Germany under Wilhelm II, and Belgium under King Leopold II – were certainly responsible, as Hannah Arendt writes, for the 'most terrible (colonial) massacres' in the nineteenth century. German Southwest Africa and the Congo, whose population she claims was 'reduced from 20–40 million to 8 million people', are examples that she sees as precursor forms of totalitarian genocide.[32] Yet there were also catastrophic outcomes deriving from the imperial expansion and colonial policies of the liberal western states. Collapses in human ecology leading to mass deaths in the settler colonies, even if unintended, were consequent on intrusion and colonial rule. The Algerian population declined by one-third, directly or indirectly eliminated during the 'pacification' campaigns, mass deportations, massacres and the subsequent breakdown of the human ecology that followed the French conquest in 1830.[33] The famines and epidemics that followed the conquest were not 'natural' phenomena unrelated to colonial rule: they resulted from it. In the worst case of all in relative terms, the collapse of the aboriginal population of Australia, from 750,000 in 1788 to 31,000 in 1911, was a consequence of western intrusion, land occupation and the large-scale forced removal of populations.[34] Even where there were no large scale catastrophic outcomes, indiscriminate, sometimes breathtaking, violence was used to suppress anti-colonial dissent. Britain recurrently committed appalling atrocities in its Crown colonies, for instance the massacres during the suppression of the Indian Rebellion of 1857–1858, the scorched earth policy in South Africa during the Second Boer War (1899–1902) and the terrible and terribly revealing last act of empire in Africa: what Caroline Elkins has called the 'campaign of terror, dehumanizing torture and genocide' in Kenya during the 'emergency' (1952–1957).[35]

Colonial imaginings of ontological racial difference and of 'empty spaces' authorised limitless violence against the de-humanised colonial subject. As the historian Jürgen Zimmerer argues,[36] the potential for genocide was implicit in the settler colonial assumption that indigenous populations were 'superfluous' and 'utterly disposable' and could hence be 'removed' from 'empty' lands. If the autocratic state was responsible for colonial genocide, millions of indigenous people were also 'removed' and destroyed by the most liberal western states. To paraphrase Zimmerer, this history of incessant war, subjugation and mass deaths calls into question the master narrative of globalisation and western global expansion as a progressive and modernising project.

THE UNITED STATES IN THE TRANSATLANTIC IMPERIAL SYSTEM

American expansion was an integral part of this general movement. The United States and the earlier British mainland American colonies were a crucial component of the transatlantic political economy. They were inserted in international commodity chains, transnational capital flows and transnational migratory flows. Prior to independence, the British mainland American colonies were integrated into the trade routes and financial networks of the expanding slave-based transatlantic economy. After independence, continental territorial expansion and economic growth were conditioned and fostered by the growth of the internationalised British economy. Rooted in material forces and racial and cultural outlooks common to all the colonial empires, expansion was consistently coercive. Like the European imperial states, the American state was constantly at war during the nineteenth century as it extended its sovereignty and territorial reach. The settler colonial project led to the century-long war and 'removal' of Native Americans and to one major interstate war of conquest (Mexico, 1846–1848). It rested on a highly effective liberal state whose 'success in claiming, protecting and extending sovereignty was unprecedented in scope'.[37] There was, writes Ira Katznelson, a 'tight fit between the military and westward settlement activity...by the positioning of its troops, the United States defined US boundaries; literally, it was a state whose shape and limits were marked by military garrisons...the nation's small military was constantly in motion, its forts often only fixed for short periods, its navy always on the move, searching for pressure points and keen to deter interference with the country's considerable commercial and geopolitical ambitions'.[38]

The Single Economic System

Continuous expansion was founded on concepts of race, space and hierarchy inherent to all the late-modern settler colonial projects. This is hardly surprising since the United States 'matured in an age of empires as part of an empire'[39] and came into being as a nation state during the early phases of the industrial revolution as a small but nonetheless increasingly important component of the emerging British-centred world economy. Along with other European colonies in the Americas, the British mainland American colonies and the later United States were part of a transatlantic economic system organised around the transatlantic slave trade and the slave-based production of colonial staples. Deepening economic linkages generated what Joseph Inikori calls 'a single system of international economic relations in the Atlantic basin',[40] of which Great Britain was the centre, that shaped the conditions of expansion of both Britain and its mainland American settler colonies. The 'single system' was built around the international commodity chains based on slave labour. Slavery is one of the major distinguishing features of the early American empire. If territorial expansion and the 'removal' of indigenous populations falls within the settler colonial norm, the institutionalisation of *domestic* despotism is a singularity of the liberal American state: while the European imperial states exported their violence and subjugated peoples overseas, the United States applied despotism within large areas of its constantly expanding sphere of continental sovereignty.

Transatlantic trade flows rose sharply as the British economy grew over the course of the eighteenth century. Britain imported colonial products for domestic consumption and re-export to the European continent, and exported semi-finished and finished products to the colonies. Between the mid seventeenth century and the end of the eighteenth century, the annual value of exports from British America[41] grew explosively, multiplying by a factor of 46 (£421,000 to £19,545,000) and then again by a factor of three over the next 50 years (£54,797,000, or 61 per cent of total exports from the Americas in 1850). Highlighting the rising importance of the western hemisphere for the early British imperial economy is the fact that while trade with the Americas grew exponentially, 'Europe's share of (British) overseas trade dropped from 74% in 1713–17 to 33% in 1803–7'.[42] The transatlantic slave and commodity trade were instrumental to early British industrialisation. In the eighteenth century, the slave trade and slavery were:

...integral though subordinate components of a growing north Atlantic economy, the expansion of which was largely dictated by forces within British society, notably rising consumer demand for colonial staples such as sugar. Rising British sugar imports in turn created enhanced export opportunities for British manufacturers in colonial and African markets and thereby made a significant contribution...to the acceleration in the rate of growth of British industrial output in the middle of the eighteenth century.[43]

By the latter part of the eighteenth century, the mainland American colonies had become a vital hub in the transnational linkages of the 'Atlantic World'. As the slave-based commodity trade accelerated British economic growth, rising British demand consonantly transformed the United States into the dominant New World exporter of colonial goods. Transatlantic trade in the colonial era rose continuously 'down to the war of Independence, survived the creation of the United States and prospered thereafter'[44] despite temporary disruptions in the first decade of the nineteenth century. The future United States' share of total exports from the Americas thus rose from 0.02 per cent in 1650, to 22.2 per cent in 1800 to just over 56 per cent in the mid nineteenth century.[45] Most of the increase from the early 1800s on was attributable to cotton, which was the 'pacemaker of industrial change'[46] during the first industrial revolution in Britain. The cotton industry in Britain had the highest rate of growth of all early industries – 6–7 per cent per annum from 1815 to 1840 – and accounted after 1815 for 20 per cent of total net imports and 'something like *one half* of the value of *all* British exports', or a sixth of total output in 1800. In 1850, textiles accounted for over half of all British exports in value terms. 'In a real sense', writes Eric Hobsbawm, 'the British balance of payments depended on the fortunes of this single industry, and so did much of Britain's shipping and overseas trade in general'.[47]

An Expansive Slave Regime

Rising British demand stimulated the spatial spread of the plantation system and hence the expansion of slavery. While the plantations of the West Indies had been Britain's primary source of sugar and raw cotton until the 1790s, the British textile industry 'acquired a new and virtually unlimited source in the slave plantations of the Southern USA...The most modern centre of production thus

preserved and extended the most primitive form of exploitation'.[48]
In the United States:

> Cotton became the predominant fact of economic life across
> much of the broad southern prairies and alluvial districts from
> the Carolinas to Texas. Within a dozen years after the cotton gin
> removed the major constraint on feasible commercial output of
> short-staple varieties, the United States was producing almost a
> tenth of the world's cotton supply. By the 1820s, it was the world's
> largest producer and also surpassed all other Western Hemisphere
> nations in the number of slaves...the expansion continued until
> the United States accounted for more than two-thirds of world
> output. In terms of the size of crop, number of producing units,
> number of forced labourers, the American Southland achieved the
> dubious distinction of being the pre-eminent plantation economy
> of its time. [49]

The South, writes Adam Rothman, became the 'leading edge of
a dynamic, expansive slave regime incorporated politically into
the United States and firmly tied to the transatlantic system of
commodity exchange'.[50] Slavery had of course been enshrined in
three clauses of the original American Constitution (1787) which
authorised the pursuit until 1808 of the transatlantic slave trade
(and which assured the dominance of the south over American
political institutions until the mid nineteenth century).[51] Well over
100,000 slaves were 'imported' to the United States between 1783
and 1808,[52] during which time two new slave states were added to
the Union (Kentucky and Tennessee (Louisiana being incorporated
in 1812); six additional slave states were admitted to the Union
between 1812 and 1845, Texas being the last). In 1790, out of
a total population of slightly less than 4 million, 757,208 were
slaves (689,000 in the southern states, whose white population was
1.27 million). Thirty years later, due to natural increase and new
slave arrivals after 1783, the total slave population had risen to 1.5
million out of a total population of 9.6 million (the slave population
reached 3,953,760 in 1860, or 14 per cent of the total population).
By the mid nineteenth century, the southern plantation economy
accounted for over two-thirds of the total value of US exports.[53]
  If international trade was not the sole determinant of early
American economic development, it is generally recognised that
it played a vital role in stimulating growth and 'proved critical to
the maintenance of national prosperity'.[54] The cotton trade not

only promoted southern expansion but also capital accumulation in the northern states, which served as the hubs of the United States' international trade and were the centre of the country's own textile industry. Northern merchants were the intermediaries of transatlantic commerce and built a significant proportion of the ships which carried the trade. Financing came from both Britain and northern US economic institutions: 'A major reason New York City emerged as America's economic capital was its dominance of the trade between Southern cotton growers and British manufacturers'.[55] As expansion southwards and westwards proceeded, the cotton industry stimulated inter-regional specialisation in the national American economy. Early economic development and aggressive US territorial expansionism – legitimated and interpreted by southern American expansionists as the country's 'Manifest Destiny'[56] – was thus in great part dependent on and shaped by the slave economy which came into existence and grew as part of the worldwide capitalist dynamic of the late eighteenth and the nineteenth centuries.

Transnational Capital Flows

Transnational capital flows, which increased rapidly if intermittently after independence, likewise promoted territorial expansion. European capital financed foreign trade and was invested in land, farming, cattle, national and local government, commercial banking and, most importantly, infrastructure development (roads, canals and railroads). While relatively small in overall volume these capital flows 'almost certainly played a critical role in shaping American development'[57] and fostering economic integration. According to the research of Lance Davis and Robert Cull, they accounted for 22 per cent of new capital formation between 1816 and 1840, 16 per cent between 1861 and 1870 and 9 per cent between 1880 and 1890. The first period 'saw the rapid development of the nation's first man-made inter-regional transportation system; the second encompasses the years of the Civil War and reconstruction and the completion of the first inter-continental railroad; and the third captures the development of the American West and its integration into the national economy'.[58] Capital flows contributed to the development of 'an integrated market in the East and upper Midwest' and played 'a major role in 'opening the American West and...integrating [it] into the developing eastern industrial economy'.[59]

Inflows stemmed predominantly from Great Britain, which from the 1820s on 'depended on rapidly increasing returns on foreign investments in Europe, North America and the Middle East'.[60] Herbert Feis, an early student of transnational finance, writes that the United States 'was the greatest foreign field of financial adventure for the British capitalist'.[61] Despite American protection of 'infant industries', wars, debt repudiations by local governments and railroads, and repeated financial panics, British-sourced investment rose constantly, albeit irregularly through the century, accounting for 'well over a third of the whole British investment outside the empire' in 1913.[62] British direct investment in the United States, Canada, Australia, New Zealand and South Africa totalled just over £2 billion in 1913, compared to £213 million in Europe and £441 million in the Crown colonies. Davis and Cull come to similar conclusions: while inflows from Germany, the Netherlands and France grew steadily in the latter part of the nineteenth century, 'the British were [without question] the largest foreign investors in the United States', accounting for 90 per cent of all foreign investment in 1861, 85.5 per cent in 1870, 77 per cent in 1890 and 71 per cent in 1900. From the end of the Civil War to 1900, the share of investment flowing to the United States averaged 22 per cent of total British sourced investment in the world.[63]

International Migratory Flows

To these factors favouring American expansion one must add one more: international migratory flows. The acquisition of new territories, whether through purchase or violence, labour shortages and economic growth generated a powerful pull for mass immigration, which in turn gave an impulse to further expansion. If the extension of slave labour made possible the massive expansion of the plantation economies in the south in the first half of the century, relatively cheap immigrant labour, primarily though not exclusively from Europe, supported land and resource development in the west and, at an accelerating pace in the latter half of the century, industrial activity in the north. The American population increased from nearly 3.9 million in 1790, to 12.8 million in 1830, 23.2 million in 1850, 50 million in 1880, 76 million in 1900 and 98 million in 1913[64] – a trajectory that was fuelled by mass immigration. More than 33 million immigrants came to the United States between 1820 and 1924.[65] In comparison, the population of Great Britain grew significantly but at a slower pace: 27 million in

1850, 37.4 million in 1890, 41.1 million in 1900 and 45 million in 1914. In 1850, the foreign-born free population in the US accounted for 13–14 per cent of total population in the United States, a ratio that remained nearly constant until the 1920s. In the first half of the nineteenth century immigrants built the transportation networks and public works and flowed to rural areas where land was available and agricultural productivity was high (55 per cent higher than Britain's in 1830 and 300 per cent higher than the European average). Europe's average level of productivity was multiplied by three between 1800 and 1910, but was multiplied by 20 in the United States, due to economies of scale made possible by land availability (once cleared of Native Americans, of course) and the large-scale introduction of agricultural machinery in the latter part of the century.

Migratory flows played a decisive role in industrialisation and urbanisation in the latter part of the century, creating a vast pool of low-cost wage-seeking labour for the rapidly expanding post-bellum northeastern and northwestern industrial economy. From 1860 to 1920, the ratio of immigrants to total population averaged 13–14 per cent but was significantly higher as a share of the total workforce. In 1900, the foreign-born population represented more than one-fifth of the workforce and was concentrated in the rapidly industrialising urban areas. In 1900, 'about three quarters of the populations of many large cities were composed of immigrants and their children, including New York, Chicago, Boston, Cleveland, San Francisco, Buffalo, Milwaukee and Detroit'.[66] Without these migratory flows, the present population of the United States would by some estimates hover around 200 rather than 300 million people.[67] Conversely, mass emigration from Europe to the 'New World' as well as to overseas colonies of settlement helped to populate the latter and answer a set of demographic and socio-political problems at home, notably social unrest caused by the rural to urban transition, poverty and the emergence of the industrial working class.[68]

These transnational linkages show not only a high degree of American integration in the Europe-centred world economy throughout the nineteenth century, but symbiotic development. Had it not been for the transnational connections spanning the Atlantic, the rise of the United States as the dominant capitalist state at the end of the nineteenth century would certainly have been far slower and far more difficult. British and European capital generally was a crucial instrument in the development of American national power: 24 per cent of global overseas investment flows went to the United

States in 1914.[69] (A similar point can be made with regard to Japan, whose rapid industrialisation following the Meiji Restoration of 1868 was promoted by British capital flows.[70]) The re-centring of the world economy from London to New York in the last two decades of the century was surely not an outcome that the British imperial elites anticipated or intended. But just as the United States' economic development depended in the nineteenth century on the European market and British investments, Britain's sustained growth rested to a significant degree on American economic success: the growth of the empire's flagship textile industry during the first half of the century, and the growing importance of the invisible earnings of the City of London derived from investment in the United States in the latter half,[71] were decisive factors in propelling Britain to global status and then keeping the empire economically afloat.

The next chapter shows how continental American expansion went hand in hand with international economic and political expansion, and argues that the two cannot be separated. The United States actively participated in the inter-imperial system and, as its relative power grew, developed world imperial aims. Accompanied by the crystallisation of imperialist outlooks, expansion culminated in the late nineteenth century with the constitution of an overseas colonial empire. The 'imperialist urge' of the 1890s constitutes a transitional moment between earlier expansion and the US' global expansion in the twentieth century.

3
A Taste of Blood in the Jungle: The Late Nineteenth Century

The United States has a record of conquest, colonization, and territorial expansion unequalled by any people in the nineteenth century...We are not to be curbed now.

Henry Cabot Lodge, 1895[1]

We want the earth – not consciously as a formulated program, but instinctively, with a desire that is too deep for consciousness, too constant and too regular ever to be questioned or thought of.

H.H. Powers, 1898[2]

There is no neat dividing line between the continental and global phases of American expansion. By the 1830s, writes William Earl Weeks, the United States 'boasted the second largest carrying trade in the world' and 'Americans fanned out around the globe in search of new markets'. International commercial expansion was encouraged by a 'national neo-mercantilist policy' and was supported by a small but very active navy that 'lent indispensable assistance to America's burgeoning overseas interests'.[3] In his valuable study of the role of the state in early American expansion, Ira Katznelson likewise notes that the US Naval Squadron, established in 1822, patrolled the Pacific 'quite routinely...linked [the United States] with Mazatlan, Callao, and Valparaiso, with New Baranof (Sitka) and Kamchatka, Canton, Tahiti, Australia and New Zealand, and pivotal to all these, the Hawaiian Islands'.[4] In fact, the US armed forces were involved in overseas imperial operations in one part or another of the world throughout the nineteenth century. The war with Mexico in the mid nineteenth century, which was financed through the Mexican war loans sold in London,[5] was synchronous with the rising frequency of armed interventions in Asia and the Pacific: five American punitive operations and/or demonstrations of force in China between 1843 and 1866, four in Japan between 1853 and 1868 and five in the Fiji islands, Samoa and the Hawaiian islands between 1840 and 1870.

Military operations were still more frequent in the western hemisphere, with 15 military operations between 1848 and 1868.

Intermittent military interventions also took place in Turkey and Africa, and coercive diplomacy was used to acquire Alaska from Russia in 1867.[6] In Asia, the United States was a prominent actor in western imperial ventures. The US won extraterritorial rights in China in 1844 under the unequal treaties that followed the first Sino-British Opium War and retained them until February 11, 1943.[7] (American traders participated in the opium trade, the profits from which were invested, among other things, in 'infrastructure for westward expansion in the United States'.[8]) The British and American settlements in Shanghai were amalgamated in 1863. Alongside the British, French and Dutch navies, the United States participated in the 1863–1864 military interventions to 'compel Japan' to re-open the Straits of Shimonoseki, an intrusion that helped to catalyse the Meiji Restoration. Continental expansion and international imperial interventions were coextensive movements.

Table 3.1   Overseas Imperial Interventions, 1846–1868

	Latin America	Asia Pacific	Near East	Africa
1846	Mexico			
1849			Smyrna	
1851			Turkey	
1852	Argentina			
1853	Argent/Nicaragua	Japan		
1854	Nicaragua	China		
1855	Uruguay	China/Fiji		
1856	Panama	China		
1857	Nicaragua			
1858	Uruguay	Fiji Islands	Turkey	
1859	Paraguay/Mexico	China	Turkey	
1860	Colombia			Angola
1863		Japan		
1864		Japan		
1865	Panama			
1866	Mexico	China		
1867	Nicaragua	Formosa		
1868	Uruguay/Colombia	Japan		

Source: Richard F. Grimmett.[9]

THE US: AN 'ACTIVE UNIT'

By the end of the century, the United States had become an 'active unit' in the international system; that is, a unit, in François Perroux' definition, 'whose program is not simply adapted to its environment but which adapts the environment to its program'.[10] In the decades subsequent to the Civil War, the United States underwent intense tariff-protected industrialisation. While in 1880 its share of world manufacturing output was still lower than Britain's, the rate of increase of that share was greater than that of any other industrialising country: the US share tripled between 1830 and 1860 from 2.4 to 7.2 per cent, and more than doubled over the next 20 years to 14.7 per cent (see Table 3.2). By the end of the following decade, the former colony had displaced Britain as the world's leading manufacturer, a trend that accelerated in following years. This ascending movement is even more clearly apparent in Paul Bairoch's estimates of per capita GNP, a better measure of the intensity of growth. In constant dollars (1960), per capita GNP of free Americans rose from $240 in 1800 to $465 in mid-century, more than doubling once again to $1,070 in 1900. American per capita GNP was only ten percentage points lower than Britain's at the height of the latter's economic primacy in 1870. From the 1890s onwards, however, there is an ever-widening differential in the US' favour (see Table 3.3). Between 1830 and 1913, the American rate of increase was double the European average.

Table 3.2   Share of World Manufacturing, Industrial Countries (per cent)

	1750	1800	1830	1860	1880	1900
Europe	23.2	28.1	34.2	53.2	61.3	62.0
GB	1.9	4.3	9.5	19.9	22.9	18.5
USA	0.1	0.8	2.4	7.2	14.7	23.6
Germany	2.9	3.5	3.5	4.9	8.5	13.2

Source: Bairoch, 'International industrialisation'

Using rising British per capita GNP as a baseline, per capita GNP in the United States was 98.9 (out of 100) in 1850, 89 in 1870, 107 in 1890, 116 in 1900 and 130 in 1913. Differentials were much wider between the US and other large European countries: in 1913, it was twice that of France and well above Germany's. Since the American population was much larger than any single European country, the United States' GNP in 1913 was greater than Britain's, Germany's and France's combined.

The United States increasingly shaped the conditions of operation of the world economy. Its industrial strength was reflected in the changing composition of exports. Having long been an exporter of primary products and a net importer of industrial goods, the United States in the late 1890s also became a major exporter of manufactured goods (by 1910, it was a net exporter of manufactured products). American commodities, industrial goods and machinery were sold throughout the world, a trend that was likened by contemporary observers to an 'invasion'. During the decade, the United States began to displace Britain in world markets as the leading source of manufactured products, including engineering equipment (for instance, oil drilling equipment). The United States, *The New York Times* reported in 1901, was 'encroaching on spheres of trade formerly considered under the exclusive control of the United Kingdom and other (European) nations'.[11] American goods and equipment competed efficiently with British manufactured products in the dominions of the British crown (in Australia and Canada in particular) and gained an increasingly large market share in the British economy itself.[12] In the late 1890s, the United States also became a new and rapidly growing source of international investment. Between 1897 and 1914, American foreign direct investment quadrupled, rising from $634.5 million to $2,652.3 million, 67 per cent of which was concentrated in nearly equal parts between Mexico, Canada and Europe (22.1, 23.3 and 21.6 per cent respectively). International portfolio investment likewise grew exponentially, rising from $50 million to $861.5 million.[13] By 1913, the United States accounted for 8 per cent of international investment. Epitomised by J.P. Morgan, British and American finance became increasingly enmeshed during the end of century internationalisation of capital flows. From 1914 to 1917, the United States went from being a debtor to a 'mature creditor' of the international economy.[14]

Table 3.3 GNP Per Capita, 1800–1913 (constant 1960 dollars)

	1800	1830	1850	1870	1890	1900
Europe	199	240	285	350	400	465
GB	240	355	470	650	815	915
USA	240	325	465	580	875	1,070
Germany	200	240	305	425	540	645
France	205	275	345	450	525	610

Source: Bairoch, *Victoires et déboires*, Vol. 2

OVERSEAS IMPERIALISM

There is no need to assign explanatory primacy to material or ideational variables in accounting for imperialist expansion. They are mutually constituting and cannot be disentangled into neatly demarcated causal factors. The 'imperialist urge of the 1890s',[15] which led to the constitution in 1897–1902 of a formal overseas colonial empire in the Caribbean, Asia and the Pacific, was the culmination of the expansionism of the previous century. It expressed a widening scope rather than a change of character in American ambitions. The 'new' international empire had been envisioned and desired long before the fact: 'Starting with William Seward if not earlier', writes Walter LaFeber, 'US policymakers designed and manoeuvred for a new empire beyond the continental empire they were already bringing to fruition in North America…The war of 1898, the colonial and informal empire that resulted, the new global presence…were a continuation of currents rooted deeply in the American experience'.[16] Soon after independence, American leaders entertained the idea of annexing Cuba and Canada. In mid-century, the southern slave states, the major drivers of the war with Mexico, advocated overseas colonial expansion in Central America, South America and the Caribbean, anticipating that an overseas empire would increase the spatial reach of slavery and hence the weight of the South in American politics.[17] After the Civil War, the north–south sectional divide gave way to a nationalist expansionist ethos that excluded slavery – though not fierce racial inequality – but supported aggressive expansion within and beyond the western hemisphere. Indeed, the late nineteenth-century turn to territorialised imperialism reunified south and north in a new common purpose.[18] The discursive repertoires of continental expansionism were thus effortlessly transposed to the new circumstances of American power.

Imperial Narratives and Interests

The key actors in this phase of international expansion were a small but cohesive and influential elite network seeking power, prestige and profit through international empire. The 'vigorous empire men'[19] who manufactured the 'splendid little war' (John Hay) with Spain in 1898 fused these motives in a mobilisation narrative designed to galvanise American society behind an agenda of war and international empire. Public opinion was rallied by an activist press that tapped into a deep reservoir of teleological representations of expansion as American destiny. Overseas territorial empire would not only secure an open door for American commerce in Asia, an agenda supported by agricultural and business interests convinced by the severe depression of 1893–1897 that American surpluses needed international outlets, but also establish the United States as a 'Great Power' and allow it to compete in the partition of the world on at least an equal footing with the European imperial states. By gaining a stepping-stone in the Philippines, the United States would be in position to penetrate China, the 'coveted empire',[20] and eventually dominate the Pacific. Theodore Roosevelt was clear on this point: 'I wish to see the United States the dominant power on the shores of the Pacific…(Our people) are eager to do the great work of a great world power'.[21] The extraordinary hubris that swept through leading social groups in the late 1890s is summed up by the statement of a prominent journalist a few years prior to the war with Spain: 'The United States is a great imperial Republic destined to exercise a controlling influence upon the actions of mankind and to affect the future of the world as the world was never affected even by the Roman Empire'.[22] Discussed in Chapter 6, there is remarkable identity between these statements and those of the apologists of global empire in the aftermath of the Cold War.

The will to power was cloaked in the language of necessity. International empire was the inevitable outcome of natural urges to expand: 'We want the earth', wrote H.H. Power, 'instinctively, with a desire that is too deep for consciousness, too constant and too regular ever to be questioned or thought of'.[23] Brooks Adams, an influential figure close to Roosevelt who thought 'imperialism the noblest passion to inflame the human mind',[24] asserted: the 'expansion of the United States is automatic and inevitable, and in expanding she only obeys the impulsion of nature, like any other substance'.[25] In an editorial published in 1898, the *Washington Post* carried the biological metaphor a step further: 'A new consciousness seems to have come upon us – the consciousness of strength – and with it a new appetite…the taste of Empire is in the mouth of the people even as the taste of blood in the jungle'.[26] Half a century later, in the early years of the Cold War, George Kennan critically attributed the war with Spain and colonial expansion to 'a very able and quiet intrigue by a few strategically placed persons in Washington…which received absolution, forgiveness, and a sort of public blessing by virtue of war hysteria'. Yet he acknowledged that 'at the bottom of it all lay something deeper…the fact that the

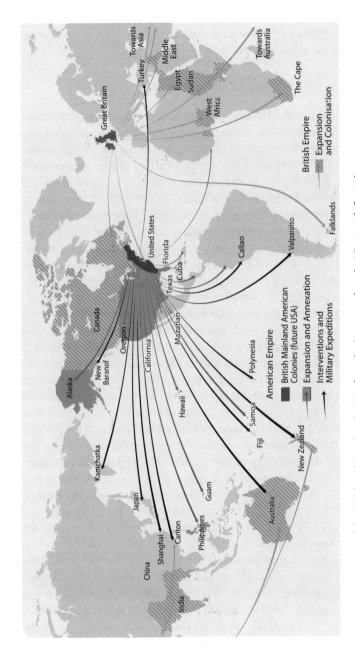

Figure 3.1   Expansion of the British and American Empires from the Seventeenth to the Nineteenth Centuries

Map by Philippe Rekacewicz

more influential spokesmen [of the American people] simply liked the smell of empire and felt an urge to range themselves among the colonial powers of the times...to bask in the sunshine of recognition as one of the great imperial powers of the world'.[27]

Endogenous and Exogenous Colonial Models

These self-appointed 'spokesmen' had been born and bred in a culture of force and expansion: hence the ease with which they slipped into their new imperialist clothes. Notwithstanding its exceptionalist idiom, American expansionism was a variant of European empire building. It proceeded from the same general causes and produced and reproduced within the continent the hierarchies that Europe imposed overseas. If anything, the colonial experience was more deeply imprinted in American society since, as has already been pointed out, despotism and subaltern-ness were established within the constantly expanding domestic space. The 'total American experience' was not characterised by 'pervasive liberalism', as the liberal-exceptionalist narrative would have it.[28] Prior to the Civil War, large parts of the population were directly, intimately involved in the master–slave relationship. European societies, with the exception of France, were mostly removed from the daily experience of colonial despotism. (It was only in the post-colonial period, with mass immigration, that European populations were confronted with a mass encounter with former colonial subjects.) In the United States, slavery was a dominant feature of society up to the Civil War as was racism thereafter. Hence Judith Shklar's essential insight that prior to the constitutional amendments passed during and after the Civil War, 'America was neither a liberal nor a democratic country, whatever its citizens might have believed'. Rather, the 'country had embarked upon two experiments simultaneously: one in democracy, the other in tyranny'.[29] Moreover, the experiment in tyranny did not end with the Civil War, since it took a century of struggle for African-Americans to obtain the end of segregation and full formal political rights. In the South, African-Americans were subjected after the Civil War to intimidation and terror. Discussing this, Robert Paxton argues that 'it may be that the earliest phenomenon that can be functionally related to fascism is American: the Ku Klux Klan... [The Klan] was arguably a remarkable preview of the way fascist movements were to function in interwar Europe'.[30] The existence over very long periods of two separate social spheres – an inclusive sphere of citizenship and rights and a sphere of exclusion and denial of rights – is at the core of the American experience.

The other tyrannical settler colonial experience – the 'removal' of Native Americans – climaxed in the immediate aftermath of the Civil War. The US government decided in 1868 to withdraw recognition of the 'Indian nations as sovereign polities' and to concentrate Native Americans in reservations. Military historian Russell Weigley notes: 'the new policy implied that the Army would be mainly on the offensive, to force the Indians into their reservations and to punish them if they did not go promptly or if they wandered astray'.[31] The aim was to open large territories in the Indian country to white settlers. The latter, said General Ulysses Grant in 1868, would be protected 'even if the extermination of every Indian tribe was necessary to secure such a result'.[32] General William Tecumseh Sherman likewise said: 'We must act with vindictive earnestness against the Sioux, even to their extermination, men, women and children.'[33] Two years later, prior to General Sheridan's winter campaign to 'force Indians into reservations' by starving them into submission, Sherman wrote: 'the more we can kill this year, the less will have to be killed the next war, for the more I see of these Indians the more convinced I am that they all have to be killed or maintained as a species of pauper. Their attempts at civilization are simply ridiculous'.[34] In the 20 years that followed, the US Army waged a 'campaign of annihilation, obliteration and complete destruction', in General Philip Sheridan's infamous words, against Native Americans that culminated in the crushing of the Sioux uprising in 1890, eight years before the war with Spain.

The practices of overseas imperialism derived directly from these prior experiences of war, while its ideology was fed by representations of racial hierarchy fostered in the suppression of African and Native Americans. Following the conquest and occupation of the Philippines, American leaders advocated unrestrained violence to subdue nationalist insurgents ('barbarians' in Theodore Roosevelt's words), who had initially welcomed the United States' victory over Spain, and to make survivors into docile colonial subjects. The war against Native Americans provided the template for colonial policy in the Philippines. Military strategy was modelled on the 'Indian Wars'. The colonial status of Native Americans as 'domestic dependent nations', set by the Supreme Court in 1831 and later reaffirmed, gave American leaders a ready-made juridical framework for ruling foreign 'dependents'.[35] In the course of the war waged against Filipino independence fighters (1899–1902), the United

States relied on the example of the 'strategy of annihilation' against Native Americans. Senator Alfred Beveridge, who considered the conquest and subjugation of the Philippines a necessary step to 'establish the supremacy of the American republic throughout the East till the end of time',[36] told the Senate during heated debate over the occupation and prosecution of the war: 'Our Indian wars would have been shortened, the lives of soldiers and settlers saved, and the Indians themselves benefited had we made continuous and decisive war'.[37] Admonishing the faint-hearted who recoiled at the atrocities being committed by American forces in the archipelago,[38] he went on to advocate the extermination of nationalist Filipino insurgents:

> The Philippines are ours forever…A lasting peace can be secured only by overwhelming forces in ceaseless action until universal and absolutely final defeat is inflicted on the enemy. To halt before every guerrilla band opposing us is dispersed or exterminated will prolong hostilities and leave alive the seeds of perpetual insurrection.[39]

A few years before the war with Spain, Theodore Roosevelt had advocated the suppression of colonised peoples with 'merciless ferocity'. In the third volume of *The Winning of the West*, published in 1894, Roosevelt derided the 'false sentimentality' of humanitarian concerns regarding non-white peoples: 'It is as idle to apply to savages the rules of international morality which are observed between stable and cultured communities…The most ultimately righteous of all wars is a war with savages though it is apt to be also the most terrible and inhuman'.[40] He added: 'It is of incalculable importance that America, Australia and Siberia should pass out of the hands of their red, black and yellow aboriginal owners, and become the heritage of the dominant world races'.[41] In his definitive study of Roosevelt's foreign policy, from which most of these citations are taken, Howard K. Beale notes that Roosevelt was 'a remarkably well informed man. He knew as few men in America did the horrors of war in the Philippines, the outrages committed by foreign troops in China'.[42] Yet he considered the Filipinos 'squalid savages'[43] and dismissed American atrocities in the Philippines by arguing that similar practices had 'happened hundreds of times in our warfare against the Indians'.[44] Alfred Thayer Mahan, the theorist of naval power and a pivotal figure in the imperialist camp, was of like mind: the Filipinos, as the 'Indians', had to be crushed before being (somewhat) civilised: 'Our Western

Indians', he wrote in 1899, 'began to be thoroughly overcome only when our troops gave up the habit of winter quarters and followed the savages through the bitter winters of the plains'.[45] Given these attitudes, undoubtedly shared by the senior officers who occupied the Philippines and ran the counterinsurgency war, 87 per cent of whom had served in the wars against Native Americans in the West,[46] the extraordinary violence of the Filipino counter-insurgency campaign is hardly surprising.

Established jurisprudence governing the domestic colonial system provided the base for the legal framework for overseas colonial rule. Like the American 'Indians', the Filipinos, once defeated, would fall under American sovereignty without citizenship rights. Basing themselves on successive Supreme Court rulings regarding the 'Indian tribes',[47] legal scholars claimed plenary powers for the government to act at will in foreign-held territories: 'In the government (of the Indian tribes)', wrote a jurist, 'the federal power has never regarded itself as circumscribed or limited by the provisions of the Constitution...Congress may therefore establish such courts and provide such procedure as it deems expedient in foreign territory or for Indian tribes'.[48] Some scholars operated distinctions among subalterns whose aptitudes for self-rule were correlated with degrees of whiteness or blackness – signifiers of civilisation and savagery. Of 'European stock' and considered in the main 'civilised', Cubans and Puerto Ricans could over time be granted some legal guarantees and partial autonomy. The Filipinos, by way of contrast, were 'utterly incapable of ruling themselves in a civilized way'. Consequently, there 'need be no question about the need of obtaining consent of the governed' or extending constitutional freedoms and protections to them.[49] The Filipinos, asserted an academic, are:

...incapable of gratitude, profligate, undependable, improvident, cruel, impatient, superstitious, treacherous...a people so averse to social order that they can only be ruled by coercion, by the demonstration of force...Cuba and Porto Rico are near our shores; the Philippines are far away. The first have long been within our sphere of influence; possession of the second, suddenly makes us an Asiatic power...The first are in the main civilized; the second on the whole savage. In the first one, white men can live and work; in the second, they can only make others work.[50]

American leaders flattered themselves that theirs was a distinctive humanitarian form of colonial rule. Once the nationalists were defeated, self-government was authorised at the municipal level. But, as Anthony Anghie points out in his study of imperialism and international law, the Filipinos were obliged to demonstrate 'an absolute and unconditional loyalty to the United States', a provision that 'rendered the whole idea of self-government extremely problematic'.[51] In fact, the United States was merely following the 'spirit and tendency of European policy', as one author put it at the time. Mahan, an early advocate of 'Anglo-American reunion', wrote that 'the impulse towards expansion which has recently taken so decisive a stride...is but one phase of a sentiment that has swept over the whole civilized European world within the last few decades'.[52]

While the subjugation of Native Americans provided the juridical framework for overseas colonial rule, European models of 'tropical colonisation' promised to yield valuable insights in the adminis-tration and economics of international empire. Encouraged and sometimes initiated by the government, comparative colonial studies became an important research agenda. Mahan, at the time a member of the Naval War Board, commissioned the President of Johns Hopkins University to undertake a study of the 'origins of British rule in India to ascertain the factors in the British success there'.[53] The President of Cornell University, who headed the First Philippine Commission, was asked to 'gather information...on the Philippines in preparation for colonial government'. The McKinley administration commissioned reports on 'Administration of British colonies in the Orient' and engaged the Treasury Department in a 'massive research program' on worldwide colonisation.[54]

Appointed Secretary of War in 1899, Elihu Root spent a few months studying the British colonial system: 'The first thing I did after my appointment was to make out a list of a great number of books which cover in detail both the practice and the principles of...colonial government under the English law'.[55] The 1899 annual conference of the American Academy of Political and Social Science was devoted to constitutional issues raised by colonisation and to comparative studies of the 'government of dependencies'.[56] The same year, the American Historical Association set up a 'Committee on the History of Colonies and Dependencies',[57] which presented some of its work in progress on the 'selection and training of colonial officials in England, Holland and France', 'tropical colonization' and the 'problems of race encountered in American colonization' at the Boston Congress of the Association in 1900.[58] A. Lawrence Lowell, an influential figure who later became President of Harvard and a leading American advocate of the League of Nations, published the results of his detailed comparative study of European colonial services the same year.[59] In 1898, *The New York Times* suggested the creation of a colonial civil service to back up and ultimately replace the first military administrators of the newly conquered territories. The 'real secret of the future of expansion', the *Times* editorialised, 'lies in the character of our "colonial" service'.[60] Rejecting the rigidities of the French and Dutch colonial systems, Lowell recommended the creation of an American colonial school modelled on the East India Company's Haileybury College, to serve as the seed form of an American colonial service. 'We find', wrote a jurist from Yale University who participated in the American Historical Association's workshop, 'the very general opinion that the British system is best worth copying…The results (of British rule in India) have been splendid' thanks to a 'picked class, drawn from the flower of the race…that makes a science of the business of governing dependent races'.[61]

A separate colonial office was never established. In 1902, Root established the Bureau of Insular Affairs within the War Department, which was entrusted with overseas colonial management. Responsibility for the management of dependencies and protectorates remained centralised in the Bureau until Franklin D. Roosevelt's decision in 1939 to de-militarise the Bureau and transfer its functions to a newly constituted division in the Department of the Interior.[62]

INTER-IMPERIAL LINKS AND RIVALRIES

The shift of opinion regarding the other 'Anglo-Saxon' empire, from hemispheric rival to model, or ally and partner, is indicative of the new role American leaders sought to play in the inter-imperialist system. The United States had carved out a partly autonomous space in the nineteenth-century imperial system by asserting hemispheric rights exclusive of the European empires, with which there were recurrent tensions throughout the century.[63] In the mid 1890s, many American expansionists saw the world as an arena of competition between rival imperial states. Soon after the 1895 Venezuela border dispute that had severely tested Anglo-American relations, and in the midst of a new rift over Nicaragua, a nationalist expansionist wrote that the United States and Great Britain were destined to clash: 'We have long been accustomed to look upon the western half of the earth's surface as ours while England's ambition seems to be to dominate the whole. To a certain extent, therefore, we both desire the same thing'.[64]

Yet a few years later rivalry over the western hemisphere gave way to convergence – albeit tainted with rivalry – over the common world-civilising mission of the two English-speaking peoples. Britain not only ceased to challenge American dominance in the western hemisphere but, in Beale's words, was 'delighted at American entry into imperialism'.[65] Kipling's 'The White Man's Burden' was of course dedicated to the United States' conquest of the Philippines (the subtitle of the poem is 'The United States and the Philippine Islands'). In his last will, Cecil Rhodes established a trust for what the *The New York Times* dubbed a 'race center' designed to promote 'Anglo-Saxon unity'.[66] Beneath the 'delight' over cultural and racial unity there was a good deal of realism. Confronted with growing German power in Europe and Russian expansion in the Far East, facing rising nationalist challenges throughout the empire and convinced that it could not defend 'English civilisation' alone, Britain gave diplomatic and material support to American overseas expansion.

If London turned to the United States to safeguard the British Empire, the United States relied on Britain to secure the establishment of the American international empire. British imperialism, formerly decried, appeared in a newly favourable light. 'We are aligned, perhaps allied somewhat, in policy with England', said an American general officer during a public conference with Mahan, 'awake to the fact that the statesmen of England have had an underlying purpose other than mere expansion and land-grabbing for its sake'.[67] Richard Olney, Secretary of State during the 1895 Venezuela dispute and a staunch nationalist, defended the new alliance as favouring American interests. The United States' 'inevitable' international expansion, he wrote in 1900, had thrown America 'into the arms of England...We join ourselves to that one of the great powers most formidable as a foe and most effective as a friend, whose people make with our own but one family...whose influence upon the material and spiritual conditions of the human race has, on the whole, been elevating and beneficent, and whose example and experience cannot help being of the utmost service'.[68] Olney was more cautious than Anglo-Saxon racialists like Beveridge, who believed that the expansion of the 'English-speaking and Teutonic peoples' was 'elemental' and 'racial'. In Beveridge's view, God had been 'preparing (these peoples) for a thousand years' to be 'the master organizers of the world where chaos reigns'.[69] Yet, as the word 'family' suggests, Olney's realism contained a cultural and racial subtext. Representations of racial and cultural kinship with

England played an important role in forging America's own imperial identity. Late nineteenth-century racial Anglo-Saxonism, writes Paul Kramer, 'resonated powerfully with American republican destinarian nationalism...Anglo-Saxonism and US nationalism were congruent enough that in the mid-nineteenth century, in discussions of the white conquest of Native Americans and Mexicans, Anglo-Saxons were proclaimed the racial embodiments and shock troops of American Manifest Destiny'.[70] By the end of the century, notwithstanding enduring American republican exceptionalist beliefs, 'Anglo-Saxon racism developed as a self-conscious bond connecting Britons and Americans...forged on their violent imperial frontiers and solidifying at points of elite Anglo-American social and intellectual contact'.[71]

The formation at the level of the elite of an informal transatlantic network with shared outlooks and congruent interests favoured inter-imperial cooperation in the suppression of nationalist anti-colonial movements (in China, for instance, where joint western expeditionary forces crushed the Boxer rebellion in 1900). Convergence at the elite level was sufficiently strong to contain widespread American republican-nationalist sympathies for the insurgent Afrikaners during the South Africa War (or Second Boer War, 1899–1902), and remained so more than a decade later when Woodrow Wilson prevailed over strong domestic opposition to the United States' entry on the side of the Allies in the First World War. 'At this juncture', writes Kees Van der Pijl, 'the looming conflict between British imperial interests and American universalism could still be reconciled on account of specific complementarities suggesting common interest'.[72] Notwithstanding misgivings in their own ranks, American imperialists supported the British war effort in South Africa just as Britain had supported the United States in the Philippines. Writing in the immediate aftermath of the two colonial wars, Mahan thought the application of power in both cases had taught an object lesson to subalterns: '[In the Philippines] and in the Transvaal a short experience of the comforts of peace and good government, coupled with a vivid recollection of the miseries of being ever on the run, will contribute to make both Boers and Filipinos careful about quarrelling with their bread and butter – their material prosperity – in the near future.'[73] While he sympathised with the Afrikaners, Theodore Roosevelt backed Britain because he thought that the future of the 'race' was at stake: 'I should regard the downfall of the British empire as a calamity to the race and especially to this country'.[74]

Imperial solidarity and imagined racial kinship never translated into a complete identity of interests. Cooperation went along with rivalry and a struggle for world economic dominance. American expansionists perceived that the balance was shifting and that the United States was supplanting Britain as the world's leading economic power. The South Africa War was a turning point, since it marked the beginning of the erosion of British imperial credibility. Fought to safeguard the routes to India and secure 'the weakest link in the imperial chain', the war wasted British wealth and blood, brought home the atrocities of scorched earth colonial policies to the British public and, most importantly, revealed the limits of imperial power. The war, which was financed by a £30 million loan secured in New York (a telling shift: half a century earlier the United States had financed its war with Mexico in London), was the 'greatest test of British imperial power since the Indian Mutiny and turned into the most extensive and costly war fought by Britain between the defeat of Napoleon and the First World War'.[75]

The unprecedented difficulty the British had in subduing the Afrikaner insurgency subtly affected American and indeed worldwide perceptions of British imperial might: it put an end to the 'unalloyed belief in British fitness to rule'.[76] In the United States, the revelation of British 'weakness' suggested that the British and American imperial trajectories were diverging in favour of the latter.[77] In 1900, when Britain was experiencing battlefield reverses, the Anglophile Secretary of State John Hay wrote: 'The serious thing is the discovery now past doubt, that the British have lost all skill at fighting, and the whole world knows it, and is regulating itself accordingly'.[78] Roosevelt likewise noted that 'England's failure in South Africa and our own success with Spain and the Philippines have been symptomatic of…changed conditions'.[79] Britain ultimately won its war, but at a very steep price. A few years later Roosevelt expressed concern over Britain's inability or unwillingness to stem the rise of the independence movements in India, and 'contempt' over her failure to decisively crush Egyptian nationalists.[80]

Changed conditions were even more clearly apparent in the economic sphere. The fact that the United States was displacing Great Britain as the world's leading economy fuelled expectations that it would in the near future become the predominant partner in a reconfigured Anglo-Saxon world imperial order. In a series of essays published in 1900 under the title *America's Economic Supremacy*, which was circulated to all members of the Cabinet and the Justices of the Supreme Court,[81] Brooks Adams argued that the 'seat of empire' had for millennia been inexorably moving from east to west: wealth and power were now shifting from the Thames to the Hudson. (The book was republished in 1947 during a new moment of ascent.) Adams supported an 'Anglo-Saxon coalition' to police the world's seas and to contain German and Russian imperial ambitions in Asia, if necessary by warring over 'the carcass of a dying civilization' (China). Nonetheless, he was convinced that Britain was 'decaying' while America was rising. In a letter to Roosevelt, Adams wrote: 'You have a greater place than Trajan, for you are the embodiment of a power not only vaster than the power of the empire, but vaster than men have ever known'.[82] In *Supremacy* he suggested that if only America showed the necessary determination to build a strong state[83] committed to world power 'there is no reason why the United States should not become a greater seat of wealth and power than ever was England, Rome or Constantinople'.[84]

WILSON, LIBERAL INTERNATIONALISM AND ULTRA-IMPERIALISM

In the introduction I argued that empire was not bounded by territories incorporated in imperial state space and that variations in the exercise of power occur within a continuum. Overseas territorial imperialism was not an anomaly in the trajectory of American empire. Rather, it was a defining transitional moment between nineteenth-century expansion and the 'globalizing of America'[85] in the twentieth century. The 'imperial explosion gave Americans a sense of self confidence, a sense that they had a special mission, a belief that they could shape international events'.[86] As Gabriel Kolko remarks, it 'scaled the objectives of American foreign policy to the capacity of American power to extend into the world'.[87] During the Second World War, Walter Lippmann approvingly wrote that international expansion under Theodore Roosevelt had instituted territorial and strategic commitments stretching 'over an immense section of the surface of the globe' that included 'the defense of territory from Alaska to Luzon, from Greenland to Brazil, from Canada to the Argentine'.[88] These international commitments generated the need for a much larger standing army, a two-ocean capable navy and an inter-oceanic canal, the construction of which began in 1904.[89] On the eve of the First World War, the United States was already a world power in strategic terms; it was also the world's leading economy, accounting for 32 per cent of world manufacturing output and 13.5 per cent of total world exports.[90]

Per capita GNP was more than double Germany's and 30 per cent higher than Britain's. As we saw earlier, it had become a major international investor, notably in Europe.

The United States had powerful economic and strategic motives to finance the Allies and then to fight on their side. Robert Lansing, legal adviser to the State Department immediately prior to the war and then Secretary of State during it, argued for American intervention on the Allies' side by warning that the United States would face 'restrictions of output, industrial depression, idle capital, numerous failures, financial demoraliza-tion and general unrest' if Europe were to fall under German control.[91] 'It may not be too cynical to suggest', write Peter Cain and Anthony Hopkins, 'that one motive for American intervention on the Allied side was to safeguard her loans and her burgeoning export markets, which would have been imperilled by an Allied defeat or by a stalemate peace among increasingly protectionist powers'.[92] Another major motive, linked to the first, was to secure the international strategic position acquired in 1898 and uphold worldwide American claims.

The war vastly increased the United States' relative power. It enriched the United States while it shattered European finance, inflicted huge human and material losses on all the European protagonists, challenged metropolitan control over the colonies and ushered in revolution in Russia. London lost its position as the world's financial centre and became a debtor to the United States. In the early 1920s, New York became the world's centre of credit; by the end of the decade, the United States accounted for 39 per cent of world manufacturing output and over a quarter of world trade. The war deeply undermined Europe's claim to cultural and racial superiority and hence its 'right' to rule, and stimulated nationalist anti-colonial resistance throughout the colonial empires. Anti-colonial movements of 'unprecedented intensity and scope' culminated in the worldwide movement that witnessed mass rebellions against colonial rule in Asia, the Near and Middle East and Africa – all of which were ruthlessly crushed.[93] 'In the course of the war', noted Lord Curzon, 'forces have been let loose, ideas have found vent, aspirations have been formulated, which were either dormant before or which in a short space of time have reached an almost incredible development'.[94] Revolution, begun in Russia, threatened to spill over into Germany and spread to the colonial areas.

Wilson's 'Fourteen Points'

Wilson's project for a new American-centred world order, expressed in the Fourteen Points, came in response to this systemic breakdown. Conflating American with universal interests, Wilson sought and failed to find a solution to disintegration and revolution by establishing and institutionalising an *entente,* under American leadership, among the major capitalist states. Karl Kautsky had imagined a solution of this kind in 'Ultra Imperialism', drafted a few weeks before the outbreak of the war. Kautsky argued that the rational interests of world capitalism might lead 'far-sighted capitalists' to forgo national monopolistic claims in favour of a 'holy alliance of the imperialists' to deal with the 'awakening of Eastern Asia and India as well as of the Pan-Islamic movement in the Near East and North Africa'. Wilson's effort to create a liberal post-war world order based on collective security and free trade, governed by a League of Nations, was designed to contain post-war revolutionary ferment in Europe and in the colonial world. A universal free trade regime was required to save world capitalism and secure American economic interests. Germany had to be reintegrated through a moderate peace settlement. At the same time, the European empires had to be liberalised to avoid revolutionary contagion in the colonies.

The Fourteen Points addressed these issues: Points II and III respectively called for 'absolute freedom of navigation upon the seas' and 'the removal, so far as possible, of all economic barriers and the establishment of an equality of trade conditions among all the nations consenting the peace'. Point V called for 'a free, open-minded and absolutely impartial adjustment of all colonial claims, based upon a strict observance of the principle that in determining all such questions of sovereignty the interests of the populations concerned must have equal weight with the equitable claims of the government whose title is to be determined'. This point stimulated great hopes among colonial nationalists that were shattered by the post-war settlement.[95] In Wilson's project, the Fourteen Points were to be enshrined in the League of Nations as binding principles of international behaviour. The whole design, however, fell apart when external and domestic resistance combined to make it impossible to implement. If they resonated with parts of liberal opinion in Europe, the Fourteen Points were interpreted in government in London as a direct challenge to Britain's 'premier position' as the leading naval carrier of the world, a threat to its planned post-war efforts to secure a tariff barrier around the Empire and guarantee raw materials supplies, and indeed as putting into question 'French and British [colonial territory] held long before the war and whose allegiance has never been called into question'.[96] Domestic resistance was based on the rejection by nationalist expansionists, led by Henry Cabot Lodge, of a binding institutional system that would have constrained American autonomy.

Means and Ends

When distinguishing Wilsonian 'liberal internationalists' from these assertive nationalist expansionists it is important to keep in mind, as E.H. Carr points out, that Wilson like his critics harboured 'visions of [American] world supremacy'.[97] While they differed sharply on the ways to achieve this aim, the Wilsonians and the nationalist expansionists shared contemporary assumptions about racial and cultural hierarchy. Both favoured the expansion of informal empire in Latin America and Asia; both had eschewed territorial imperialism beyond the Philippines (Lodge rejected the idea of a 'widely extended system of colonization'[98] and by 1906 Theodore Roosevelt was complaining that the Philippines had become America's 'Achilles Heel') in favour of protectorates and indirect rule; both concurred on the need to use force to curb social revolutions that endangered American economic interests;[99] and both sought a predominant role for the United States in the post-war order. Where the liberal internationalists and the assertive nationalists parted ways was on how, not whether, the United States should exercise its world power. The international empire builders of 1898 who brought down Wilson's project had not suddenly become 'isolationists'. Rather, they advocated unbounded American autonomy and therefore rejected a collective security system that would have been binding on the United States. 'Far from espousing isolationism', writes Michael Hunt, 'they agreed in broad terms with Wilson that the United States had achieved an eminence in world affairs (and had no problem with making new international commitments)... Lodge could not accept a League that would infringe on American sovereignty'.[100] In other words, the nationalist expansionists around Lodge were seeking to acquire a position of national dominance in the inter-imperial system while Wilson made an attempt to secure an American-led world order transcending the rivalries and segmentations of the international capitalist system.

First systematically put forth by E.H. Carr, the core of the realist critique of Wilson rests on the case that the President veiled the fundamental purposes of the state by enveloping them in illusory humanitarian democratic rhetoric and thus failed to obtain the domestic political consensus required for the actual exercise of American world power. Yet the 'Wilson offensive', to borrow Kees Van der Pijl's formulation, with its 'transcendent scheme of bourgeois universalism',[101] was a 'far-sighted' project prefiguring the United States' 'imperial universalism' during and in the immediate aftermath of the First World War. Wilson's failure in the struggle over the League gave way to American economic and political nationalism that had international expansionist aims. Walter Lippmann, a fierce critic of both Wilson and the 'isolationalists', writes that 'almost none of the so-called isolationists declared that the commitments of the United States should be reduced – that the Monroe Doctrine should be revoked, that the Philippines should not be defended, that Japan should be given the free hand in China which she demanded...The isolationalist party adhered, on the whole, to our vast trans-oceanic commitments.' However, they opposed the alliances with the European imperial powers that 'we needed in order to validate those commitments'.[102] After the failure of the League, Anglo-American cooperation gave way to intense economic and financial rivalry. While Britain sought to preserve London's status as the world's financial centre by 'persuading American leaders to use their surplus capital cooperatively rather than competitively', the United States imposed stringent conditions on the repayment of British war debt and dealt with the question of reparations in a way that 'showed American determination to preserve its [post-war] dominance over Britain'.[103] To paraphrase Carr, if British leaders were hoping for a post-war *Pax Anglosaxonica*, their American counterparts were already dreaming of *Pax Americana*.

At the same time, the terms of the Treaty of Versailles extinguished the prospect of liberalisation, much less independence, in the European colonies. Imperial trade blocs were solidified and the 'absolutely impartial adjustment' of colonial claims sought by Wilson gave way to the mandate system of the League of Nations (from which the US had extricated itself) and to the expansion rather than the contraction of the British and French empires. In a revealing moment of inter-imperialist bargaining, in the 1920s, the United States fought bitterly for equal rights for the burgeoning oil industry in British-administered Iraq, rights which the American oil companies obtained in 1929. In Europe, the terms of the peace set the stage for the rise of integral nationalism[104] in Germany and elsewhere. All of the latent tensions of the war and the settlement exploded into the open during the world depression, which inexorably led to protectionist blocs and the unravelling of the world trading system in the 1930s. Virulent fascist social forces were set into motion, tearing apart the remaining threads of international cooperation. The outcome of this long breakdown of the European world order was, in Karl Polanyi's words, 'wars of an unprecedented type in which scores of states crashed and the contours of new empires emerged in a sea of blood'.[105]

The collapse of Europe opened the way for the *Pax Americana*. We will see in the next chapter that it is misleading to apply uniformly the notion of hegemonic leadership to distinguish the American from the European imperial system. Hegemony in its proper definition is synonymous with the construction by a dominant social group of a system of rule that differs from forms of domination that coercively impose a normative order from on top, in that it secures widespread social consent.[106] Transposed to international politics, world hegemony denotes a configuration in which a dominant state creates an interstate order that generates international public goods, mutualising its interests with the interests of subordinate states. If it differed in some important respects from the nineteenth-century imperial system, the post-1945 American order, outside of the Soviet bloc, was only hegemonic in the western core and Japan. Beyond these two strategic frontiers, the US acted as an imperial power even if it did not seek to establish direct territorial control.

4
The Hierarchies of *Pax Americana*

From Darius I's Persia, Alexander's Greece, Hadrian's Rome, Victoria's Britain... No nation or group of nations has had our responsibilities.

Harry Truman, 1946[1]

Calling an empire a 'hegemony' does not change its nature or objectives in the slightest.

Moses I. Finley[2]

The contours of the post-war American empire became fully apparent in the late phase of the Second World War. Yet well before the United States' official entry in the conflict American observers were convinced that the European era was coming to a close. 'In the lifetime of the generation to which we belong', wrote Walter Lippmann in 1939, 'there has been one of the greatest events in the history of mankind. The controlling power in western civilization has crossed the Atlantic.' What 'Rome was to the ancient world, what Great Britain has been to the modern world, America is to the world of tomorrow'.[3] On December 10, 1940, the President of the National Industrial Conference Board told the Investment Bankers Association that a 'vast revolution in the balance of power' was in progress. The United States, he said, would become the:

...heir and residuary legatee or receiver for (the) economic and political assets of the [British] Empire...Even though, by our aid, England should emerge from this struggle without defeat, she will be so impoverished economically and crippled in prestige that it is improbable she will be able to resume or maintain the dominant position in world affairs which she has occupied so long. At best, England will become a junior partner in a new Anglo-Saxon imperialism, in which the economic resources and the military and naval strength of the United States will be the center of gravity... the scepter passes to the United States.[4]

Two months later, Henry Luce announced the coming 'American Century'. In his famous essay in *Life* magazine, Luce wrote that

'America's first century as a dominant power in the world' was at hand. The American people should 'accept wholeheartedly our duty and our opportunity as the most powerful and vital nation in the world and in consequence to exert upon the world the full impact of our influence, for such purposes as we see fit and by such means as we see fit'. Like other interventionists, Luce anticipated victory and a post-war settlement in which Great Britain and other allied European imperial states would become subordinate partners of the United States: 'In any sort of partnership with the British Empire… America should assume the role of senior partner'.[5] The First World War had highlighted Europe's inability to manage the balance of power. The Second would open the way for global American leadership. Unlike in 1918–1919, when Wilson's world leadership effort collapsed, after the defeat of the Axis the exhausted European imperial powers would be incorporated in a new American-led world order. The Pacific would become an 'American lake'. The United States would henceforth, Lippmann wrote in 1944, be at 'the centre, no longer on the edges…of the first universal order since classical time'.[6]

SUPPLANTING BRITAIN

American leaders never lost sight of this: being at the centre became the cosmological constant of US wartime and post-war policy. During the war the US set itself the dual objective of defeating the Axis and supplanting the European imperial states. Nationalists and internationalists were agreed that the US should 'take advantage of the position of power in which it finds itself' to 'dictate to England'.[7] If this attitude was attenuated by the imperatives of wartime coalition politics, Franklin Roosevelt was absolutely clear on the point that the US had what he called 'the whip hand' in the bilateral relationship.[8] Wartime economic planning reflected the American ambition. Gabriel Kolko emphasises that the administration developed 'a clear, explicit and well-outlined agenda' and that in no other area 'was the United States so determined to have its way in attaining its post-war aims'.[9] The economic challenge to Britain took the form of constant pressure to open world trade and dismantle closed imperial trading blocs, a point over which Secretary of State Cordell Hull displayed what Dean Acheson called 'fanatical single mindedness',[10] but which was broadly agreed upon in the administration.[11] Under conditions of great and growing economic disparity between Europe and the United States, an open and non-discriminatory trading system would lock in American comparative advantages in the post-war world economy, 'glorify the principles of liberal capitalism, provide the markets for American agricultural and industrial production, and stymie the accretion of strategic power by other nations'.[12]

The US' principal instrument of influence and control was the conditional aid supplied under the Lend-Lease programme, which was understood as a 'device that could be used to alter the structure of international trade and finance, and determine the global balance of power in the post-war world'.[13] The US consistently used Lend-Lease to assert American preferences. Going into the Atlantic Conference that led to the Atlantic Charter, the State Department 'desired to take advantage of Britain's precarious position by inducing London to commit to pledges of [colonial] self-determination and the open-door policy regarding resources'.[14] To digress briefly, the anti-colonial dimension of the policy was far more ambiguous than US economic aims. While the Roosevelt administration frequently invoked colonial self-determination, a policy supported by progressive New Dealers such as Sumner Welles, it was very careful not to stimulate revolutionary trends in colonial areas. Throughout the war, the US played a balancing act, simultaneously leading nationalists in the colonies to believe that it supported their cause while assuring their wartime allies, including the Dutch and French governments in exile, that they would recover full colonial sovereignty. The US never asked 'Britain, France or the Netherlands for an immediate grant of self government to their colonies'.[15] As a critic of this policy noted in 1944:

> Because of our silence we are tacitly committed to the support of an imperial system which will inevitably come to an end... We appear to millions of Asiatics to be fighting [not only to defeat Japan] but to restore colonialism in Asia...Failure to clarify our position in unequivocal terms may bring us into a future alignment where we shall be ranged with a dying imperialism against a united and vigorous Asia.[16]

To come back to Lend-Lease, the creation of a financial dependency relationship constrained British wartime and post-war autonomy. 'Great Britain', writes Randall Bennett Woods, 'received enough aid to enable it to survive and to play a role in the war against the Axis, but not enough to preserve its overseas investments and markets, to maintain its military outposts, or to participate in a system of multilateral commerce.'[17] In the war's immediate aftermath, John Maynard Keynes bitterly remarked that the 'US administration was very careful to take every possible precaution to see that the British were as near as possible bankrupt before any assistance was given'.[18]

New 'Strategic Frontiers'

The strategic dimension of post-war planning surfaced in the later phases of the conflict when it became clear that the US would emerge with a new global network of military bases stretching from the Arctic to the Cape, the Atlantic to the Pacific. In 1943–1944 'military planners devised elaborate plans for an overseas base system [which] presupposed American hegemony over the Atlantic and Pacific oceans'.[19] These bases, which prefigured the worldwide Cold War military archipelago, were the unbounded, expanding edges of the United States' new 'strategic frontiers' and delimited a vast new area of *de facto* American sovereignty. They were/are the territorial nodes of the American post-war empire. Their security function was spelled out by Lippmann in 1943: 'The strategic defenses of the United States extend across both oceans and to all the trans-oceanic lands from which an attack by sea or by air can be launched... American security at sea has always extended to the coast line of Europe, Africa and Asia. In the new age of air power, it extends beyond the coast lines to the lands.'[20] But the more significant and far-reaching imperial functions of the military structure became apparent during the Cold War: policing world resource flows, guaranteeing access to raw materials, curbing revolution in colonial and post-colonial areas and limiting the autonomy of subordinate allied states – in short, securing America's new globalised position, in Harry Truman's words, as 'the greatest and most powerful nation in the world'.[21]

THE TRIPARTITE IMPERIAL SYSTEM

Given the conditions under which it emerged, *Pax Americana* necessarily differed in significant respects from the nineteenth-century European-centred imperial order. The overriding need to restore the capitalist world economy and the related effort to contain the USSR and inhibit revolution in Europe and the colonial areas made for a 'new kind of global empire', in Susan Strange's formulation, which had no need for extensive territorial commitments. That empire could be achieved 'by a combination of military alliances and a world economy opened up to trade, investment, and information'.[22] While functionally distinct, the security and economic institutions erected in the aftermath of the war became interlaced parts of a single system of power that was consolidated by the Cold War and the strategy of global containment. The existence of a counter-system, hostile to liberal capitalism, gave purpose to American power (the 'evil empire' presupposes a 'benevolent empire') and played important domestic and international functions. Domestically, it unified the power elite behind the strategy of global military supremacy outlined in NSC 68, the foundational 1950 Cold War policy document that advocated permanent mobilisation to attain 'superior overall power'.[23] At the same time, anti-communism and threat-inflation[24] were determining factors in generating popular consent for the large-scale extraction of resources required to sustain permanent mobilisation and the US' expanding international commitments. US military expenditures from 1948 to 1991 totalled $13.1 trillion (1996 dollars), resources that were spent 'as part of an arithmetic of power and world hegemony'.[25] Richard Perle, a prominent organic intellectual of empire, acknowledges that the Soviet Union provided a rationale for permanent mobilisation and international expansion: 'The fear of the Soviet Union...was certainly an animating factor and we would not have voted the budgets we did or supported the activities we did without that. In its absence, we probably would not have expanded into places that we went, in order to contend with and confront the Soviet Union'.[26] At the international level, the Soviet Union acted, in Zbigniew Brzezinski's words, as a 'unifier of the [non-communist] international system' behind the United States.[27]

The economic and political objectives of containment – maintaining the world capitalist economy, policing the international system, curbing revolution and securing leverage over the United States' subordinate allies – were interconnected insofar as securing the *Pax Americana* required the construction not only of regional security structures under US control, but also of an economically and politically sustainable belt of prospering, hence socially stable, capitalist countries around the Soviet Union and the People's Republic of China that would defer to American preferences. Given revolutionary post-war conditions, American economic policy was adjusted to meet these objectives. Rather than the universal free trade regime envisaged by wartime planners, the United States supported the creation of a multilateral system accommodating domestic developmentalism in European and east Asian allied states.

This modified liberalism translated as support for developmental states with pre-existing endogenous roots (the European social state, the neo-mercantilist east Asian developmental state) which were enmeshed in the wider American order. The 'essence of the embedded liberalism compromise', in John Ruggie's well known formulation, was to:

> ...aid the quest for domestic stability without, at the same time, triggering the mutually destructive external consequences that had plagued the interwar period: unlike the economic nationalism of the thirties, it would be multilateral in character. Unlike the liberalism of the gold standard and free trade, its multilateralism would be predicated upon domestic interventionism.[28]

Mixed economies with strong government intervention became the norm within the Atlantic core and in northeast Asia, the new 'strategic frontiers' of American power. At the same time, multilateralism was upheld by the set of institutions created at Bretton Woods (1944), which gave a preponderant say to the United States in the management of the world economy.

The political terms of *Pax Americana* were, however, very far from uniform: there were multiple and unequal jurisdictions in what David Calleo has called the 'Near Empire' and the 'Far Empire' (the 'Near' being western Europe and Japan, the 'Far' being the post-colonial world).[29] That distinction needs to be amended, since the United States in fact established distinct patterns of relations in western Europe, northeast Asia and the rest of the colonial and post-colonial periphery. In Europe, *Pax Americana* rested mostly on pluralist politics and liberal democratic states (even this judgment has to be qualified somewhat since the US supported dictatorships in Spain and Portugal for decades, as well as in Greece in the late 1960s and early 1970s, and sustained one-party rule in Italy until the end of the Cold War). In northeast Asia it rested on semi-sovereign authoritarian or semi-democratic developmental states. 'Nations', writes Bruce Cumings referring to the European and northeast Asian jurisdictions, were enmeshed 'in a hierarchy of economic and political preferences whose ideal goal was free trade, open systems and liberal democracy but which also encompassed neo-mercantile states and authoritarian politics'.[30] In the colonial and post-colonial periphery it rested on interventionism and predatory imperial politics.

EUROPE: THE HEGEMONIC FRONTIER

In northern Europe, the United States acted as a world hegemonic state, in the Gramscian sense of the term, that is as the leader of a coalition of states whose ruling elites shared fundamental interests with the US – reviving the liberal economy, attenuating class struggle and containing the Soviet Union – and which, in the main, recognised the US as a legitimate source of authority. The domestic legitimacy of these elites was established through the social compact between the state, capital and labour. The United States upheld or, in the case of the Federal Republic of Germany, helped to construct some liberal-democratic constitutional states, encouraged European economic integration, erected transatlantic security institutions and provided significant resources to back up the effort. Whether or not the 1948–1952 Marshall Plan was the primary cause of Europe's rapid economic recovery rather than endogenous factors, it was crucial in leading 'Western Europe progressively toward trade liberalization and exchange convertibility'.[31] Moreover, US financial assistance to Europe in the form of grants and loans did not terminate with the Marshall Plan: from 1948 to 1960, western Europe received more than half of total US worldwide aid, $43 billion out of a total of $84 billion, of which 67.7 per cent was for non-military purposes.

The central strategic importance attributed by the United States to the Atlantic core and northeast Asia, and conversely the near complete indifference to economic development elsewhere, notably in Latin America and sub-Saharan Africa, is manifest in the asymmetry of aid flows. US public financial flows to Europe were more than double the aid provided to east Asian Cold War allies during the same period ($18.9 billion), three times the volume of flows to the Middle East and south Asia ($13.4 billion), ten times the flows directed to Latin America ($4.4 billion) and 50 times the aid to sub-Saharan Africa ($822 million).[32] These public flows were complemented by private capital flows that grew at an accelerating pace along with Europe's economic recovery: American-sourced direct foreign investment in European manufacturing rose from $932 million in 1950 to $8.8 billion in 1966, or 40.3 per cent of total US foreign direct investment at the time.[33] These flows generated an integrated transatlantic economy: US investment, public and private, stimulated investment and consumption in Europe, which in turn generated outlets for American industry and finance. Western Europe became enmeshed in the increasingly internationalised

American economy. By the mid 1960s, US multinational companies accounted for a large, sometimes dominant, share of west European industrial output in most manufacturing sectors.[34]

Webs of economic interdependence were complemented by the transatlantic security system which gave the US ultimate authority over war and peace. Until France developed its own autonomous nuclear arsenal and then withdrew from NATO's military command in 1966, Washington had exclusive authority over the use of nuclear weapons. NATO provided the United States with a legal framework for the network of sovereign bases it established throughout Europe and which gave the United States leverage over allied security and military policies. Seymour Melman emphasises that the 'US general-purpose forces emplaced in Western Europe and Japan are there on behalf of US political objectives and not primarily for the military defense of these lands'.[35] As part of the new Cold War division of labour, the United States gave a role, if not an effective say, to the still standing but much diminished European imperial states in regional spheres of global system management. As a Cold War proxy, France received significant American financial and military aid during its colonial war in Indochina until defeat at Dien Bien Phu in 1954. Though its aims often clashed with those of the United States in North Africa,[36] France also became a regional *gendarme* in sub-Saharan Africa. Great Britain, which had 'abdicated from the Middle East [in 1947] with obvious implications as to their successor', in navy Secretary James Forrestal's famous words, was accorded a junior partner role, sometimes acting jointly with the United States to suppress nationalist movements and to secure control of strategic raw materials. The two policies were co-extensive, exemplified in the 1953 *coup d'état* against the nationalist Mossadegh government in Iran, the reverberations of which are still being felt today.

Walking a Tightrope

At the same time the United States set boundaries to the sovereign action of the declining European imperial states. Both the United Kingdom and France were shown the precise outer limits of their post-war autonomy during the 1956 Suez crisis when the Eisenhower administration used public diplomacy[37] and coercive economic diplomacy (selling sterling and threatening to withhold vital oil shipments to Britain) to force the Anglo-French-Israeli expeditionary forces to withdraw.[38] The Suez crisis, as William

Roger Louis and Ronald Robinson point out, is a 'touchstone of the enquiry into the nature of post-war imperial power'.[39] It revealed the depth of the disparity of power between Europe and the United States. While not pushing aggressively for decolonisation, indeed sustaining the European empires in revolutionary east Asia and in Africa, the United States engaged some nationalist forces in some European colonies, as they had during the war. Washington established informal ties with the Algerian National Liberation Front, thereby giving it implicit recognition.[40] Like the Roosevelt administration, which had pressed the European imperial powers politically to liberalise their empires, but had no 'idea of urging an immediate grant of independence to peoples not fully prepared for it',[41] the Eisenhower administration attempted to balance its Cold War commitment to the imperial states of the Atlantic Alliance and its effort to co-opt nationalism in the colonial or formerly colonial countries, powerfully expressed in the 1955 Bandung Conference of Non-Aligned countries.

Speaking before the US National Security Council in 1956 John Foster Dulles said that the United States 'has been walking a tightrope between the effort to maintain our old and valued relations with our British and French allies on the one hand, and on the other trying to assure ourselves of the friendship and understanding of the newly independent countries who have escaped from colonialism'.[42] Though it did not hesitate to intervene coercively when its own interests were perceived as being directly at stake (Iran, Guatemala, etc.), the United States, as Eisenhower put it, could not condone '*extreme* colonialism'[43] [author's emphasis], for fear that it would stimulate revolutionary social forces, pit the United States against the rising tide of Third World nationalism and favour the Soviet Union. Eisenhower believed that the European colonial systems were ultimately doomed and thought that the colonial powers would be wise to 'transform a necessity into a virtue' by insisting on their commitment to independence within 25 years: 'by that time everyone of these peoples should have attained the intellectual and economic capacity to serve their own needs. My own belief is that their experience would be much like ours with Puerto Rico – in most cases, faced with such prospects of responsibilities and increased costs, these peoples would insist upon retaining their connections with the mother country'.[44] In September 1956, Eisenhower warned British Prime Minister Anthony Eden against military action in the following terms: 'The peoples of the Near East and of North Africa and, to some extent, of all of Asia and all of Africa, would be consolidated against the West to a degree which, I fear, could not be overcome in a generation and, perhaps, not even in a century particularly having in mind the capacity of the Russians to make mischief'.[45] When the Suez expedition was nonetheless launched against US advice, Washington reacted severely. Territorialised imperialism and 'extreme colonialism' had no place in the new global American order. What mattered was the maintenance of American imperial power and authority. But American attitudes were ambiguous. In an editorial published in 1958, Henry Luce's *Time Magazine* endorsed colonialism:

> No US administration has ever found a means of capitalizing on its anti-colonialism in Asia and Africa without bitterly antagonizing the colonial powers of Europe. Overriding all others is the new fact that leadership of the free world has thrust upon the US responsibilities and commitments that neither Roosevelt nor Wilson ever confronted. Ten years ago most US citizens could share the traditional American concept of colonialism as unrelieved oppression and exploitation. Today's US leaders are aware that colonialism has often been an instrument of progress.[46]

A Hierarchical Interstate System

After Suez, the United Kingdom and France sought to restore their shaken authority and obtain a greater say in world politics by respectively aligning with and separating from the United States. Hoping to influence American decision-making from the inside, and thereby regaining some of its lost autonomy, the United Kingdom adapted its foreign policy after 1956 to American preferences, fulfilling Clement Attlee's 1948 forecast that 'the British Isles [would henceforth have to be considered] as an easterly extension of a strategic arc the centre of which is the American continent'. After 1956, the 'special relationship' became a faint and, as is plainly apparent today, largely illusory substitute for empire. The Gaullist state pursued the same general aim – recovering France's world influence *after empire* – by adopting the opposite policy, that is, by contesting American hegemony. De Gaulle sought to re-invent a world role for France by playing on the contradictions of the two superpowers, working towards a semi-autonomous Europe under French leadership and appealing to post-colonial nationalism in the name of a French 'Third Way'. Designed to restore their positions at least in part, both strategies failed to produce the desired effects in the long run. The United Kingdom never gained decisive influence over US policy-making. France, for its part, never achieved predominant leadership in continental Europe and lost its ability to dance between the blocs when the Soviet Union collapsed in 1991. Meanwhile, the United States' wartime foes, Germany and Italy, semi-sovereign states in the Atlantic system, were given powerful economic and security incentives to stay within the American fold. US control was much more direct than in France or Britain. Though Italy was nominally sovereign, it was, like Germany, thoroughly penetrated by the United States' military and intelligence apparatus. The German pre-war position as the industrial workshop of continental Europe was quickly restored. Like Japan, though in a more liberal environment, it was encouraged to accumulate wealth, not power.

On the whole, the United States constructed a hierarchical interstate system in which, for most European states most of the time, the benefits of hegemony outweighed the costs measured in their loss of political autonomy. The United States set the agenda and became the dominant actor in European security, as well as an important and controversial actor in European domestic politics.[47] Political rivalries and economic competition were muted by common Cold War security interests. The outcome, a system of hegemonic authority that preserved the fiction of equality under conditions of asymmetry, proved lasting during the Cold War and beyond. At elite level, wealth accumulation and interpenetrated economic interests provided the glue that held the Atlantic system together. Over time, institutionalised cooperation helped to forge a networked transatlantic ruling class with converging interests and worldviews. At societal level, the Atlantic system was consolidated and legitimated by the Keynesian compromise that proved largely successful in curbing class conflict. The 'social state' underpinned liberal democratic political norms that legitimised the American hegemonic order. Horizontal intra-European cooperation, coordination and integration was not inhibited but encouraged by the United States.

AUTHORITARIAN MERCANTILISM: THE EAST ASIAN FRONTIER

In east Asia, the United States pursued analogous strategic aims but implemented them in radically different ways. In a 1948 policy memorandum, George Kennan suggested that in the Far East the United States should 'cease to talk about vague and unreal objectives such as human rights, the raising of the living standards, and democratization'. Instead, it should 'deal in straight power concepts' and seek to 'maintain disparity':

> We have about 50 percent of the world's wealth but only 6.3 percent of its population. This disparity is particularly great between ourselves and the peoples of Asia. In this situation, we cannot fail to be the object of envy and resentment. Our real task in the coming period is to devise a pattern of relationships which will permit us to maintain this position of disparity without positive detriment to our national security. To do so, we will have to dispense with all sentimentality and daydreaming; and our attention will have to be concentrated everywhere on our immediate national objectives. We need not deceive ourselves that we can afford today the luxury of altruism and world-benefaction.[48]

The imperial pattern of relationships that developed in east Asia was based on a vision of 'Asians as part of an alien, and in important ways, inferior community'.[49] An extraordinarily telling example of this racialised attitude is the statement made by Paul Nitze after the war, that 'the emotional effect of seeing what happened in Darmstadt was greater, in a surprising way, than it was in Hiroshima and Nagasaki'.[50] The transpacific alliance system differed from the transatlantic hegemonic system in three crucial respects.

'Unfit For Democracy'

First, on the political level, *Pax Americana* in east Asia was consistently illiberal. In contrast with Europe, where the exercise of hegemony was generally bound with pluralism and liberal democracy, in east Asia the United States instituted alliances that rested on authoritarian or, in Japan's case, formally democratic developmental states (Bruce Cumings defines them as 'Bureaucratic-Authoritarian Industrializing Regimes') inextricably intertwined with and subordinate to the American national security state. Pre-war and immediate post-war plans to destroy the foundations of Japanese militarism were rapidly discarded and were superseded by a security policy centred on the restoration of Japanese industry as part of the global containment project. Senior American officials considered Japan, and *a fortiori* other east Asian states, as unfit for democracy: 'I am certain', said Acting Secretary of State Joseph C. Grew in 1945, 'that we could not graft our type of a democracy on Japan because I know very well they are not fitted for it and that it could not possibly work'.[51] Starting in 1947, the US reversed policies 'regarding the purge program, decartelization, reparations of equipment, limits on industry, and promotion of the rights of organized labor'.[52] After 1948, Japan was perceived, writes Bruce Cumings, as an 'American defined economic animal' within the American security system. According to a 1949 document of the State Department's Policy Planning Staff, Japan would be reconstructed and reshaped to become an 'American satellite…without an identity of its own'.[53] While formally a constitutional democracy, from the end of the American occupation in 1952 until 2007 the country has been ruled by a one-party state. Japan's experience was far more benign that that of South Korea or Taiwan, the management of which the United States took over after Japan's defeat. Until the end of the Cold War both were ruled by militarised authoritarian regimes that kept 'civil society in the tight grip of the state'.[54] In southeast Asia, as in Latin America, the United States relied on predatory military dictators and/or autocrats (General Suharto in Indonesia, the series of military governments in South Vietnam and Thailand, Ferdinand Marcos in the Philippines, Lee Kwan Yew in Singapore, etc.), many of whom used ferocious violence to suppress domestic opposition from the left. Like in northeast Asia, democratisation occurred only in the very late phases of the Cold War or in the post-Cold War, with mixed results.

Single Market Dependency

Second, unlike the transatlantic economic system, the Cold War political economy in capitalist east Asia was structured around bilateral relations with Washington rather than horizontal integration. The east Asian countries, former enemies reluctantly bound together through their alliance with Washington, communicated 'with each other through the United States'.[55] In the early years of the Cold War, the State Department envisaged east Asia's integration into the world multilateral system: a 'great crescent' of containment stretching from Japan in the Far East through southeast Asia and south Asia to the Gulf that would have tied all of the key raw materials production zones to the centre and sub-centres of capitalism. This was seen as crucial for containment in Asia but also for the revival of the economies of Europe. The Economic Recovery in Occupied Areas (EROA) was aimed to be 'tightly meshed' with the European Recovery Program (ERP) 'through the medium of the

European colonies in the Far East'.[56] In the first decades of the Cold War, however, the capitalist east Asian economies were inserted not in the multilateral world trading system but in exclusive bilateral trade relationships with the United States. As part of its compact with east Asian dependent states in which the latter traded off their political autonomy for access to the American market, the United States encouraged bilateralism and export-led industrialisation by keeping its market open to east Asian commodities and industrial products. This stimulated growth but also generated a single-market dependency that acted as a constant and major constraint on autonomy. Throughout the Cold War, the five major east Asian capitalist economies (Japan, South Korea, Taiwan, Hong Kong and Singapore) were, in Robert Wade's words, 'addicted to the American market'.[57] Writing in the early 1990s, Meredith Woo-Cumings noted that despite their growing financial autonomy, the American market still 'absorbed more than one third of all Japan's exports, about forty percent of South Korea's exports, and forty four percent of Taiwan's exports'. She added: 'For all the East Asian economies…the United States still looks like the only game in town, and this is where the United States has wielded unilateral influence, making and breaking the essential fabric of political economy in the region'.[58] As we shall see in Chapter 7, deepening regional integration since the mid 1990s and China's emergence as a pole of the new regional political economy is gradually altering this configuration: east Asia's export dependency on the American market has lessened over the past decade but still remains an important, if diminishing, constraint.

War Making and State Building

Third, America's Far Eastern 'strategic frontier' was almost constantly at war. In Asia, the Cold War was anything but cold: though statistics vary according to different sources, the death toll in post-1945 east Asian interstate wars and civil wars in which the United States was overtly or covertly involved is appalling. Anywhere from 2.5 million to 3.5 million people, military and civilian, died during the Korean War (1950–1953), 1 million in North Korea alone; 2 to 3 million during the Vietnam War (1963–1975); many hundreds of thousands, possibly as many as 1 million during the Indonesia civil war (the 1965 overthrow of President Sukarno and the subsequent liquidation of the Communist Party by the Indonesian Armed Forces led by General Suharto); 200,000 to 300,000 during Indonesia's invasion of East Timor in 1975 which was sanctioned by the United States and tens of thousands in the suppression of insurgencies in Thailand and the Philippines. One might add the millions who died in Cambodia at the hands of the Khmer Rouge, a genocidal regime that received tacit diplomatic support from the United States after 1975 as a 'counterweight to North Vietnam'.[59] Total casualties during the Cold War in east Asia are thus equivalent to the human cost of the First World War. Moreover, the violence was indiscriminate: Walter Russell Mead points out that the 'ratio of civilian to combat deaths' in Korea and Vietnam surpassed 'the ratio observed in Germany's eastern theatre of operations during World War II'. He concludes that the US 'is the most dangerous military power in the history of the world'.[60] The point is not to apportion blame for the origins of Cold War conflict in east Asia, a subject beyond the scope of this enquiry, but to highlight the sharp contrast between the United States' action in its Asian and European post-war 'frontiers'.

War-making, under American auspices, shaped the northeast Asian developmental state. For Japan, the Korean war was a 'gift of the gods' in the oft-quoted words of then Prime Minister Shigeru Yoshida. It fuelled Japan's economic take-off in the 1950s, American demand creating favourable conditions for the mobilisation of endogenous productive capabilities.[61] Likewise, the Vietnam War stimulated the South Korean economy's rapid growth and indus-trialisation in the 1960s and 1970s. Ranked 99th in World Bank per capita GDP country rankings in 1962, South Korea became a platform of American investment (as well as a source of manpower for the battles in the jungles and rice paddies of Vietnam). By 1975, it was ranked 61 and per capita GDP had been multiplied by three – an escape from the 'Third World' made possible by forced-paced industrialisation under a militarised neo-mercantilist state. The price paid for this successful rush into modernity was a decades-long crushing of the democratic aspirations of civil society.

DISCIPLINING THE FAR EMPIRE

These particular developmental circumstances, linked to the creation of a Cold War political economy in northeast Asia (contradicting cultural or free market accounts of east Asia's 'economic miracle'),[62] were not to be found elsewhere in post-colonial areas of lesser economic or strategic interest. There, war and/or authoritarian-ism with unbalanced or minimal development were the Cold War norm. Allied states in southeast Asia such as the Philippines, a colony of the United States until 1946, or in the Middle East, such as Jordan and Egypt after Nasser, received military and political support but very little in the way of development. In both regions, the United States consistently sustained authoritarian regimes and local rentier and oligarchic elites. The same was the case in the Caribbean and South America where the United States supported predatory dictatorial regimes and local elites who confiscated and concentrated wealth to an extraordinary degree. More generally, American overt and covert interventions to check social transformation, secure strategic raw materials or sustain the 'credibility' of US power, or all three, caused significant disruptions in post-colonial societies. (The same argument can of course be made of Soviet interventions though they were fewer than those of the US.) The long and dreary list, over 50 major interventions,[63] many of them lasting for years, need not be detailed here. But even a cursory glance shows that from the early 1950s until today, the United States has either been at war, supporting war-making or sustaining predatory states almost constantly in one or another part of the 'Far Empire': the Philippines, 1948–1954; Iran, 1953; Guatemala, 1954; Indonesia, 1955–1975; Congo/Zaire 1960–1965; Cuba, 1961; Brazil, 1960s; Vietnam, Laos and Cambodia, 1963–1975; Chile, 1973; Angola, 1975–1992; Nicaragua, 1980s; Grenada, 1983; Panama, 1989–1990; Afghanistan, 1980–1988; Iran–Iraq war, 1980–1988; Iraq, 1990–1991…). Over the past three decades, the Gulf region, which has come to play a functional role as an economic keystone of empire analogous to the one India played for the British Empire, has become the major focus of American military operations. Following the pattern of ever-rising American external energy dependency there has been a continuous escalation of commitments, culminating in the invasion of Iraq in 2003.[64] To cite an American academic who in the late 1960s imagined the United States as a bigger and better Roman empire, these 'routine imperial wars'[65] or interventions fought 'at the remote frontier of empire' were in fact dictated less by anti-communism than by 'the concern for upholding minimum world order globally while raising issues of virtually direct rule locally'.[66]

The Dual Face of Empire

The differential assertion of American authority in Europe and the plural post-colonial worlds reveal the colonial archaeology of the *Pax Americana*. At best, the post-war American power elite was convinced that non-western peoples were unprepared and unfit for self-rule. Deeply embedded assumptions about cultural hierarchy and race translated into paternalistic policies predicated on the idea that non-western societies had to go through decades of tutelage and 'modernisation'. This was manifest, for instance, in the United States' dealings with democratic India after independence, when the State Department reproduced the racially tinged cultural gaze and stereotypes of the British.[67] As one of Eisenhower's aides, exasperated over India's policy of non-alignment, put it: 'The Western world has somewhat more experience with the operation of war, peace and parliamentary procedures than the swirling mass of emotionally super-charged Africans, and Asiatics and Arabs that outnumber us'.[68] At worst, the United States used extraordinary violence to impose its will and preferences when American imperial interests were challenged in the colonial or post-colonial periphery. Like the liberal British empire, which, in J.R. Seeley's well-known words, supported 'despotism in Asia and democracy in Australia' (once cleared of its indigenous peoples),[69] the American empire sustained authoritarian regimes and oligarchical rule in the 'Third World' and democracy in northwestern Europe. In the former world regions, the 'Cold' War warped development pathways, bred local militarization[70] and altered social systems. In so doing, the American empire, like all earlier empires, sets social forces into motion which challenge and undermine imperial order and which have 'modernising' or 'anti-modernising' and national or transnational agendas depending on their specific cultural and political histories.

Since American authors and political actors often use Rome as a mirror, it is heuristically useful to recall that Roman imperialism too had a dual face. Rome expanded quite differently in the Hellenised East and along the 'barbarian' frontier. The classicist Ernst Badian points out that Rome adapted its 'urge for domination'. In the Hellenistic East it established 'hegemonial' control 'in a cautious and, on the whole fairly civilized way, without violence…[or] direct control and major wars, abandoning annexation [in favour of] subordination by treaty'. Elsewhere, wars of conquest were waged 'against the barbarians' and 'policy was openly brutal and aggressive'. Badian accounts for this 'puzzling contradiction of Roman policy' by noting that the Hellenised provinces were peopled by 'cultural equals or superiors' and were thus areas where Rome could avoid 'burdensome and inconvenient commitments'.[71] Closer to our times, Britain avoided annexation when it could, for instance in the Gulf and the Middle East where, 'chary of taking on the management of more Orientals' after the first Indian War of Independence in 1857, it sought instead to 'create friendly buffer states' and local clients rather than direct dependencies.[72] To paraphrase Gallagher and Robinson, British policy was informal empire where possible, formal empire where necessary. In sum, like *Pax Britannica*, which favoured liberalism and peace in the core and despotism in the periphery, *Pax Americana* has not been predominantly liberal and was/is only selectively democratic. While it eschewed territorialised imperialism in favour of informal empire and indirect rule, the United States established a worldwide imperial system with different patterns of relations in Europe, northeast Asia and the 'Third World'. The system cannot properly be described as world-hegemonic. To paraphrase Peter Cain's and Anthony Hopkins' apposite remark on the British empire, *Pax Americana* has been predatory and developmental, liberal and authoritarian at different times and in different places. During the Cold War it was all of these, often at the same time, in different places.

The following chapter discusses the post-Cold War transition. It focuses on the military and monetary structures of *Pax Americana* and the way in which they were used to assert US 'primacy' during and after the Cold War. The new configuration of world politics generated different options, with various combinations of actors engaging in different forms of international intervention and imperial policies.

5
Power and Plenty in the Post-Cold War

We remain uniquely positioned, not only geographically, but strategically, politically and economically at the center...and that is where we must stay.

Senator Jesse Helms, 1996[1]

Pax Americana has rested on overlapping international social structures: the worldwide security structure and the economic and monetary structures of the post-1945 world capitalist economy. While functionally distinct, these structures were/are interlaced parts of an imperial system that has ensured the United States' continuing, though not unchallenged, dominance of the international system. As we shall see in this chapter, these structures are a constraint inhibiting change at the international level, limiting the autonomy of states enmeshed in the imperial or the hegemonic systems. Hence the fact that the centrifugal economic movements starting in the 1960s did not lead to a de-concentration of power or an attenuation of control. In this chapter I re-examine the debate on 'hegemonic decline' and the post-Cold War transition, analysing the mechanisms that, until very recently, have inhibited an effective diffusion of power. The imperial system is now fraying as a result of novel centrifugal forces – the rise of relatively autonomous state actors not historically enmeshed in the security structures of *Pax Americana*, such as China, deepening economic regionalisation in east Asia and Latin America, the slowly emerging role of the euro as an international reserve currency and the multifaceted crisis of American power. Examined further in Chapter 7, these are very recent transformations, the systemic effects of which will have to be assessed over time.

THE IMPERIUM BELLICUM AMERICANUM[2]

The pivotal role of the *Imperium Bellicum Americanum* in the reproduction of American world power has become fully apparent since the end of the Cold War. Notwithstanding the absence of a strategic rival comparable to the Soviet Union, the internationalised American security structure has remained in place. Since 2000 it has been significantly expanded. On average, during the Cold War one-quarter of the US armed forces were permanently deployed, ashore and afloat, in Europe, the Far East, the Near East and the Mediterranean, Latin America and the Pacific (during the Korean and Vietnam wars this rose to 30 per cent). It fell to 15 per cent in 1995, with 238,064 defence personnel deployed outside of the US and US territories, rising in 1999 to 18 per cent. Today, as a result of the Iraq and Afghanistan wars, it has risen to 30 per cent once again (see Figure 5.1) with 510,927 personnel deployed worldwide.[3] US defence spending fell in absolute terms in the 1990s, from $398.9 billion in 1989 to $282.4 billion in 1998 (in constant 2000 dollars), not far below the Cold War average ($319 billion) (see Table 6.1). Nevertheless, the US *share of world defence spending* rose considerably in the 1990s, from 28.4 per cent in 1984, during the Reagan build-up, to 34 per cent a decade later due to the precipitous decline of expenditures in the rest of the world (see Table 5.1). NATO expansion, still ongoing, simultaneously extended the reach of the American alliance system in Central and Eastern Europe.

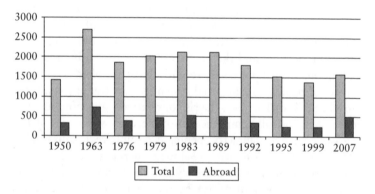

Figure 5.1 US Military Personnel (thousands)

Source: Derived from Statistical Tables US Department of Defense, 'Active Duty Military Personnel Strengths by Regional Area and by Country', Department of Defense, Washington, D.C.

The expansion of the security structure since 2001 has, in the words of an influential American defence theorist, transformed the US into a 'military Leviathan' whose primary global function, as 'system administrator of globalization', is to police the world political economy and safeguard 'the core' by 'exporting security' to discipline 'the gap' – the unruly or unsettled parts of the post-colonial periphery (so called rogue states, failed states, or non-state enemies of the American-*cum*-western world order).[4] The United States today accounts for nearly half of world defence spending. The NATO countries, the United States included, account for nearly 70 per cent. When non-NATO, US allies or 'friendly' states are added, the total reaches 85 per cent.[5] Military expansion has occurred in the absence of state actors capable of, or willing to, challenge American global predominance. For reasons I explore in Chapter 7, the People's Republic of China (PRC) is neither willing nor yet able to challenge the United States' post-1945 strategic position in east Asia, much less its global strategic role. Likewise, while Russia has recently defied the United States in the Caucasus, it is not about to restore its pre-1991 place as a global actor. While Russia's economy has recovered from the depression of the 1990s, its gross domestic product, in purchasing power parity, is today equivalent to France's. As far as smaller and weaker states are concerned, the handful of 'potential threat states', in the US' nomenclature, are hardly in a position to upset the basic structures of world order. The same applies to non-state actors, however much damage they may cause. Moreover, large conventional military capabilities are not suited to dealing with covert, decentralised transnational networks, and indeed do not provide security against 'asymmetric warfare'.

The *Raison d'être* of the Security Structure

The inescapable conclusion, then, is that the security structure is not designed to provide security. Rather, its *raison d'être* is, indeed has always been, independent of any of the threats, real or supposed, that it ostensibly was/is designed to deter or fight. As US officials have at times quite frankly acknowledged, its function is to create frameworks and generate outcomes that promote American interests. Commenting on the post-Cold War defence strategy of the George H.W. Bush administration, elaborated in the aftermath of the 1991 Gulf War, the then US Deputy Assistant Secretary of Defense for Special Operations and Low Intensity Conflict remarked: 'The new strategy is less concerned with a specific threat than with giving the US the military capabilities with which to move the post Cold War international order in a favorable direction'.[6]

This does not mean that there are no post-Cold War threats and challenges as far as the United States is concerned, or that these are always contrived. Some clearly are, such as Iraq in 2001–2003.

Many, however, are generated by the imperial system itself: they emerge as direct or indirect responses to the historical impacts of empire in varying local cultural and political contexts (the 1979 Iranian revolution, as I have already pointed out, and the emergence of the Taliban state in Afghanistan, are paradigmatic instances of challenges that emerge as a consequence of earlier imperial actions or pressures). Following the classical imperial pattern, expanding commitments generate new threats and challenges, which in turn generate new commitments. As a structure of imperial order rather than security or defence, the United States' internationalised security apparatus performs an array of global functions of discipline and control – maintaining favourable regional balances, keeping allies in check, curbing challenges, securing unhindered access to resources – designed not to answer any specific menace but to inhibit centrifugal change and to obtain desired international outcomes, i.e. to secure American primacy.[7] The fact that it cannot always guarantee such outcomes does not alter its basic function.

Table 5.1 US Defence Spending as a Share of World Spending (%)

	1986	1994	2007
USA	28.2	34.3	45.00
Non-NATO World	56.0	44.0	32.24
NATO + other allies*			84.56
PTS**	42.4	19.8	Insignificant**

Adapted from Project on Defense Alternatives (PDA figures 1986 and 1994), Washington, D.C., available at www.comw.org/pda/; Stockholm International Peace Research Institute (SIPRI), SIPRI Military Expenditure Database and SIPRI Yearbook 2008, available at http://yearbook2008.sipri.org/.

* 'Other allies' in my nomenclature refers to friendly states that have close or cooperative security ties with the US. For the list selected by the author, see endnote.[8]
** PTS (Potential Threat States) refers to states that the US designated or designates as potential threats. In 1986, this included the Soviet Union, the Warsaw Pact countries, China and so-called 'rogue states' or alleged 'state sponsors of terrorism'. In 2007, the US Department of State listed five 'state sponsors of terrorism': Cuba, Iran, North Korea, Sudan, and Syria. North Korea was taken off the list in 2008. The four remaining countries account for a tiny share of world defence spending.[9] Russia and the PRC, neither of which are in fact 'threats', accounted for 7.7 per cent of world defence expenditures in 2007.

From 2001, the security structure became the blunt instrument of a new effort of formal imperial expansion, designed not to maintain the international status quo but to upset it. The invasion of Iraq was hardly a 'routine imperial war', much less an imperial police action. Rather, it was the result of the decision by a coalition of nationalist and internationalist expansionists to make use of the United States' overwhelming post-Cold War dominance of the international security structure to reshape the international system and, in their own words, to establish a global empire. This extraordinary ambition, I argue below, was a potential though not a necessary outcome of the post-1991 asymmetry of power, which generated the conditions of its possibility. Before turning to this, I step back and examine the primary function played by the security structure and its relationship with the monetary structure during the latter part of the Cold War: averting the diffusion of power that was widely, if erroneously, considered unavoidable in the 1970s and 1980s. The discussion provides necessary background to the post-Cold War transition and the new phase of imperial expansionism that began in 2001.

AVERTING DECLINE

There was a broad consensus in the 1970s and 1980s among American scholars and policy-makers that the United States, after having briefly enjoyed a position of global pre-eminence, had entered a period of decline. Declinism cut across the spectrum of social scientific opinion and became an issue of intense public debate. Notwithstanding varying theoretical perspectives and quite different normative concerns, neo-realists, neo-liberals and world systems theorists concurred that the United States was losing or indeed had lost its centrality in and its control of the international system.[10] 'Hegemonic decline' was identified at multiple levels. In the security sphere, it was evidenced by the Soviet Union's attainment of nuclear parity and the US' defeat in Vietnam (1973–1975). In the economic and financial spheres, it was evidenced by Europe and Japan's rising position in the world economy, the dollar crisis of the late 1960s and early 1970s, the breakdown of the Bretton Woods fixed exchange rate system (1971–1973) and the oil price hikes of 1973 decided by the Organization of the Petroleum Exporting Countries (OPEC). The fact that the oil price increases had been engineered by Saudi Arabia and Iran, the latter still an American client state, highlighted the extent of the United States' loss of control, further evidenced by Saudi participation in the 1973 oil embargo, and even more spectacularly by the 1979 Iranian revolution, a reversal more significant than Vietnam in terms of its long-term outcomes.[11] At the same time, a broader ideological challenge to the liberal economic foundations of the

Pax Americana had emerged in the 'Far Empire': the Non-Aligned countries' call for a New International Economic Order (NIEO), which had revolutionary implications since it aimed fundamentally to restructure the post-war international economic order.[12]

American perceptions of 'ruin and retreat'[13] were amplified by the sharp domestic economic crisis of the 1970s: high and lasting inflation, generated by financing the deficit incurred during the Vietnam War; the depreciation of the dollar and the oil price rises of 1973 (the annual average of the Consumer Price Index was 7.7 per cent between 1969 and 1981); weak growth and rising mass unemployment (average annual unemployment rose from 5.4 per cent in the first years of the decade to 7.9 per cent between 1974 and 1979). The reversal after 1971 of the merchandise trade balance, which had been positive since 1894, and the reversal in the early 1980s of the US' post-1918 position as the world's creditor signalled a shift in the balance of world economic power. By the early 1980s, the consensus view inside and outside the academy was that the 'American Century' had lasted a mere two decades.[14] In an emblematic statement, Robert Gilpin asserted in 1981 that 'power is diffusing at an unprecedented rate to a plurality of powers... The relative decline of American power could well signify a change from the America-centered global system to a more nearly equal bipolar system, and, perhaps eventually, a multipolar global system'. Centrifugal movement, in his view, was risk-laden, since 'the redistribution of military power in favor of Russia as the rising state in the international system and the possibility of further redistributions of power to other states pose serious threats to the stability of the system'.[15]

In spite of mounting evidence of a simultaneous systemic Soviet crisis,[16] the failure of the Non-Aligned states to obtain substantive modifications in the international economic order and persisting European and Japanese impotence in the face of unilateral American monetary and trade decisions, declinism did not subside in the latter part of the decade. In 1987, Paul Kennedy published a broad historical survey of imperial rises and falls in which he diagnosed American 'imperial overstretch', that is a mismatch between contracting economic resources and global imperial commitments:

> It has been a common dilemma facing previous 'number one' countries that even as their relative economic strength is ebbing, the growing foreign challenges to their position have compelled them to allocate more and more of their resources into the military

sector...In the largest sense of all, therefore, the only answer to the question...of whether the United States can preserve its existing position is 'no'.[17]

Two years later, echoing Robert Gilpin's 1981 assessment, John Ikenberry wrote: 'The historically unprecedented resources and capabilities that stood behind the American Century have given way to a remarkable and rapid redistribution of international wealth and power'.[18] (Highlighting the time bound character of social scientific judgments, these two authors argued in 2002–2003 that, thanks to its unrivalled control of the international security structure, the United States dominates the international system to a historically unprecedented degree. This reversal is examined in the next chapter as symptomatic of a wider ideational shift in the post-Cold War.)

As the Soviet Union faded in the late 1980s, Japan became the prime focus of American concerns. A slew of alarmist articles, books and reports portrayed Japan as surging ahead of the United States, whose 'technological leadership and international [manufacturing] competitiveness [was portrayed] as imperilled and probably on the decline'.[19] *Made in America: Regaining the Productive Edge*, published by the MIT Commission on Industrial Productivity, which began its work in 1986, identified 'systematic and pervasive' American manufacturing decline not only in rust belt sectors, but also in innovative knowledge-intensive sectors such as pharmaceuticals, computer hardware and software.[20] Summing up the 1980s *Zeitgeist*, Ethan Kapstein writes: 'The future seemed grim. Studies detailing falling productivity, drops in research spending, a lack of innovation, poor quality control, shortages of qualified workers, rising raw material prices, the absence of supporting industrial policies, and myriad other factors that were driving American firms downhill'.[21] At the end of the 1980s, critiques of Japanese neo-mercantilism, many of which contained barely concealed racial subtexts,[22] took on an increasingly hysterical tone. A striking but hardly unique example is the 1989 statement by Lawrence Summers that 'an Asian economic bloc with Japan at its apex is in the making. This raises the possibility that the majority of American people who now feel that Japan is a greater threat to the US than the Soviet Union are right'.[23]

Dissident Voices

During the period there were remarkably few dissident voices.[24] A notable exception was Fernand Braudel's early though unelaborated scepticism over American economic decline. In a series of lectures at Johns Hopkins University in 1977 he argued that 'New York would not succumb to the durable crisis [of capitalism]' and would most likely emerge 'strengthened from the ordeal'.[25] Susan Strange, who humorously dismissed the 'weeping and wailing and wringing of American hands over the fall of the imperial republic as something quite exaggerated', made the most trenchant early critique in 1982. She attributed ubiquitous concerns over decline to American-centric visions that simultaneously overestimated 'America's capacity to remake the whole world in the image of the USA' and understated the real-world operations of American empire: 'In this vision Washington was the center of the system...from which radiated military, monetary, commercial, and technological as well as purely political channels carrying the values of American polity, economy and society...out to the ends of the earth'.[26] American reticence to '[acknowledge] their imperialism' accounted for the sharp contrast between American perceptions and those of the rest of the world: 'The decline of imperial republic', she wrote, is 'not how it looks to us in Europe, in Japan, in Latin America or even in the Middle East'.[27]

Strange reiterated and amplified her critique in the late 1980s. Analysing the United States' 'undiminished' structural power in the security, credit, knowledge and production spheres, she concluded that the 'decline of US hegemony is a myth...In every important respect, the US still has the predominant power to shape frameworks and influence outcomes. This implies it can draw the limits within which others can choose from a restricted list of options, the restrictions being in large part a result of US decisions'.[28] Moreover, as Stephen Gill pointed out contemporaneously, since the US shapes the global environment simply by virtue of its position and weight, intentional purpose is not always necessary to generate outcomes: 'Since the United States possesses a unique structural dominance within the global political economy, other nations' potential actions, welfare and prospects may be constrained by or affected by the United States, irrespective of any conscious design by American policy-makers. In other words, the very size and weight of the United States in the international system substantially affects the conditions under which all other states and interests must operate'.[29]

ACTOR DESIGNS AND STRUCTURAL CONSTRAINTS

This is an important observation, suggesting that the United States, by being at the centre of the system, exercises gravitational pull on the rest of the world. Nonetheless, it is hard to ignore the less subtle but recurrent purposeful use of structural power to obtain favourable outcomes. American decisions and actions in the 1970s and 1980s to reverse perceptions of decline and to restore power reflected conscious design. For important sectors of the American power elite, declinism played a useful function as a contra-fulfilling prophecy.[30] Aiming to recover control and restore imperial authority by demonstrating that the United States was 'a power that cannot be abused with impunity',[31] successive governments used as leverage the United States' central position in the world political economy to lift external economic constraints, extract resources from dependent allies and to reinstate American strategic supremacy. Diffusion was effectively inhibited by a series of actions that revealed the structural dimensions of American power. The series of non-cooperative monetary decisions taken by the US in the last two decades of the Cold War and the rearmament of the 1980s showed how various mechanisms of dependence effectively limited the options of states subject to hegemonic or imperial control.

Externalising Adjustment Costs

Starting with the decision of the Nixon administration to end the convertibility of the dollar into gold (1971) and to abandon the fixed exchange rate regime set up at Bretton Woods, the United States used its dominance in finance and security to alter the conditions of operation of the world economy. The unilateral monetary decisions taken in the 1970s and the 1980s transferred the costs of American macroeconomic and financial imbalances to the rest of the world by manipulating the dollar's exchange rate. Having the world's sole reserve currency gave the US the 'exorbitant privilege', in Charles de Gaulle's words, of financing its deficits in its own currency. By ignoring or discarding rules it had itself erected, the US was in effect able to extract resources from security-dependent allies by externalising adjustment costs. John Braithwaite and Peter Drahos write:

> The era of flexible and floating exchange rates that followed the breakdown of the Bretton Woods exchange regime was not really a victory for the principle of national sovereignty as much as a triumph of US financial hegemony…[In hegemonic currency systems] other states are left without any real disciplinary recourse when the hegemon defects from the order.[32]

George Ball makes a similar point about the 'Nixon Doctrine': 'Advertised as a design for shrinking American commitments... [its] objective was to increase America's reach...by increasing our freedom of action through the stripping off of irksome obligations to consult and act collectively'.[33]

The 1971 monetary decision, which left the United States' allies sitting on large depreciated dollar reserves, was merely the first of a series of instances of US actions that altered global market conditions to American gain. In 1973, the US government signed secret accords with the Saudi Arabian authorities to recycle 'petrodollars' through the US banking system to exclusive American advantage.[34] (The acquiescence of Saudi Arabia and other Gulf countries to this scheme was preceded by public threats of the use of force and contingency planning for an invasion of the Gulf and the seizure of oil fields, threats that the British government took extremely seriously. One presumes that the Saudi monarchy took them equally seriously.[35]) This was followed in 1979 by the far more consequential decision to increase US interest rates sharply, a sustained action that redirected world capital flows to the United States (the prime rate peaked in 1981 at 21.5 per cent, eight points above inflation). The last monetary action of this type during the Cold War was the engineered currency realignment of 1985 (the Plaza Accord) which was cooperative only in appearance and led to a sudden sharp appreciation of the Japanese yen, the South Korean won and the Deutschmark.

These swings of monetary policy cannot be simply interpreted as *ad hoc* efforts, influenced by domestic interest groups, to resolve cascading economic and financial dilemmas generated by previous decisions. They were ultimately part of a calculus of world power. In the face of a 'broad systemic and dynamic crisis',[36] the United States abandoned the 'fiction of equality'[37] and of collective decision-making that had made the alliance systems of the *Pax Americana* appear less hierarchical and asymmetrical than in fact they were. If the motive of the 1971 decision was to lift external financial constraints, the central motive of the 1979 monetarist shift was, as its architect Paul Volcker retrospectively acknowledged, to restore American predominance:

> I was certainly worried about the future of the United States in terms of its place in the world...We were the dominant economic power, the dominant military power, the dominant security power. By and large we were in favor of the right things, and [if] we

weren't strong economically, we weren't going to be able to carry out what I saw as reasonable responsibilities in the world.[38]

Giovanni Arrighi emphasises that the 'stunningly successful monetarist counter-revolution...allowed the United States to achieve through financial means what it could not achieve by force of arms – to defeat the USSR in the Cold War and tame the rebellious South'.[39] The re-routing of global financial flows made possible the deficit financing of the military build-up of the late 1970s and early 1980s (American defence expenditures fell slightly between 1975 and 1979 from $262.7 billion to $257.4 billion, but then rose sharply from $267.1 billion to $398.9 billion between 1980 and 1988) and dampened efforts by the Non-Aligned countries to achieve a new international economic order. The two policies were part of a reformulated post-Vietnam power elite consensus on the need, in Richard Falk's words, to 'avoid the impression of decline and geopolitical withdrawal, neutralize the Non-Aligned challenge, and reverse the slide of global hegemony'.[40]

Three Types of Dependency Relations

The United States' ability to change the rules of the game – or to discard them altogether – and, at the same time, the rest of the world's inability to set rules binding on the United States, reflects the various dependency relations established across structures in different parts of the world political economy. Three different types of dependency relations are highlighted below: the conditioning of peripheral economies by core countries emphasised by dependency theory,[41] the security dependence of the European NATO states and other US allies and the single-market dependence of northeast Asian countries.[42]

Post-colonial countries inserted in the capitalist world economy were to varying degrees caged in structures of trade and finance dominated by the US-*cum*-western economies and exhibited the greatest vulnerabilities. Evidenced in the Mexican debt crisis in the early 1980s, as well as the later emerging market crises brought on by capital account liberalisation and volatile globalised capital flows, decisions taken by the United States government, or economic and financial shifts induced by dominant markets, provoked systemic effects over which they had neither voice nor control. The 1979–1983 monetary shock brought Latin American countries, which had contracted large volumes of dollar-denominated debt, to their knees, calling into question regional 'neo-corporatist' developmental strategies.[43] With internationalised economies and single-market dependency on the US, these and other post-colonial countries were faced with an extraordinarily difficult dilemma. If they wished to avoid exogenously driven shocks their only choice was to exit the dominant economic system, with high attendant costs: loss of access to the markets of the advanced industrialised countries. Yet if they remained within the system, they were subject to intense pressure to liberalise and open their economies still further, accentuating their exposure to international markets and hence increasing their vulnerability to future shocks. Indeed, the social and economic adjustment costs of the major emerging market crises of the 1980s and 1990s, all of which derived from this structure of dependence, were borne by post-colonial societies.[44]

Security dependence (in Japan's case coupled with deep single-market trade dependence) acted as a powerful restraint on western Europe and Japan. The alliances were/are instrumentalities of control, keeping American allies firmly enmeshed in the *Pax Americana*. In the words of Stephen Peter Rosen, a leading exponent of American empire, 'NATO, ANZUS and the US–Japan defense agreement are not really alliances among equals...but mechanisms for codifying interstate hierarchy'.[45] With the partial exception of France,[46] Europe was neither willing nor able to challenge the hegemonic order, '[accepting] chronic US payments deficits and a dollar centered international monetary system as yet another aspect of the security umbrella'.[47] Security was never a free international public good. During the first two decades of the Cold War, the European and east Asian allies 'paid' for security through a loss of political autonomy; in the later years they were made to pay more directly, through resource extraction in ways sketched above. Treasury Secretary John Connally, an actor in the 1971 decision to break the gold peg, succinctly made the point when famously telling a visiting European delegation that 'the dollar may be our currency but it's your problem'. In testimony to Congress, Connally justified the break of the gold peg to the balance of payments problem caused by 'net military expenditures abroad' (the Vietnam war and the costs of maintaining the archipelago of US bases in Europe and East Asia) that supposedly served the general western interest.[48] On August 15, 1971, the day the decision was announced, Richard Nixon was even more explicit:

At the end of World War II the economies of the major industrial nations of Europe and Asia were shattered. To help them get on their feet and protect their freedom, the United States has provided over the past 25 years $143 billion in foreign aid... Today, largely with our help, they have regained their vitality. They have become our strong competitors...The time has come for them to bear their fair share of the burden of defending freedom around the world.[49]

Japan's, and *a fortiori* South Korea and Taiwan's, dependence on the United States was/is deeper than Europe's since it combined a lesser degree of political autonomy, a greater security dependence and a constraining single-market dependency. On average, between 1963 and 1999, the North American market absorbed 30.9 per cent of Japanese merchandise exports, but only 8.92 per cent of European exports.[50] From the 1970s on Japan was subjected to intense mercantilist pressure and, in spite of its ever-growing role as a creditor of the United States, could do little but acquiesce to successive *faits accomplis*. 'The implications', François Godement noted in the late 1990s, 'are astonishing. Japan is a major industrial power and the largest source of financial surpluses in the world. But it is not a veritable financial power since it has very little influence on its own currency'.[51] Europe's somewhat greater autonomy manifested itself in the decision of the European Commission, at French and German initiative, to found the European Monetary System in 1979 and create the European Currency Unit, the seed-form of the euro, which came into being 20 years later. Nonetheless, on the whole Europe, like Japan, demonstrated extreme passivity in the face of successive American offensives. As far as the allies were concerned, the non-cooperative economic policies and actions of the United States during the latter part of the Cold War were manifestations of power rather than signs of loss of control.

POST-COLD WAR OPTIONS

The end of the Cold War relaxed the set of constraints bred by the security structure at both international and domestic level. The disintegration of the Soviet Union left the United States with near-monopoly control of the international security structure. But it also radically reduced the importance of traditional security issues and hence the rationale for the global defence structure and the domestic 'National Security State'. In the absence of a

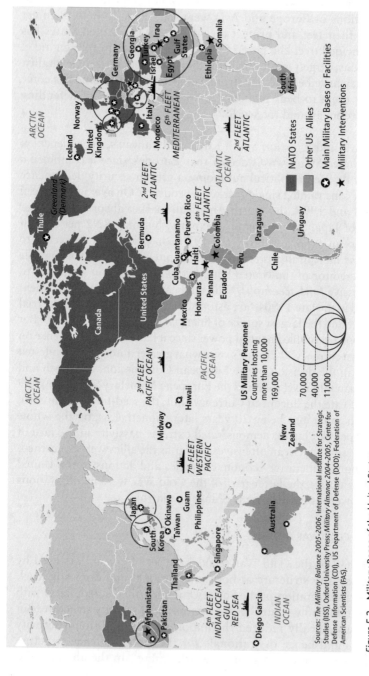

Figure 5.2 Military Bases of the United States
Map by Philippe Rekacewicz

Sources: *The Military Balance 2005-2006*, International Institute for Strategic Studies (IISS), Oxford University Press; *Military Almanac 2004-2005*, Center for Defense Information (CDI), US Department of Defense (DOD); Federation of American Scientists (FAS).

US Military Personnel
Countries hosting
more than 10,000

169,000
70,000
40,000
11,000

NATO States   Other US Allies

⊕ Main Military Bases or Facilities

★ Military Interventions

ARCTIC OCEAN

ARCTIC OCEAN

Thule

Greenland (Denmark)

Canada

United States

Bermuda

2nd FLEET ATLANTIC

ATLANTIC OCEAN

Puerto Rico

4th FLEET ATLANTIC

Cuba Guantanamo

Haiti

Honduras

Mexico

Panama

Ecuador

Colombia

Peru

Chile

Paraguay

Uruguay

3rd FLEET PACIFIC OCEAN

PACIFIC OCEAN

Hawaii

Midway

New Zealand

Australia

7th FLEET WESTERN PACIFIC

Japan

South Korea

Okinawa

Guam

Taiwan

Philippines

Thailand

Singapore

Afghanistan

Pakistan

Diego Garcia

INDIAN OCEAN

5th FLEET INDIAN OCEAN GULF RED SEA

Iceland

Norway

United Kingdom

Germany

Georgia

Turkey

Iraq

Gulf States

Israel

Egypt

Somalia

Ethiopia

South Africa

Morocco

Italy

6th FLEET MEDITERRANEAN

2nd FLEET ATLANTIC

94

unifying security threat, the Cold War alliances were expected to wane. 'When there is no longer a single threat and each country perceives its perils from its own national perspective', wrote Henry Kissinger, 'those societies which had nestled under American protection will feel compelled to assume greater responsibility for their own security'.[52] German reunification (1989), the Treaty of the European Union (1992) and the creation of the single currency (1999–2002) all indicated that one of the fundamental inhibitions to European autonomy had indeed been lifted. The relaxation of security pressures likewise created the conditions for democratic domestic political transitions in east Asia favouring greater political autonomy.[53] The globalisation of the capitalist world economy had even more far-reaching implications since it shifted the grammar of international relations from 'high politics', issues of war and peace, to an array of post-Westphalian economic and human security issues transcending the national state and not soluble without deepened international cooperation and international legal regimes set by mutual consent.

Under these circumstances, it was reasonable to expect that the end of the Cold War would usher in a plural international order. At domestic level, it offered the prospect of a very substantial military demobilisation, a redirection of resources to domestic improvements and a change of cultural paradigm. Peter Katzenstein points out that the United States' collective identity was being transformed by transnational flows of people, goods and ideas and multicultural hybridisation, and could no 'longer be reinforced by the invocation of an overpowering foreign enemy unless, of course, one was to reinvent that enemy for political reasons in a new cultural gestalt'.[54] In a word, the dissolution of the Soviet Union concentrated military power to an extraordinary degree, significantly augmenting US foreign policy and security autonomy. But it simultaneously made the security structure of the *Pax Americana* increasingly irrelevant at both international and domestic level.

Three Major Options

This contradiction lies at the heart of the policy divides that came to the fore in the immediate aftermath of the Cold War and explains the hesitations of American foreign and security policy in the 1990s. Restating and reformulating the typology of elite groups, outlooks and options I proposed in July 2001,[55] three major options emerged out of the post-Cold War configuration, expressing the contending outlooks and interests of different elite social groups. This typology, which overlaps with the one formulated by Richard Falk in the mid 1970s,[56] excludes post-international and cosmopolitan perspectives not because they are theoretically or normatively insignificant but because they were never contemplated at power elite level. It therefore only includes the dominant strands of thinking within the American policy-making elites. It should be kept in mind that if they differ considerably in terms of their impacts and outcomes, to varying degrees and in different ways they are intrusive, involving the coercive affirmation of American power.

Neo-liberal globalism

Founded on the primacy of economics,[57] neo-liberalism encompassed various strands of liberalism, from commercial pacifists to liberal interventionists, and framed the end of the Cold War as an opportunity for the United States to establish a new position of global leadership by expanding the 'democratic peace' and consolidating or creating new institutional frameworks and regimes of governance that would secure and support the emergence of a global American-centred liberal economic order. In practice, neo-liberals proposed a shift in the hierarchy of international priorities from military security to trade, international competitiveness and larger issues of human security. Rather than centring exclusively on the balance of power, foreign policy would refocus on the promotion of US economic interests, human rights, democratisation and 'humanitarian interventions'.[58] Recognition of interdependence meant that American 'national interests' had to be more closely aligned with collective concerns and emerging global issues. Nonetheless, the United States would remain the guarantor of world order. Liberal internationalist interventionists advocated the use of force to support democratisation and curb potential threat states. At the same time, since it implied international convergence around a hegemonic economic model, neo-liberalism was/is highly intrusive.

Realism

Realists expected a gradual diffusion of power at international level as 'economic power gradually replaced military power as the *ultima ratio* of state relations',[59] and as new major state actors such as China and India appeared on the world scene. In keeping with their basic assumptions regarding international anarchy, they argued that military capabilities and power politics would remain an important, albeit not the sole, determinant in world politics. Concerned about the conservation of American authority, and of the 'primacy' of the United States, realists argued in favour of deterrence, containment of 'rogue states' and a classical balance of power policy in the regions of the world of strategic and economic import to the United States (Europe, East Asia and the Middle East). This policy, mixing cooperation and coercion, would preserve the fiction of equality among allies and allow the United States to 'function in much the same way that Great Britain did in maintaining the European balance of power',[60] that is, as *primus inter pares* of the international state system. The corollary of this idea was that the US should be prepared to use force selectively to preserve the status quo rather than as a transformational tool.

Imperialism

The imperialist vision was/is founded on the primacy of force. The imperialists interpreted the disintegration of the Soviet Union as an historic opportunity to rely on the new monopoly of force to lock in and extend the United States' lead and reach with the purpose of securing a second global 'American Century'. Unlike the realist prescription for American preponderance, they envisioned the US as 'the standard-bearer of moral, political and military might and right',[61] an empire no longer constrained by an 'illusory international community', having no need to abide by international law or to mask its international power aims. The imperialist prescription was that the United States should seek neither to preserve the status quo nor accommodate plurality but, as the sole legitimate source of order and law, to found a new world order under exclusive American control, 'unashamedly laying down the rules of world order and being prepared to enforce them'.[62]

These ideal-typical categories of course simplify reality. There are important distinctions within and some fluidity between groups. Realists and imperialists inhabit the same social milieu: the national security establishment. For their part, the imperialists encompass anti-internationalist 'sovereignists' and neo-conservative 'internationalists'. The former, ideological heirs of the nationalist expansionists of the late nineteenth century, traditionally grouped in the Republican Party, assert the supremacy of American over international law and reject international institutional constraints, however weak, on US autonomy.[63] They meet Peter Alter's criteria for 'integral nationalism' in that they are 'prepared to assert unscrupulously the interests of their own nation at the expense of others' in the name of religious ideas of the nation that makes 'absolute demands on the individual'.[64] As Alter points out, the 'marriage between nationalism and imperialism' was a common feature of all the expansionist nation states of the nineteenth century.[65] The essential concern of the internationalist expansionists, the neo-conservatives originating in the Cold War foreign policy and defence establishment of the Democratic Party, is the assertion and expansion of American global power and authority. The neo-Wilsonian rhetoric of the internationalist interventionists clashes with the purely Hobbesian philosophical outlook of the ultra-nationalists. But they strongly converge in their commitment to American power and a shared belief in the value and virtue of force. In the late 1990s, Samuel Huntington proposed a synthesis of these two strands of American conservatism, calling for a 'robust nationalism' that would unite nationalists and neo-conservatives behind a Trinitarian credo – God, the nation and the armed forces – the purpose of which would be to avert domestic disintegration, maintain the United States' global role and assure that American power would remain 'at its peak'.[66] The two were indeed fused in the first George W. Bush administration. There is also some fluidity between groups, evidenced in the support given by many prominent 'liberal internationalist' intellectuals as well as a few realists (such as Henry Kissinger) to the George W. Bush administration's strategic agenda in the Gulf or, conversely, in the defection of some leading neo-conservatives from the imperialist camp (for example, Francis Fukuyama). The typology nonetheless provides a broad guide to the scope of the debate in the United States in the post-Cold War era and the options of US international policy.

THE LIBERAL INTERLUDE

The imperialist coalition, centred in the civilian hierarchy of the Department of Defense (DOD) and leading parts of the Republican Party in Congress, became an influential but not dominant force in the George H.W. Bush administration (1988–1992). Under Clinton it initially lost ground and then regained momentum when the Republicans gained control of both houses of Congress in 1994. Overall, under George H.W. Bush, realists shaped the first years of the post-Cold War transition. In Europe, the administration proceeded cautiously, in consultation with a declining Soviet Union, regarding German reunification and the Yugoslav crisis. In the Gulf, it went to war with Iraq but decided to avoid shattering the Iraqi state, upsetting the regional balance in Iran's favour and engaging in 'an indefinite occupation of a hostile state'.[67] In the Middle East, it co-sponsored the 1991 Madrid Conference with the Soviet Union which led to the Oslo Accords in 1993. In east Asia, the administration demonstrated restraint towards China after the 1989 Tiananmen repression and also in the Korean peninsula. US nuclear weapons were withdrawn from South Korea and post-Cold War *détente* between the two Koreas led to the signing of two North–South agreements in 1991, which have provided the framework for inter-Korean relations ever since.[68] The guiding principle was to secure regional balances favourable to the United States. In a particularly clear statement of American aims, a senior Department of Defense official wrote in 1992 that 'in a transitional phase of international politics comparable to 1789–1815 during which the established configurations of power are changing before new structures of order are securely in place', the United States had a 'dramatic opportunity to redefine its global role'. The US, he wrote, should emulate 'Great Britain in much of the eighteen and nineteenth centuries' and seek to become the 'holder of the balance'. To avoid 'decentralisation and anarchy', the US should: a) 'Maintain a global balance of power favourable to the US and its allies'; b) oppose 'attempts by hostile states to gain regional hegemony' in areas 'critical to long-term US security'; c) promote 'an international trading and monetary system conducive to American economic prosperity' through the free movement of capital and goods, and d) encourage democratisation where possible and strengthen the 'frameworks and norms' of international order. While the United States could not and should not try to 'remake the world in its image', American 'political and economic diplomacy must be pre-eminent, with American military power playing a supportive but nonetheless important role'.[69]

Clinton: The Primacy of Economics

Under the Clinton administration the pendulum swung from classical security concerns to a global agenda centred, in Secretary of State Warren Christopher's words, on advancing 'America's economic security with the same energy and resourcefulness we devoted to waging the Cold War'.[70] In 1992, C. Fred Bergsten wrote that 'America's national interests have shifted sharply in the direction of economics'.[71] The administration developed a 'core strategy of encouraging the deeper integration of countries into global financial markets'.[72] This choice led to a partial, though never-completed, shift in the centre of institutional gravity in the executive branch from the national security apparatus to the Treasury and Commerce Departments. Closely tied to internationalised Wall Street banking and investment firms,[73] as well as to sectors of the 'new economy', the Clinton administration considerably amplified the global liberalisation agenda of its predecessors: 'Previous administrations had pushed for financial liberalization principally in Japan, but under President Clinton it became a worldwide effort directed at all kinds of countries, even smaller ones much less able to absorb it than Japan'.[74] On January 25, 1993, the President signed an Executive Order instituting the National Economic Council (NEC) within the Executive Office to 'coordinate the economic policymaking process with respect to domestic and international economic issues'. With a status equivalent to the National Security Council, the NEC became the nerve centre of an aggressive campaign, global in nature but primarily focused on east Asia, to reshape local regulatory frameworks and give American financial firms access to east Asian financial markets.

The intensity of state intervention directed at obtaining this result was remarkable. The administration set up a 'war room' in the Department of Commerce to advance American trade, developed a 'big emerging markets plan to identify ten rising economic powers and push relentlessly to win business for American companies there'.[75] The White House mobilised the CIA and other intelligence agencies to promote US economic interests, making that the US' foreign policy priority. R. James Woolsey, Clinton's first Director of Central Intelligence, stated publicly in 1993 that industrial espionage and economic forecasting had become the 'hottest topic in intelligence policy', a position reiterated in 1994 during a conference in Washington, D.C.[76] 'The Clinton administration', wrote the *Christian Science Monitor* in 1999, 'has attached especial importance to economic intelligence...The NEC routinely seeks information from the National Security Agency and the CIA...The NSA, as the biggest and wealthiest communications interception agency in the world, is best placed to trawl electronic communications and use what comes up for US commercial advantage'.[77]

A Transnational Agenda with an American Core

Global liberalisation was not simply a national American project. There was a broad transnational elite consensus during the 1990s that barriers to capital flows should be broken down, an agenda assiduously implemented and furthered by international institutions in which the US has a dominant say[78] (the IMF, World Bank and OECD) and private transnational elite clubs (such as the World Economic Forum[79]) in which, until recently, the US had a very large constituency (Strange's apposite expression). The Washington Consensus reflected the diffusion and institutionalisation of a set of hegemonic ideas and norms, originating in a dominant state and accomplished through a combination of coercion and consent. The cultural critic Rob Kroes noted at the end of the 1990s that 'like Rome in the days of the Roman Empire, the US is the center of webs of control and communication that span the world', the source of an ubiquitous language and 'visual lingua franca conveying American culture to the rest of the world'.[80] The analogy with Rome appropriately underscores the fact that international acculturation to the norms and outlooks of a dominant society results less from its intrinsic attractiveness ('soft power'), a notion dependent on the side of the looking glass one is peering through, than from the hierarchical structure of the international political economy. If transnational elite constituencies feel culturally at home in empire it is because empire generates transnational constituencies with a vested interest in empire, just as it creates its antagonists, in the process of its construction.[81]

Global liberalisation was thus a transnational agenda with an American core. Resulting from the position of the US financial industry at the centre of world capital flows, global liberalisation primarily advanced the interests of the most internationalised segments of American capital. Considered by the Clinton White House as being coterminous with US 'national interests', liberalisation had power-political effects in that it weakened alternative growth and development models. The spread of the global free market affirmed the US' comparative advantages in post-industrial sectors (finance, insurance, real estate, communications, entertainment, etc.) and generated a global culture of business and social practices the norms of which were set by the American financial industry. During the 1990s, the US laid down the regimes – the dominant economic norms, procedures and frameworks – of the global economy.[82] US capital thus operated in a universe of rules it had defined and which reflected its interests. Given the differential distribution of power and sovereignty of the international system, neo-liberal globalisation constrained the autonomy of states in asymmetric fashion, challenging the economic systems of 'emerging' countries. 'Intense political pressure was exerted by advanced industrialized countries on developing countries to open their economies...along a variety of dimensions, the national economic regulations of developing countries were called into question by powerful states'.[83] This remark must be extended to the east Asian developmental states whose national economic systems were also relentlessly challenged.

The United States was not subject to the restraints liberalisation set on others. As Robert Wade argues, the 'increasing mobility of information, finance and goods and services frees the American government of constraints while putting everyone else under tighter constraints'.[84] When favourable outcomes could not be obtained through the 'natural' workings of the market or indirect institutional pressures, they were secured through direct coercive political interventions.[85] During the 1997–1998 'Asian' financial crisis, the US Treasury 'quickly and brutally crushed'[86] Japan's initiative to create an Asian Monetary Fund (AMF). The AMF would have pooled regional financial resources and provided much needed liquidity to south and northeast Asian countries facing critical conditions caused by massive and time-compressed capital outflows. Motivated by concerns that the AMF might become the kernel of an autonomous regional financial system rivalling the IMF, US action provoked a strong nationalist backlash at both elite and popular levels in east Asia and played an important if unintended role in the subsequent choice of regional leaders who would deepen regional integration. (This is examined in Chapter 7.) In east Asia, US behaviour was not interpreted as a policy 'mistake' but as a form of liberal imperialism, a design to break developmentalism and use the crisis to acquire valuable local industrial and financial assets at much depreciated prices.[87] Eisuke Sakakibara, Deputy Finance Minister of Japan at the time, rejected western suggestions that it was, properly speaking, an 'Asian crisis'. Rather, he argued, it was part of a 'global crisis of capitalism'.[88] In the United States, the crisis was interpreted as a defining moment in the balance of world economic power: it supposedly 'destroyed the credibility of the Japanese or East Asian model of economic growth',[89] in the words of one commentator, and represented, in Alan Greenspan's formulation, a defeat of state-led modernisation models and 'an important milestone in what evidently has been a significant and seemingly inexorable trend toward market capitalism'.[90]

Contingent factors also played a role in re-establishing the US' relative economic position. During the decade, Japan and the European Union respectively suffered a long period of economic stagnation and weak growth: the former as a result of the collapse of the financial bubble generated by the appreciation of the yen following the 1985 Plaza Accord, the latter because of the costs of German reunification and the restrictive fiscal and monetary corset of the European Unification Treaty. These circumstances meant that the American economy found itself facing a much reduced competitive challenge at a moment when it had a renewed strong growth trajectory. The growth of the US economy was supported by favourable monetary conditions (a sustained low interest rate regime due to capital inflows and the price deflation of consumer products due to the global relocation of production in emerging economies), as well as innovation and investment in the information and communications technology (ICT) sector. Government, it should once again be emphasised, played an important role. The new technologies emerged out of Cold War defence related research[91] and the Clinton administration created the institutional frameworks for renewed American technological dynamism in the ICT sector.[92]

During the 1990s, global liberalisation proved a potent instrument in advancing American agendas and spreading the reach of the informal empire. At the turn of the century, the United States not only enjoyed undisputed dominance of the security structure but was setting the norms and constraints of the newly globalised capitalist economy.[93] Discussed in the next chapter, these new circumstances led to widespread triumphalism and, on the right of the political spectrum, the crystallisation and affirmation of imperialist outlooks. The Bush administration's drive for empire was, in other words, a possible but not a necessary outcome of this new set of international circumstances. Yet if the proximate cause can be traced to the conjunction of a new configuration of structure and a group of agents, the new expansionism should be seen as part of a wider historical continuum. What differentiates it from earlier exercises of imperial power is neither its discursive contents nor the underlying cosmology, but its limitless aims.

6
Striving for Global Monopoly

We're an empire now, and when we act, we create our own reality. And while you're studying that reality – judiciously, as you will – we'll act again, creating other new realities, which you can study too, and that's how things will sort out. We're history's actors... and you, all of you, will be left to just study what we do.

Senior US official, 2002[1]

It is not hard to see how the configuration of the late 1990s led to the crystallisation and expression of latent imperial outlooks. Evidence of the United States' economic and strategic ascendancy rekindled imaginings of American global supremacy. Declinism gave way to extraordinary hubris and, in some cases, to illusions of omnipotence. By the end of the decade empire suffused elite American discourse. In 1998, soon after an American bombing raid on Iraq, Secretary of State Madeleine Albright asserted: 'If we have to use force, it is because we are America. We are the indispensable nation. We stand tall. We see further into the future'.[2] Zbigniew Brzezinski, a sharp critic of the 2003 Iraq war, was more precise:

> The scope and pervasiveness of American global power today are unique. Not only does the US control all of the world's oceans and seas, but it has developed an assertive military capability for amphibious shore control that enables it to project its power inland in politically significant ways. Its military legions are firmly perched on the western and eastern extremities of Eurasia, and they also control the Persian Gulf. American vassals and tributaries, some yearning to be embraced by even more formal ties to Washington, dot the entire Eurasian continent.[3]

He added: 'To put it in terminology that hearkens back to the more brutal age of ancient empires, the three grand imperatives of imperial geostrategy are to prevent collusion and maintain security dependence among the vassals, to keep tributaries pliant and protected, and to keep the barbarians from coming together'.[4] A few years later Henry Kissinger wrote:

At the dawn of the new millennium, the United States is enjoying a pre-eminence unrivalled by even the greatest empires of the past. From weaponry to entrepreneurship, from science to technology, from higher education to popular culture, America exercises an unparalleled ascendancy around the globe.[5]

'American pre-eminence', in his view, would be 'a fact of life for the near and almost certainly the mid-term future'.[6] In 2002, Joseph Nye opened his book *The Paradox of American Power* with a chapter entitled 'The American Colossus'. The first lines read:

Not since Rome has one nation loomed so large above the others. In the words of *The Economist*, 'the United States bestrides the globe like a colossus. It dominates business, commerce and communications; its economy is the world's most successful, its military might second to none'...The United States is undoubtedly the world's number one power, but how long can this situation last, and what should we do with it?[7]

A BROAD IDEATIONAL TREND

I cite these few examples not because they articulate the views of the elite social group that I have defined as imperialist but precisely because they do not. While Brzezinski, Kissinger and Nye inhabit the same sphere of influence and power at the intersection of the academy, think tanks and government as the imperialists, the first two are classical realists, the latter a prominent neo-liberal international relations theorist. They argued that the United States could only preserve its position of 'unique global power' and avoid the 'erosion of [its] pre-eminence' by transforming it 'into increasingly institutionalized global cooperation' (Brzezinski), by emphasising 'soft power' (Nye), and by 'avoiding a deliberate quest for hegemony' and demonstrating prudence (Kissinger).[8] (Stephen Walt likewise argued in 2002 in favour of US self-restraint, for the same reasons.[9]) Their statements nonetheless draw attention to the pervasiveness of imperial representations in the late 1990s. In that sense, the overt affirmations of imperialist purpose that flourished in the 1990s on the right of the political spectrum and within parts of the national security establishment were an extreme manifestation of a broad ideational trend. The distinction between imperialist and realist or neo-liberal prescriptions for post-Cold War world order resided in the relative emphasis placed on military power and the role of alliances and international institutions. The imperialists were not satisfied with simply managing the favourable post-Cold War interstate balance, much less with promoting global economic integration under US auspices. Rejecting classical realism and liberalism in favour of a strategy of global primacy relying on force, they sought to take advantage of the post-1991 power asymmetry to remove constraints, however tenuous, on the exercise of American power. Military expansion would be the means to secure 'global empire', a limitless objective. Eliot Cohen, an academic who was appointed Special Adviser to Secretary of State Condoleezza Rice in 2007, wrote in 1998:

> The Cold War ended in 1990...no formidable new foe looms on the horizon...The Pentagon's pallid substitute for 'containment' is a requirement to be ready to fight two major theatre wars 'nearly simultaneously' – an artificial standard driven by short-term concerns. A better strategic concept would embrace some uncomfortable truths, not least of which is the reality of an America that now acts as a global empire, rather than as one of two rival superpowers, or a normal state.[10]

The United States, he added:

> ...needs an imperial strategy. Defence planners could never admit it openly, of course, and most would feel uncomfortable with the idea, but that is, in fact, what the United States at the end of the twentieth century is – a global empire. Talk of 'cooperative security' masks the reality that in any serious military confrontation, the central question is whom the United States asks to cooperate.[11]

Soon after, the Project for a New American Century (PNAC), a neo-conservative 'think tank' founded in 1997, published *Rebuilding America's Defenses*, a report that recommended substantially increasing defence spending, modernising the United States' nuclear arsenal, investing in R&D to extend the US' military–technological lead, as well as building larger expeditionary forces capable of dealing with 'multiple constabulary missions [requiring] a permanent allocation of US armed forces'. The goal was to secure and extend the 'American peace' through 'unquestioned US military pre-eminence'.[12] Gazing back to the 1890s to see into the future, the columnist Charles Krauthammer wrote in December 1999: 'Last week's handover of the Panama Canal neatly brackets the American Century. It begins with Theodore Roosevelt conceiving the canal and, with it, America ascending to the rank of Great Power. It ends with America so great a power, so serenely dominant in the world, that it can give away T.R.'s strategic jewel with hardly a notice'. America, he concluded, 'bestrides the world like a colossus... Not since Rome destroyed Carthage has a great power risen to the heights we have'.[13] Said another neo-conservative author: 'On the brink of the 21st century, the United States is at a point reminiscent of its entry into the twentieth...France had the seventeenth century, Britain the nineteenth, and America the twentieth. It will also have the twenty-first'.[14]

GLOBAL EXPANSIONISM AND NATIONALISM

The imperialist 'party' regrouped different social forces (I use the past tense because the coalition has now broken apart). It constituted a coalition between neo-conservative internationalists who emerged as an intellectual community out of the Cold War containment project, and ultra or integral nationalists – the Christian Right, sovereignists and militarists – who make the cult of the nation an 'end in itself', see the nation as absolute, and fuse nationalism and imperialism.[15] The coalition thus united the two historical strands of US expansionism around a set of different international and domestic goals. The international goals, discussed below, were to use the post-Cold War strategic asymmetry to expand US power, establish an unchallengeable military lead and restore dominance in the Gulf. The nationalist domestic goal, clearly articulated by Samuel Huntington in 1999, was to avert the cultural and political disintegration supposedly induced by liberal cosmopolitanism and multiculturalism by unifying the country around God, the nation and the armed forces. Advocating a 'robust nationalism' as the 'alternative to divisive multiculturalism, xenophobic isolationism and wimpy universalism', Huntington denounced the 'denation-alized elites' – the 'international class of businessmen, officials, academics, journalists and others' whose ideology and interests 'run counter to the economic interests and cultural concerns of the mass publics in their societies'.[16]

Imperial expansion synthesised these goals by asserting the US' exclusive global authority. If the neo-conservative component of the coalition provided the intellectual resources of the drive for empire, it was made possible only by the fact that their agenda converged with the main goals of the national-expansionists who actually wielded power and were in decision-making positions (President Bush, Vice President Dick Cheney, Secretary of Defense Donald Rumsfeld). Condoleezza Rice voiced the core agenda of the coalition during the 2000 presidential campaign. Prefiguring the military mobilisation that followed in 2001, she denounced the Clinton administration's supposed subordination of American 'national interests' to an 'illusory international community', and advocated a return to force-based 'power politics':

> The next president should refocus the Pentagon's priorities on building the military of the 21st century...US technological advantages should be leveraged to build forces that are lighter and more lethal, more mobile and agile, and capable of firing accurately from long distances. In order to do this, Washington must reallocate resources, perhaps in some cases skipping a generation of technology to make leaps rather than incremental improvements in its forces...The American military must be able to meet decisively the emergence of any hostile military power in the Asia–Pacific region, the Middle East, the Persian Gulf, and Europe.[17]

Permanent strategic supremacy had been one of the longstanding objectives of the Cold War global military containment project. Influential sectors of the American foreign and security policy-making elite had virulently opposed *détente* with the Soviet Union in the early 1970s and campaigned to have the US return to the vision of 'superior overall power' articulated in NSC 68, the foundational policy document that set the US on the path of permanent mobilisation during the cold war.[18] For like reasons they also vigorously opposed the set of policies centred on trade, arms control and economic convergence espoused by the Trilateral Commission in the latter part of the decade for the 'management of interdependence'.[19] Rather than deterrence or cooperation, they advocated offensive worldwide action, short of war, to challenge the Soviet system and 're-establish objectives of victory'.[20] They shaped the offensive strategy of the first Reagan administration, which aimed to achieve nuclear superiority and dominance of space (the Strategic Defense Initiative) and engaged in high-risk clandestine operations to test Soviet reactions and defence capabilities.[21] Having gained senior positions of responsibility in the George H.W. Bush administration, the protagonists of permanent mobilisation who 'wished for a military posture approaching mobilization [and who] would create or invent whatever crisis were required to bring this about',[22] interpreted the dissolution of the Soviet Union as resulting from US pressure rather than domestic causes[23] and crafted a post-Cold War agenda to seize the opportunity to establish 'unchallengeable' military supremacy.

The 1991 Gulf War was a defining moment in the elaboration of this agenda. As the Cold War came to a close, it remobilised the US armed forces, justified continued high levels of military spending, and created a new rationale for military interventions. Testifying to the Senate Armed Services Committee in February 1991, Defense Secretary Dick Cheney told Congress that the war against Iraq:

> ...presages very much the type of conflict we are most likely to confront again in this new era – major regional contingencies against foes well armed with advanced conventional and unconventional weaponry. In addition to southwest Asia, we have important interests in Europe, Asia, the Pacific, and Central and Latin America. In each of these regions there are opportunities and potential future threats to our interests. We must configure our policies and our forces to effectively deter, or quickly defeat, such future regional threats.[24]

The war also demonstrated that 'military power remained as significant as ever in interstate relations' and dealt 'a possibly fatal blow' to pluralism by revealing that the US' European and East Asian allies were 'as dependent as ever' on the security structures of the *Pax*.[25] Bruce Cumings noted at the time: 'If Korea was the alpha of the military-industrial complex, Iraq was the omega. The end of the Cold War had done nothing by mid-1990 to dismantle the enormous machine set in motion in the 50s, a perpetual motion machine that was built for war and that advances its interests in making war'.[26] With hindsight, we know that the 1991 war was merely one step in the elaboration of an expansionist military doctrine and the crystallisation of an imperialist coalition of forces that came to power in 2000.

A Strategy of Supremacy

In the immediate aftermath of the war, senior officials in the Department of Defense drafted *Defense Planning Guideline (FY*

1994–1999) outlining the United States' post-Cold War strategic doctrine in systematic form. According to the National Security Archive (NSA), which recently obtained partial declassification of the document, the guidance was written, and then later amended in the face of strong criticism, to meet Defense Secretary Dick Cheney's 'requirements for a strategy of military supremacy'.[27] Notwithstanding the disappearance of the Soviet Union, the original version of *DPG 1994–1999* warned: 'There are other potential nations or coalitions that could, in the further future, develop strategic aims and a defense posture of region-wide or global domination'. It therefore recommended that the US should refocus its strategy 'on precluding the emergence of any potential future global competitor', 'maintaining the mechanisms for deterring potential competitors from even aspiring to a larger regional or global role' and avoiding regional hegemonies in 'Europe, East Asia, the Middle East and Southwest Asia, and the territory of the former Soviet Union'. Having additional 'important interests at stake in Latin America, Oceania, and Sub-Saharan Africa', the US 'will be concerned with preventing the domination of key regions by a hostile power'. As far as Europe was concerned, *DPG 1994–1999* recommended that the US should 'seek to prevent the emergence of European-only security arrangements which would undermine NATO, particularly the alliance's integrated command structure' and consider 'extending the east-central European states security commitments analogous to those we have extended to Persian Gulf States'. The overall aim was to '[convince] potential competitors that they need not aspire to a greater role or pursue a more aggressive posture to protect their legitimate interests' and to 'sufficiently account for the interests of the advanced industrial nations to discourage them from challenging our leadership or seeking to overturn the established political and economic order'.[28] Collective security would be supplanted by 'ad hoc assemblies' and, when necessary, unilateral American military action. Ronald Steel aptly summarises the doctrinal shift: 'Whereas the American arsenal was once directed primarily against the Soviet Union, it would now be directed against everybody'.[29]

The most inflammatory recommendations of the *Guidance* were shelved when parts of the document were leaked to the *New York Times* in 1992.[30] Throughout the 1990s they nonetheless remained core neo-conservative and ultra-nationalist commitments. In a 1995 report written for the US Air Force, Zalmay Khalilzad, a senior official of the George W. Bush administration, reiterated many of the central arguments of the *Guidance*: 'US global leadership and deterring the rise of another hostile global rival or a return to multipolarity for the indefinite future is the best long term guiding principle and vision [for the United States]. Precluding the rise of a hostile global rival is a good guide for defining what interests the United States should regard as vital'.[31] To achieve this, Khalilzad recommended consolidating the 'zone of democratic peace [while] avoiding conditions that can lead to "renationalization" of the security policies of key allied countries such as Japan and Germany'; avoiding the emergence of a 'European superstate'; 'precluding hostile hegemony over critical regions' since 'a global rival could emerge if a hostile power or coalition gained hegemony over a critical region'; hedging against the 'reimperialization of Russia', which 'in the near term can pose a major regional threat'; discouraging the 'emergence of a robust Commonwealth of Independent States'; and 'discouraging Chinese expansionism'. Above all, wrote Khalilzad, the US had to preserve its 'military preeminence' to be able to 'carry out the strategy outlined' and 'size its forces by requiring them to have the capability to defeat nearly simultaneously the most plausible military challenges to critical US interests from the two next most powerful military forces who are not allied with the United States'.[32]

Table 6.1   US National Defence Expenditures 1940–2009
(billions, constant 2000 US dollars)

Year	Spending	Year	Spending	Year	Spending
1940	19.9	1988	393.1	1999	283.6
1950	129.6	1989	398.9	2000	294.4
1955	320.1	1990	382.7	2001	297.2
1962	315.9	1991	333.7	2002	329.3
1968	420.3	1992	354.3	2003	364.4
1975	262.7	1993	340.3	2004	394.3
1977	250.6	1994	322.8	2005	407.3
1981	282.2	1995	305.9	2006	412.4
1985	356.5	1996	289.2	2007	426.4
1986	380.7	1997	288.4	2008	463.9
1987	387.1	1998	282.4	2009	504.7

Source: Historical Tables, Budget of the US Government, fiscal year 2009[33]

His was merely one voice among many within the national security and defence establishment. In 1996, Senator Jesse Helms, an influential ultra-nationalist closely linked to the Pentagon, declared: 'We remain uniquely positioned at the center and that is where we must stay...by being the standard-bearer of moral, political and military might and right, an example to which all others aspire'.[34] As noted above, in the latter part of the decade there was a sustained campaign by the Republican dominated Congress and the security complex to shift national priorities from the global economy to military remobilisation and power politics. Clinton's early and ephemeral efforts to curtail the institutional power of the national security apparatus met with fierce resistance from the Pentagon, which 'dreaded the prospect of demobilisation and despised the new President for his youthful activities as an anti-Vietnam War activist',[35] and from Congress, which in 1994 came under the control of Republican ultra-nationalists. Clinton proved unable and unwilling to override the defence and security structure. As a result, in the second half of the decade two centres of power co-existed in Washington: the White House and the Pentagon. Supported by Congress, the Pentagon behaved in the latter part of the decade 'increasingly as a sovereign agency, animated by a deep distrust of limitations imposed by foreigners'.[36] Congress and the Pentagon successfully protected defence programmes and engaged in a broad and sustained offensive to assert US primacy.

After 1994, the Republicans in Congress launched a vigorous assault on the international institutional system. That campaign took various forms: the refusal to pay United Nations contributions, relentless attacks on Secretary General Boutros Boutros-Ghali, the imposition of unilateral economic sanctions against 35 UN member states, the passage of extraterritorial legislation infringing international law and customary rules of conduct (Iran–Libya Sanctions Act, Helms–Burton law) and the refusal to ratify important international conventions. After 1994, the US Senate and the Pentagon worked together to block the ratification of the Ottawa Convention banning the production, trade and use of anti-personnel land mines (1997) and the Comprehensive Test Ban Treaty (1999). While it ratified the Chemical Weapons Convention in 1997, Congress inserted exemptions that effectively undermined the Convention. By the end of the decade the 'culmination of resurgent unilateralism was and is the campaign against the United Nations. The U.N. was an American vision...but it is today under unrelenting attack'.[37] Like Condoleezza Rice a few years later, House Speaker Newt Gingrich (a member of the Pentagon's Defense Planning Board during the first years of the George W. Bush administration) expressed the views of the congressional majority when he accused President Clinton of wanting to 'subordinate the US to the United

Nations'.[38] During the 1994 Congressional Campaign, President Clinton was denounced, in the words of the Republican Party's *Contract With America*, penned by Gingrich, for 'saluting the day when American men and women will fight, and die, in the "service" of the United Nations'.[39]

These trends were well established when George W. Bush came to power in 2000. He formed an administration almost exclusively composed of figures historically linked to the national security complex, a curious but revealing choice in a period of globalisation and interstate peace. Prior to September 11 the Bush administration renewed and expanded the 1990s Republican campaign against the United Nations, launching a methodical effort to deconstruct the rules-based international institutional order. In its first few months, the new administration repudiated the Kyoto protocol that had been signed by President Clinton, rejected a draft UN programme of action to control the trade in small arms and light weapons, blocked efforts to add a verification protocol to the Biological Weapons Convention, discarded the Anti-Ballistic Missile Treaty (ABM), a pillar of the international security architecture since 1972, and bitterly fought and rejected the International Criminal Court and the Rome Statute, an action that John Bolton, then Under-secretary of State for Arms Control, notoriously characterised as the 'happiest day in my government service'.[40] Condoleezza Rice had defined the contours of these policies in 2000 when decisively rejecting the idea that 'the support of many states, or even better of institutions like the UNO, is essential to the legitimate exercise of power'.[41] According to Strobe Talbott, Undersecretary of State in the Clinton administration, the word globalisation was banned in the Bush White House: 'any mention of "globalization" was declared taboo...Bush adhered, and still adheres to an uncompromising and extreme variant of exceptionalism [that] posits, explicitly, that the United States is strong enough to make one set of rules for itself and a different set for everyone else'.[42] In a particularly telling act soon after the administration was sworn in, the Office of the Secretary of Defense commissioned a still classified comparative study of ancient and modern empires to ascertain how they had 'maintained their dominance'.[43] From what evidence is publicly available, the administration also planned to go to war and invade Iraq. Former Treasury Secretary Paul O'Neill claims that discussion of Iraq began ten days after the inauguration and that the National Security Council discussed a possible occupation of Iraq as early as January and February 2001.[44]

LIMITLESS GOALS

The hierarchy of motives behind the invasion of Iraq in 2003 has been the subject of intense but inconclusive debate. Realist and neo-realist scholars, following in the footsteps of Hans Morgenthau's scathing critique of the escalation of the Vietnam War in 1965,[45] overwhelmingly opposed the war, on the grounds that it was an ill-advised and unnecessary adventure contrary to American national interests.[46] Yet their explanations vary as to why the war occurred. Kenneth Waltz offers a clear if deterministic structural answer by asserting that the drive for empire resulted from the unavoidable will to power of a state freed from systemic constraints. Simply, 'disparity of power spawns despotic rule at home and abroad'.[47] In like manner, Robert Jervis argues that while the 'adoption of a preventive war doctrine may be a mistake, especially if taken too far, it is not foreign to normal state behavior'.[48] The attempt to establish 'American hegemony, primacy or empire'[49] was the normal reaction of a 'normal state that has gained a position of dominance'.[50] But if this is so, then why did the drive for global empire not occur under the Clinton administration when the US' predominance was arguably even greater at the economic and cultural levels, and just as great at the military level? Moreover, there is no way to rigorously specify how far is 'too far'. The extraordinary military asymmetry of the post-Cold War may have generated the conditions of possibility for expansion but it does not explain much else. Other prominent realists, such as Stephen Walt and John Mearsheimer, have abandoned the realist framework altogether by resorting to domestic level explanations rather than international structure to account for US foreign policy.[51] They make the 'Israeli Lobby' the main explanatory variable of recent US behaviour, thereby eliding American imperial structures and the long history of American expansion. Even if there is a broad ideological and political convergence between the US and Israel, and sometimes a symbiosis of interests, this does not mean that Israel was the determining motive.

Economic mono-causality is not much more persuasive. The hypothesis that the war was a military Keynesian response to endogenous economic crisis (the burst of the dot com bubble and the recession of 2000), or a solution to the falling general rate of profit, cannot in our opinion be seriously entertained. War necessarily boosts the fortunes of the corporate sectors of the military-industrial complex, which at the same time are the sectors of the economy most closely tied to the state. But these only represent a small fraction of the overall economy, which is overwhelmingly driven by the service sector and consumption. Some neo-Marxist authors have argued that the US oil and armaments sectors were the 'leading fraction' of 'dominant capital' in the 1970s and 1980s. This fraction was superseded by finance and a 'new coalition led by civilian high-tech companies' in the 1990s.[52] When the 'new economy' became exhausted, this coalition was itself superseded by a 'pro-inflation coalition' led once more by the oil companies. War was the solution, meaning the 'end of the global village and...a serious blow to liberal capital mobility'.[53] However, other Marxist scholars such as Gérard Duménil and Dominique Lévy argue to the contrary that 'the new militarist trend is highly autonomous'.[54]

A stronger though not entirely convincing case can be made for a strategy designed to control oil resources given the role of fossil fuels in the world political economy. Constantly growing world demand for and rising American external dependence on a strategic non-renewable resource suggests a structural motive for opportunistic intervention in a country weakened by a decade of international sanctions and sitting on a significant share of world fossil fuel reserves.[55] Understood as a 'resource war', Iraq would constitute an instance of what Michael Klare has called the 'economization of international security affairs'.[56] Access to and control of Iraqi oil was certainly one motive in American war planning, as former Federal Reserve Chairman Alan Greenspan has candidly admitted. 'I am saddened', he recently wrote, 'that it is politically inconvenient to acknowledge what everyone knows: the Iraq war is largely about oil'.[57] Nonetheless, this explanation fails to account for other important motives and aims: reshaping the 'Greater Middle East', securing Israel, encircling the Islamic Republic of Iran and changing its regime, or setting a 'cautionary example of what can happen to other states that refuse to abandon their programs of weapons of mass destruction'.[58]

There is no compelling evidence that any one of these motives was primary. What is more, they do not account, singly or together, for the extraordinary military mobilisation that has occurred since 2001 and which was explicitly designed to establish 'unchallengeable' global US military supremacy. The White House's National Security Strategy 2002 (NSS), which formalised the US' adoption of a doctrine of preventive war, unambiguously asserted:

It is time to reaffirm the essential role of American military strength. We must build and maintain our defenses beyond challenge...The US must and will maintain the capability to defeat any attempt by an enemy to impose its will on the US, our allies or our friends...Our forces will be strong enough to dissuade potential adversaries from pursuing a military build-up in hopes of surpassing, or equaling, the power of the United States.[59]

This commitment to permanent strategic supremacy cannot be considered a response to September 11. It was articulated in the early 1990s and is a state-centric approach that has no bearing whatsoever on transnational terrorism. Moreover, no large-scale mobilisation was required to deter or destroy 'rogue states'. For that, pre-existing military capabilities were, as Afghanistan and Iraq proved, largely sufficient.

In an article published in July 2001, I argued that rather than behaving like a 'normal state', the Bush administration was bent from the very start on a course of expansion and empire.[60] Analysis of the public statements by senior administration officials after September 11 leaves little doubt that the underlying purpose of administration policy, encompassing all ancillary motives, was to alter the basic configuration of world order. On October 12, 2001, Defense Secretary Donald Rumsfeld hinted at the global transformational nature of American goals: 'It is possible', he asserted in an interview to the *New York Times*, 'that [the events of September 11 may represent] the kind of opportunities that World War II offered to refashion much of the world'.[61] Condoleezza Rice told *The New Yorker* in early 2002 that the US should 'capitalize on [the opportunities offered] by the shifting of the tectonic plates in international politics...It's important to try to seize on that and position American interests and institutions and all of that before [the plates] harden again'.[62] Comparing the mobilisation and force structure changes decided by the administration to the 'decisions that faced Harry Truman at the outset of the Cold War', Vice President Dick Cheney told the Los Angeles World Affairs Council in 2004 that 'one of the legacies of this administration will be some of the most sweeping changes in our military and our national security strategy as it relates to the military and force structure, and how we're based, and how we used it in the last fifty or sixty years, probably since World War II'.[63]

Similarly sweeping views were widely disseminated in supportive parts of the academy and the press. Soon after the invasion of Afghanistan, Charles Krauthammer wrote: 'The greatest sovereign is the American superpower...[In 1990 I wrote that] unipolarity could last thirty or forty years. That seemed bold at the time. Today, it seems rather modest. The unipolar moment has become the unipolar era'.[64] Stephen Peter Rosen, a scholar of military and security affairs at Harvard University and a former senior Department of Defense official, asserted in 2002 that the United States was now in the business of 'bringing down governments', leaving in place 'imperial garrisons for decades' and planning for 'imperial wars' using 'the maximum of force…to demonstrate that the empire cannot be challenged with impunity'. In the longer run, the US' aim, he wrote, must be to prevent the 'emergence of powerful, hostile challengers to the empire, by war if necessary but by imperial assimilation if possible. China is not yet powerful enough to be a challenger to the American empire, and the goal of the US is to prevent that challenge from emerging'.[65] Following the invasion of Iraq in 2003, he restated his argument in more general terms: 'The organizing principle of empire rests on the existence of an overarching power that creates and enforces the principle of hierarchy, but is not itself bound by such rules…If an American empire does endure, we may, in retrospect, come to understand the era of independent nation-states as something of an historical anomaly'.[66]

E.H. Carr would no doubt have recognised these statements as expressing an extreme variant of the 'ideology of predominant powers which find the sovereignty of other states a barrier to the enjoyment of their own predominant position'.[67] They certainly challenge the idea that the administration and its supporters were reacting out of a sense of vulnerability or fear. Rather, as Stanley Hoffmann points out, the Bush administration was 'drunk with power'.[68] They imagined, as the citation at the head of this chapter makes clear, that imperial will sufficed to change the course of history. The adoption of a doctrine of preventive war, the invasion of Iraq and the unmistakeable intent to then carry the campaign of 'regime change' to other states and territories, Iran in particular, should hence be seen as part of an extraordinary ambition, mixing philosophical idealism and Machiavellian purpose, to assert exclusive global American authority. If this is accepted, the synchronous effort to deconstruct the United Nations system was not a side effect of the war but rather an integral component of the same commitment and effort. As already noted in the introduction the US was, in Stanley Hoffmann's words, methodically destroying 'the main schemes of co-operation that have been established since 1945' with the aim of establishing a new world order under exclusive American control.[69]

There is a continuum between this effort to obtain monopoly control of the international system and the concomitant effort to concentrate power at the domestic level. September 11 is an explanatory factor here in that it lifted domestic constraints on executive autonomy, transforming an initially politically weak figure, whose legitimacy was tainted by the controversial way he attained the presidency,[70] into an American Caesar. The events created the conditions for an unchecked concentration of executive power and for the unification of a bitterly divided society behind and beneath the state. War and the permanent undeclared state of emergency that followed September 11 allowed the executive to assert 'presidential power at its absolute apex' and to claim 'virtually unlimited authority on matters of torture'.[71] While previous presidents also endeavoured to expand the autonomy and authority of the 'imperial presidency', the Bush administration went much further by claiming the arbitrary power to act at whim to abandon international humanitarian law, break international conventions and override domestic constitutional norms. The 2002 'torture memos' of the Office of the Counsel of the White House had implications that went beyond the question of torture as such: they affirmed the constitutional power of the president to use whatever means necessary in the accomplishment of his wartime mission as Commander-in-Chief. 'On this reasoning', writes the jurist David Cole, 'the president would be entitled by the Constitution to resort to genocide if he wished'.[72]

Since the 'Global War on Terror' (GWOT) was framed by the executive from the start as having no spatial or temporal boundaries, as 'a generational struggle', as a 'new condition of life',[73] the executive's 'unlimited authority' would extend indefinitely into the future. The Pentagon's 2006 *Quadrennial Defense Review* (QDR) renamed the 'global war on terror', calling it the 'Long War', a 'struggle that…will be fought in dozens of countries simultaneously and for many years to come'.[74] Donald Rumsfeld said that the 'Long War' would, like the Cold War, be a 'generational conflict [that] might last for decades'.[75] As Judith Butler points out, this temporal indeterminacy implied an indefinite extension of the undeclared state of emergency into the future, hence an indefinite exercise of 'lawless state power'.[76] Even if it had not been for September 11, writes a student of the US presidency, 'the Bush administration would have acted unilaterally whenever it could, consistently pushing the boundaries of presidential power'.[77] However, after those events, the executive claimed, and for a few years enjoyed, unbounded authority. Denouncing the 'accumulation of executive, judicial and legislative powers in a single branch and under a single individual', legal scholar Jack M. Balkin insisted in 2006 that this 'is the very essence of tyranny'.[78]

Authoritarian state transformation reconfigured sovereignty. Under the undeclared timeless state of emergency that followed September 11, the constitutional safeguards protecting the individual from arbitrary action on the part of the state were overridden. In classical liberal theory, rulers can only deviate from constitutional norms guaranteeing the individual against the arbitrary coercive power of the state in exceptional circumstances for a circumscribed period of time. In time-bound conditions of emergency or 'necessity', such as war, rulers of democratic states may suspend parts of the law but not the constitutional order itself. The state of emergency, or 'prerogative power' of the ruler in Locke's formulation, is an exception designed to save the norm and the constitutional order. In a permanent state of emergency, however, the exception becomes the norm. In the early part of the twentieth century, the state of exception and emergency rule were systematically theorised by Carl Schmitt who argued that the State, as the highest expression of the political, discovers its true essence in situations of emergency when it chooses the enemy and decides to combat him. That choice concentrates power, unifies the nation and depoliticises civil society. The state of emergency allows the state to transcend society and establish dictatorial autonomy. Having thus acquired the monopoly of political action and decision, the state, embodied by the dictator who decides the exception and who by so doing becomes truly sovereign, enjoys limitless powers, the most important of which is the power to override the 'existing legal order'. Since war is the purest form of the state of emergency, war forms the ontological foundation of the state.[79]

LIBERAL IMPERIALISM, COLONIAL REPRESENTATIONS

The administration's will to power was cloaked in Wilsonian rhetoric. Framed by the administration as the latest of a series of global struggles against barbarism and tyranny, the expansion of US power was conflated with the universal democratic interest.[80] This inversion of meaning is one of the invariant if constantly reformulated rhetorical devices of empire: 'Every single empire', writes Edward Said:

in its official discourse has said that it is not like all the others, that its circumstances are special, that it has a mission to enlighten, civilize, bring order and democracy, and that it uses force only as a last resort. And, sadder still, there always is a chorus of willing intellectuals to say calming words about benign or altruistic empires, as if one shouldn't trust the evidence of one's eyes watching the destruction and the misery and death brought by the latest *mission civilisatrice*.[81]

The chorus that Said was referring to were the many prominent liberal internationalist intellectuals, of whom one might have expected critical distance, who were either awed (though not shocked) by the demonstrations of American power in Afghanistan and Iraq, or who converged with the administration's imperial agenda. As the statements below suggest there was more to this than a simple suspension of critical judgment. Indeed, Joseph Nye told this author in 2001 that there were 'rhetorical rather than substantive differences'[82] between the neo-conservatives and liberal internationalists. There has always been a fine line between 'liberal imperialism' and 'liberal internationalism'. After 2001, that line was crossed.

Soon after the invasion of Afghanistan, Michael Ignatieff, then Director of the Carr Center for Human Rights Policy of the Kennedy School of Government, Harvard University, asserted:

> The contemporary situation in global politics has no precedent since the age of the later Roman Emperors...Britain's prime minister can shuttle usefully between Islamabad and New Delhi, but the influence that determines outcomes comes from Washington. This is a painful reminder for Europeans, who like the Japanese believed the myth that economic power could be equivalent of military might. Events since 9/11 have rubbed in the lesson that global power is still measured by military capacity... The US uses its power to enforce a new international division of labor in which America does the bombing and fighting, the French, British and Germans serve as police in the border zones, and the Dutch, Swiss and Scandinavians provide humanitarian aid.

In short, a 'new international order is emerging, crafted to suit American imperial objectives'.[83] Paul Kennedy, reversing his declinist judgments of a decade earlier, wrote:

Nothing has ever existed like the [present] disparity of power...
The *Pax Britannica* was run on the cheap...Napoleon's France,
Philip II's Spain had powerful foes and were part of a multipolar
system. Charlemagne's empire was merely western European in
stretch. The Roman empire stretched further afield, but there was
another great empire in Persia and a larger one in China. There
is no comparison.[84]

As American tanks rolled into Baghdad, Ignatieff celebrated the
'empire lite':

Multilateral solutions to the world's problems are all very well,
but they have no teeth unless America bares its fangs. America's
empire is not like empires of times past, built on colonies,
conquest and the white man's burden. We are no longer in the
era of the United Fruit Company, when American corporations
needed the Marines to secure their investments overseas. The 21st
century imperium is a new invention in the annals of political
science, an empire lite, a global hegemony whose grace notes are
free markets, human rights and democracy, enforced by the most
awesome military power the world has ever known.[85]

In a discussion paper drafted for the National Intelligence Council
(NIC) in 2003, John Ikenberry wrote: 'What the 1990s wrought
is a unipolar America that is more powerful than any other great
state in history'. Noting 'extreme and unprecedented disparities of
power', he argued that:

American power advantages are multidimensional, unprecedented,
and unlikely to disappear any time soon...The recent exercise of
American military power – in Afghanistan and Iraq – has shown
the world how extraordinary and effective that power is. In effect,
the exercise of power has created even more power – or at least
revealed that power to the world. The United States can take
down entire regimes without sustaining high costs of manpower
or national treasure.[86]

Even if Ikenberry argued that the United States should use its power
advantages to establish and institutionalise world 'hegemony with
liberal characteristics' rather than 'hegemony with imperial characteristics',[87] these are not innocuous statements. If demonstrations of
power generate more power, it is hard to see why the imperial state

would set restraints on its use. Intentionally or not, these paeans to military might could only reinforce the determination and increase the freedom of those wielding power to exercise it.

One plausible reason for the support given by liberal interventionists for empire was the resurgence of the figure of the 'barbarian'. September 11 released the colonial imagination and relaxed liberal internationalist inhibitions about conquest and empire. Reflecting the historical ambivalence of liberalism over western colonial expansion, a number of influential authors framed imperialism not as the historical source of but as the solution to global problems. Reviving John Stuart Mill's distinction between zones of intervention and non-intervention, American and British authors argued that September 11 evidenced the 'spreading collapse of state order in the postcolonial border zones',[88] hence the need for intervention in and long-term occupation and tutelage of 'disintegrating' Third World societies. In a much commented upon apology for liberal imperialism, Sebastian Mallaby, a *Washington Post* columnist and fellow at the Council on Foreign Relations (CFR), painted an apocalyptic picture of generalised entropy in the Third World. In his undifferentiated and undocumented rendering, the Third World was depicted as a realm of chaos, failing states, uncontrolled demographic growth and social disintegration. These factors, he argued, produced endemic violence that was spilling over and threatening world order. Imperialism thus became an historical necessity:

> None of these threats would conjure up an imperialist revival if the West had other ways of responding. But experience has shown that nonimperialist options [are not] altogether reliable…The rich world increasingly realizes that its interests are threatened by chaos, and that it lacks the tools to fix the problem…The logic of neoimperialism is too compelling for the Bush administration to resist. The chaos in the world is too threatening to ignore…A new imperial moment has arrived, and by virtue of its power America is bound to play the leading role.[89]

Max Boot, a neo-conservative journalist and fellow at the Council on Foreign Relations, made a similar case:

> It is striking – and no coincidence – that America now faces the prospect of military action in many of the same lands where generations of British colonial soldiers went on campaigns… Afghanistan and other troubled lands today cry out for the sort

of enlightened foreign administration once provided by self-confident Englishmen in jodhpurs and pith helmets.[90]

Jeffrey Garten, former Undersecretary of Commerce for International Trade who at the time was Dean of the Yale School of Management, called for the creation of an American Colonial Service to 'handle the aftermath of US military intervention in other countries'. Echoing A. Lawrence Lowell's 1900 proposal to the same effect, Garten wrote:

> Such an endeavor would recognize the reality that our nation will be forced to intervene militarily in many other countries in the coming decades and that the success of those operations depends on our ability to establish minimum conditions for stability and lay the foundation for subsequent political and economic progress. In short, as an empire in all but name, the United States must create an institution akin in its professionalism, its focus and its skills to the former British Colonial Service.[91]

The aim then would be the long-term colonial tutelage of societies left by the wayside of western modernity. On the other side of the Atlantic, Robert Cooper, then Prime Minister Tony Blair's senior diplomatic adviser, made a carefully thought-through case for 'liberal imperialism'. Cooper distinguished between post-modern, modern and pre-modern states. The first group, in his classification, encompasses countries that have chosen interdependence, renounced the use of violence and adopted a cosmopolitan ethos: Europe and Japan. Given its mixed record, the United States is 'the more doubtful [western] case'. The second is made up of states such as 'India, Pakistan and China' which act according to the dictates of the 'classical state system' and the 'supremacy of national interests'. The third is a broad group of failed and rogue states which emerged 'precisely because of the death of imperialism', a heart of darkness where 'chaos is the norm and war a way of life'. To deal with the latter group Cooper argued:

> Among ourselves, we operate on the basis of laws and open cooperative security. But when dealing with more old-fashioned kinds of states outside the postmodern continent of Europe, we need to revert to the rougher methods of an earlier era – force, pre-emptive attack, deception, whatever is necessary to deal with those who still live in the nineteenth century world of every state

for itself. Among ourselves, we keep the law but when we are operating in the jungle, we must also use the laws of the jungle.[92]

'What is needed then', he concluded, is 'a new kind of imperialism, one acceptable to a world of human rights and cosmopolitan values. We can already discern its outline: an imperialism which, like all imperialism, aims to bring order and organisation but which rests today on the voluntary principle.' Cooper, like his American counterparts, leaves unsaid how one might reconcile cosmopolitan values with force, pre-emptive attack and *whatever is necessary* to curb 'chaos' in the Third World. Neo-imperialism was accompanied by a rehabilitation of empire. Gordon Brown, then Chancellor of the Exchequer, told the *Daily Mail* in 2005 that 'the days of Britain having to apologise for its colonial history are over. We should move forward [and] celebrate much of our past rather than apologise for it'.[93]

The synchronism of the revival of colonial outlooks on both shores of the Atlantic is too striking to be overlooked. It highlights a regularity over long periods of representations of the imperial self and the colonial other that were submerged but not erased by the end of formal empires and which resurfaced and were reformulated under new historical circumstances as part of a new agenda of empire. In the US case, our main concern, the language of power and global destiny of the American imperial elites at the end of the twentieth century, bears remarkable kinship with the magnified sense of self and world ambitions of the late nineteenth-century expansionists. It is ontogenetically related to the visions and aims of the architects of *Pax Americana* who developed an 'extravagant imperial creed of global responsibility and perfected the techniques of expansionism'.[94] Imaginings of imperium surfaced during each of these moments of real or perceived ascent. The distinguishing feature of the imperialist urge of the twenty-first century, which is hence not an aberration but a variation in a wider imperial trajectory, was its limitless aim – the attempt to secure global monopoly. In the aftermath of the Cold War, a segment of the American power elite, filled with visions of omnipotence, sought through force to vastly widen the reach of US power and indefinitely expand its temporal horizon.

7
Losing Control

At this stage of history we are the greatest power in the world – if we behave like it.

Walt Rostow, 1964[1]

At the end of the nineteenth century, the British-centred liberal international economic order began to fall apart. On the wane since the 1870s, free trade gave way to protectionism and mercantilism: 'From the early 1890s, protectionism became a much more pronounced trend and by 1913 all the large countries had adopted a protective stance. Even some of the smaller European economies, such as Sweden, made a decisive move in this direction...By 1913 trade policy in the developed world is best described as islands of liberalism surrounded by a sea of protectionism'.[2] Under the guiding hand of a strong state that created the institutional frameworks for modernisation, Germany, the emblematic European 'late industrialiser', saw its share of world manufacturing output rise from 4.9 per cent in 1860 to 14.8 per cent in 1913, a point higher than Great Britain (13.9 per cent). The shifting economic balance and intensifying inter-imperialist rivalries ultimately overcame Britain's ability to 'hold the centre', bringing *Pax Britannica* and the first cycle of western globalisation to an end. Exacerbated nationalism, militarism and inter-imperialist rivalries combined to shatter the long post-1815 intra-European peace.

In his account of the collapse of liberalism and the nineteenth-century world order, Karl Polanyi argues that transnational capitalist cooperation, embodied by pan-European networks of *haute finance*, ultimately succumbed to national power politics: 'Power had precedence over profit. However closely their realms interpenetrated, ultimately it was war that laid down the law to business'.[3] Despite dense intra-European economic linkages and a high degree of market integration in the late nineteenth and early twentieth centuries, evidenced in cross-border investments, capital flows, intra-European migratory movements and price convergence,[4] the tenuous webs of economic interdependence were swept away in the rising nationalist wave.

WAR AND GLOBALISATION

We should not expect identity between the unravelling of late nineteenth-century world order and the mounting disorder of the world political economy today. Polanyi's discussion of the tension between national power and world market logics nonetheless provides a useful entry point to discuss present disintegrative trends. There has been a manifest contradiction between the pursuit of limitless American national power expansion of recent years and the processes of economic transnationalisation and supra-statal institutional construction that have been the main characteristics of contemporary globalisation. As David Harvey emphasises, 'the territorial and the capitalist logics of power are distinct from one another [and] frequently tug against each other, sometimes to the point of outright antagonism'.[5] The constitution of a global liberal market in the aftermath of the Cold War may well have required an imperial state overseeing system regulation and setting systemic disciplines and constraints.[6] Indeed, that is how American policy-makers interpreted the US post-Cold War position. Yet, this contemporary version of nineteenth-century free trade imperialism is hardly coterminous with the attempt to establish 'unilateral world domination through absolute military superiority'.[7] Hence Eric Hobsbawm's remark that 'there is no rational justification'[8] for the Bush administration's monopoly-seeking in terms of the interests of US and global capitalism.

In the late 1980s and in the early 1990s the pursuit and deepening of global market liberalisation became the dominant policy agenda of the United States, the European Union, the multilateral institutions and the transnational private constituents of the American empire: the mobile internationalised social groups which participate in borderless flows, profit from and have a vested interest in an open liberal world economic system and look to the United States as a centre of political, economic and cultural gravity. A decade and a half ago, the set of ideas and practices encompassed in the 'Washington Consensus' was so pervasive that globalisation under American auspices and convergence around a single economic and social model was widely if erroneously assumed to be an irreversible trend. Yet, much like the ephemeral Wilsonian moment, the post-Cold War liberal paradigm turned out to be an interlude. Today, the movement towards global market integration, liberalisation and democratisation is exhausted. The Washington Consensus has fallen apart. Launched in 2001, the Doha 'development' trade round, which was supposed to have been completed in 2005 and provide the last cornerstone of the global liberal multilateral trading order, stalled in 2006 and has not been successfully revived. Largely at American initiative, trade multilateralism has been superseded by proliferating bilateral or regional Free Trade Agreements (FTAs).[9] Most recently and spectacularly, the intellectual and material edifice of global liberalisation has collapsed with the outbreak in 2007–2008 of the systemic financial crisis.

According to IMF and WB estimates, the 'virulent' financial upheaval has already provoked the most severe contraction of world economic activity in the advanced economies since 1945. Along with the decline of global demand, international trade contracted in 2008–2009 for the first time since 1982. The social transmission of the crisis has been equally rapid, with a sharp rise of unemployment worldwide and an expected erosion of real wages for hundreds of millions of workers, producing what the International Labour Organization (ILO) has called a 'global jobs crisis'.[10] The amplitude of this time-compressed social shock varies from region to region, but if the world's largest economy is anything to go by, it will be severe. Official US unemployment rose from an average 4.5 per cent in 2007 to 6.7 per cent in November 2008 and 10 per cent in late 2009.[11] The crisis will thus test the ability and the will of governments and international institutions to find domestic solutions to temper its social effects while not accentuating the fragmentation of the international system along national and/or regional lines. It is too early to say whether they will meet the test.

It is of course conceivable that late twentieth-century globalisation would have stalled or even unravelled over time, independently of the US' imperialist turn, as world market expansion reached its spatial and social limits. The series of financial shocks of the past two and half decades – the 1987 worldwide stock market crash, the 1994 Mexican peso crisis and the 1997/1998 'Asian' financial crisis – pointed to growing global market volatility and mounting systemic risk. Still, in much the same way that nineteenth-century world market expansion and integration flowed out of a centre that set the dominant norms of the age, the pursuit of late twentieth-century global capitalist expansion and world market integration flowing out of the American core required/requires the continued commitment of the United States to the institutions, the sets of ideas, the frameworks and the rules that made the intergovernmental and transnational elite convergence over world market integration possible in the first place. At the very least it required, on the part of the US, behaviour consistent with the interests and expectations of public and private stakeholders in the world market system who rely on the US to enable global flows and to govern the liberal system in which they prosper and operate. They share the US' interest in international stability and can accept and sometimes applaud an empire that enforces their interests, if necessary by policing the 'barbarian' periphery. But, as world reactions to the invasion of Iraq showed, the type of militarised empire proposed by the least cosmopolitan parts of the US power elite does not constitute an acceptable global political–military regime for even a good many core constituents.[12]

Contrary to what the imperialists thought in the 1990s, the US was never in a position to enforce a new world order based on exclusive American authority. To the contrary, the US demand for unquestioned deference proved unacceptable to a majority of states which were aware that the subtext of the war in Iraq was 'whether the future world order [would be] unipolar or a multi-polar system in which others have an influence on the sole superpower'.[13] It has definitely invalidated the assumption that a unipolar distribution of world power would be stable, durable and normatively desirable.[14] Rather than producing order and stability, US monopoly-seeking has produced fragmentation and instability. As a *Harvard Business Review* article noted in 2004, the 'new world order of Bush *père* and his successor, Bill Clinton, has been replaced with the new world disorder of Bush *fils*. Under the second Bush's administration, the economic and political rationale behind the Washington Consensus of the 1990s has unravelled…The second President Bush put the final nail in the coffin of the new world order'.[15] Ironically, the administration has thus provoked outcomes in sharp contradiction with the aim of securing lasting American global primacy.

The US presently faces a dual legitimacy crisis which bears surface analogies to the crisis of the 1970s when it was confronted with a failed war, a prolonged economic downturn, a worldwide questioning of its international authority and legitimacy and a diffusion of economic power in Europe and Japan's favour. As we saw in previous chapters, the US recovered from the 1970s crisis and found itself in a position of restored power and authority in the 1990s. While remaining agnostic as to ultimate outcomes, it is unlikely that the present crisis will resolve itself in similar manner. The main difference with the 1970s resides in the fact that diffusion is not occurring within but outside of the 'western state block'.[16] The emerging or re-emerging powers of the twenty-first century –

China, India, Brazil, South Africa, Russia, etc. – are not subordinate components of the international security structure of *Pax Americana*. They enjoy far greater relative autonomy than did Germany or Japan during the Cold War and are not subject to the dependencies and mechanisms of control generated by the hegemonic alliance systems. To be sure, all exhibit various types of vulnerabilities: global market exposure, uneven domestic social and economic development and environmental constraints. Yet, as their growing voice and role in multilateral institutions such as the WTO shows, they are not simply conditioned by global forces outside their control. China in particular has become an active international unit shaping the world economic environment as much as it has been shaped by it. This movement towards polycentrism, which has altogether different implications than the diffusion of economic power within the Triad that occurred in the 1970s, was accentuated by the drive for world empire of the George W. Bush administration.

THE CRISIS OF AMERICAN POWER

To judge the extent of the US' loss of control one must look more closely at the different dimensions of the crisis of American power and authority. The first and most obvious is that the administration's wars have produced regional outcomes opposite to those intended. The United States has not secured political or economic control of Iraq.[17] It has failed to effect 'regime change' in Iran and Syria or to alter the behaviour of those states, to curb Hezbollah in Lebanon, to secure Israel or establish minimal framework conditions for peace in Palestine or to stabilise Afghanistan. It has proved unable to reconfigure what it once, blurring cultural and political distinctions to the extreme, dubbed 'The Greater Middle East'. Evidenced very early on and acknowledged by the US military and intelligence establishment,[18] failure in Iraq led to a concomitant rise of Iranian regional influence that the US has been attempting to counter since 2006–2007 through a classical imperial policy of divide and rule, pitting the Shiite and Sunni communities within Iraq and, more broadly, in the Gulf and the Middle East against one another.[19] Designed to re-establish US control, the 'strategic realignment' operated by Condoleezza Rice aimed to create 'a de facto alliance between Israel and moderate [Sunni] Arab states against Iranian extremism'.[20] In Iraq, the policy has translated into support given to former Sunni insurgents (the 'awakening councils'). While the Bush administration has claimed, contrary to expert opinion,[21] that the new policy explains falling levels of violence, it leaves unresolved the fundamental problems caused by the invasion within Iraq or in the region more broadly. The US, under the new Obama administration, appears to be on a pathway of gradual withdrawal from Iraq, but the war has left the country torn along sectarian lines, in a state of economic disrepair and facing a humanitarian crisis.[22] A similar assessment can be made of Afghanistan, where the United States and NATO have failed after six years of occupation to meet their minimal political and military objectives – the consolidation of the Afghan state, the containment of the Taliban and the stabilisation of the border areas between Afghanistan and Pakistan.[23]

More so than Vietnam, if only because of the strategic sensitivity of the Gulf, these multiple failures will have lasting effects. In an insightful essay written in 1972, Hannah Arendt remarked that the United States escalated the war in Vietnam to 'keep intact an image of omnipotence'.[24] Quoting the *Pentagon Papers*, she emphasised that the US sought to demonstrate 'the will and the ability…to have its way in world affairs' and 'to behave like the greatest power in the world for no other reason than to convince the world of this simple fact'. As the war dragged on, the goal 'became the image itself'.[25] By the late 1960s a good part of the American population came to the conclusion that the 'establishment was out of its mind'.[26] Failure in Vietnam of course caused a major fracture within the power elite, with figures such as Dean Acheson, the architect of global military containment, breaking with the escalation course.[27] Today, the image of omnipotence has again been shattered and a similar fracture has occurred within the American security and foreign policy elite. The consensus among realist scholars and US policy practitioners is that the Iraq war has caused 'enormous and possibly irreparable damage to the United States' position in the region and the world'[28] and may well lead to the end of 'American supremacy in the Gulf and Middle East'.[29] Their dismay over the outcomes of the past six years is hard to overstate.[30] The realist assessment is exemplified by Zbigniew Brzezinski's terse critical statement in testimony before the Senate Foreign Relations Committee in early 2007 that the invasion of Iraq has proved a 'historic, strategic and moral calamity'.[31]

These institutional critics, it should be stressed, were/are guardians of American power, managers of the National Security State and sometimes central actors in the imperial interventions during the Cold War and the post-Cold War. Whatever their political affiliations and personal beliefs, they were/are system managers of a self-perpetuating security structure (first analysed by C. Wright Mills) whose function is the production and reproduction of power. As a social group, the realists within the institutions of state and the broader national security establishment cannot be distinguished from the object of their criticism in terms of their willingness to use force or their historically demonstrated ruthlessness in achieving state aims – the bombing of Cambodia, the overthrow of Salvador Allende and the support given to General Suharto's invasion of Timor in the early 1970s being notorious cases in point. Nor can the primary cause of dissent of this social group be attributed to conflicting convictions over ethics, norms and values (though this may indeed be a motivating factor for individuals). It lies rather in the realisation and concern that the Bush administration's agenda has 'nearly broken the US army',[32] fundamentally weakened the United States' position in the Middle East and Gulf and, in Brzezinski's words, severely damaged 'America's global legitimacy' (that is, the ability to shape world preferences and set the global agenda). In a word, the Bush administration has squandered the US' Cold War 'victory'. The most sophisticated expressions of dissent, such as Brzezinski's, reflect the understanding that power is not reducible to the ability to coerce, and that, once lost, authority is difficult to restore.

Breakdown of Legitimacy

Monopoly-seeking has indeed caused a precipitous collapse of the US' longstanding claim to be a legitimate world authority. Though that claim was never credible in the Third World, 'the disaster area of [US] foreign policy' in the late John Kenneth Galbraith's words,[33] it was widely accepted among American allies and transnational constituents. Susan Strange rightly noted that the American empire would 'remain strong and stable as long as there are shared interests between the dominant center and important sections of society in the peripheral parts of empire'.[34] Neither she nor other analysts expected a situation in which the power political purposes of the American state would come into sharp contradiction with the needs and expectations of allies and the cosmopolitan economic elites. Despite rhetorical claims to universality, the Bush administration could not credibly claim that the expansion of the United States' reach and power provided international public goods since the legal frameworks, the norms and the rules governing world affairs that it abandoned are themselves essential international public goods.[35]

The decision to abandon international law and international humanitarian law, supplanting them with the arbitrary, illiberal and illegal[36] or lawless exercise of national power was understood for what it was, the expression of an authoritarian drive to achieve limitless US autonomy. The ultimate expression of this was the authorisation of torture at the very highest levels of government.[37]

Hence the refusal by many of the US' historic allies to bend to the ultimatum 'either you are with us or against us'. Unlike the 1991 Gulf war, the US made no serious effort to obtain widespread consent, either because the administration knew that support would be withheld or, more plausibly, because it simply did not care (Condoleezza Rice told Chile's ambassador to the UN that the US would 'go in [Iraq] with, or if needed, without the U.N.'[38]). As the clash over Iraq at the United Nations Security Council in January and February 2003 showed, the US' demand for undiluted global authority was unacceptable not only to countries outside the structures of *Pax Americana*, but also to historic American allies in western Europe and Latin America. The administration's response was to threaten countries that refused their support such as France that they would 'suffer the consequences'[39] and would be 'punished'.[40] In response, the French Foreign Minister Dominique de Villepin humorously asked Colin Powell whether he 'wanted the US to declare war on France'.[41] More potentially vulnerable countries such as Mexico, Chile and Angola – members of the Security Council at the time – which also refused to back the invasion, were threatened with economic and political reprisals and repeatedly warned that they would suffer serious costs.[42] Notwithstanding the fact that President Bush 'spouted threats like a movie gangster'[43] these countries withheld their support.

This refusal signifies that they feared the prospect of an unconstrained and unpredictable military Leviathan acting at whim more than the potential 'focused enmity of the United States'.[44] While it is very imperfect, the post-1945 international legal and institutional order sets some restraints on the arbitrary exercise of force through collective rules and norms governing interstate behaviour. The United Nations Charter bans imperialism, wars of aggression and preventive war. The fact that the spirit and the letter of the Charter have often been transgressed by one state or another does not invalidate the principles enunciated, or reduce their importance. It points instead to the need for a more binding rules-based system of post-hegemonic global governance. Given power asymmetries and the differential distribution of effective rather than formal sovereignty in the international system, weaker states rely on these rules and norms, and the institutions embodying them, for minimal protection from direct coercion by stronger states. As South African President Thabo Mbeki said at the time, the risk posed was that authorisation of the war would have legitimised the right of 'the powerful...to use the authority of the U.N. and its prestige as a peace agency to legitimise a pre-determined decision to wage war'.[45]

ACCENTUATING CENTRIFUGAL TRENDS

Failure in Iraq further aggravated the US' legitimacy crisis. As in the 1970s, signs of loss of control are everywhere apparent: in the Gulf and Middle East; in Latin America, where US influence is at its lowest ebb in decades; in the former Soviet Union where, as the Summer 2008 Russian–Georgian crisis highlighted, the United States, after having gained significant influence in central Asia and the Caucasus in the 1990s and the early years of the new century, is no longer in a position to dictate its terms; in east Asia, where the US has been obliged, reluctantly, to settle with North Korea[46] and to recognise China as an indispensable actor in regional security; and in the international institutions, which the administration attempted to make 'irrelevant' but where neither the US (nor any other state or group of states) is able to drive the agenda any longer. Coming on top of all of this, the systemic crisis of the American financial system has torn apart the credibility of previously hegemonic American economic and financial discourse.

Latin American Regionalism

Many of these trends pre-date the Bush administration and therefore cannot be directly attributed to it. The erosion of the Washington Consensus on global liberalisation was already underway in Latin America and east Asia when the Bush administration came to power.[47] But by 'breaking away from the system of international relations that it did the most to promote and which it benefited from',[48] the Bush administration unwittingly accelerated and accentuated centrifugal movements that were already underway. In Latin America, beginning with election of Hugo Chávez in 1998, the backlash against the policies that had generated the 'lost decade' in the 1980s and the widening social inequalities of the 1990s[49] paved the way for the election of a series of left-leaning leaders who represent a political break with the past: Luiz Inácio Lula da Silva in Brazil in 2002; Néstor Kirchner in Argentina in 2003; Tabaré Vázquez in Uruguay in 2004; Evo Morales in Bolivia in 2005; Michelle Bachelet in Chile, Daniel Ortega in Nicaragua and Rafael Correa in Ecuador in 2006; most recently, Fernando Lugo in Paraguay in 2008. To varying degrees, these new leaders have pulled away from the neo-liberal model. Notwithstanding continuing dependence on the US market and shallow regional economic integration (intra-regional trade accounts for a mere 25 per cent of total South American trade), the trend unmistakably reflects growing political autonomy.

The expansion of the Common Market of the South (Mercosur, or Mercosul)[50] reflects a renewed effort to intensify regional economic integration. Of note is the 2007 decision by Mercosur countries to create the *Banco del Sur* (Bank of the South) whose stated purpose is to promote 'a space devoted to the promotion of economic and social development...[and] to the convergence and comple-mentarity of processes of economic integration'. The Bank was conceived as the seed-form of autonomous institutions not subject to the American-*cum*-western dominated international financial institutions, notably the IMF, which has been much weakened over the past decade and has 'lost most of its power over middle income countries'.[51] More recently, on May 23, 2008, the Union of South American Nations (UNASUR) was founded in Brasilia, a political and economic community regrouping the countries of the Mercosur and the Andean Community. Political and economic relations of the countries of UNASUR with China and Russia, the first in particular, have been significantly amplified in recent years.[52]

The Bush administration's behaviour amplified the backlash. The administration, writes Heraldo Muñoz, Chile's Ambassador to the United Nations, 'tore multilateralism to pieces', leaving 'deep mistrust and bitterness...between the US and its allies in Europe, Latin America and beyond'.[53] Brazil, the continent's largest economy, has in recent years been an initiating actor in south–south cooperation: in 2003, India, Brazil and South Africa established a trilateral partnership (IBSA), the aim of which is to work out common responses of the Global South to global issues (trade negotiations, food security, energy, etc.).[54] President Lula da Silva's reaction in September 2008 to the financial crisis was to say: 'People ask me about the crisis, and I answer, go ask Bush. It's his crisis, not mine'.[55] This may not be an accurate economic assessment given the global nature of the crisis, but it certainly reflects a widespread and deeply held political sentiment in societies that for many years have been on the receiving end of intense pressures to restructure their economic and social systems. In October 2008, Lula said that 'we need to learn from the crisis to construct a new world economic order'.[56]

East Asian Regionalism

Centrifugal movement has if anything been more pronounced in east Asia, where regional economic integration has been deepening and has become increasingly formalised over the past decade. This is reflected in the rapid growth of intra-regional trade, which as a share of total trade has been rising constantly since the 1970s (20 per cent in 1970, 32 per cent in the early 1980s, 47 per cent in the early 1990s, 54.8 per cent in 2000, 58.5 per cent in 2007),[57] but also in the movement towards protective 'monetary regionalism' that followed the 1997–1998 financial crisis and which is designed to insulate regional markets from exogenous disruptions.[58] The United States played an instrumental if unintended role in both these movements. Like contemporaneous changes in Latin America, the new east Asia regionalism was a response to successive US mercantilist interventions to reshape the regional economic landscape. The first wave of regionalisation under Japanese auspices was stimulated by the Plaza Accord of 1985, which led to a sharp appreciation in the value of the Japanese yen (JPY). A hegemonic action designed by the Reagan administration to boost American exports and decrease Japan's industrial competitiveness, the appreciation transformed Japan overnight into the world's leading creditor and generated a major expansion of worldwide Japanese foreign direct investment

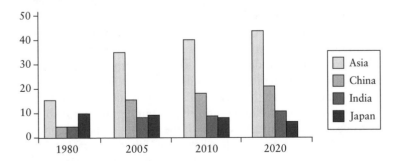

Figure 7.1   Asia Share of World GDP (PPP)

Derived from: United Nations Statistics Division and Economist Intelligence Unit[59]

(FDI). At the regional level, to restore their price competitiveness, Japanese firms redeployed their lower value-added manufacturing activities to southeast Asia and some higher value-added activities to the newly industrialised economies (NIEs) of northeast Asia.

Japanese investment flows tripled between 1985 and 1989 in the NIEs (South Korea, Singapore, Taiwan, Hong Kong) and were multiplied by seven in the emerging countries of southeast Asia (Malaysia, Thailand, Indonesia, the Philippines). Between 1985 and 1995, the regional share of total Japanese FDI rose from 8 per cent to 35 per cent (in value from JPY109 billion to JPY753 billion).[60] Unlike Japanese investment in Europe and the US, a significant share was designed to meet demand in the Japanese domestic market (one-fifth of total Japanese manufacturing imports come from regional subsidiaries of Japanese firms). Over a short period of time this generated a concatenated Japan-centred regional division of labour in east Asia reflecting the growing importance of intra-firm trade of Japanese multinational companies in the regional division of labour. Claude Pottier, a scholar who has carefully analysed the new division of labour, points out that the integration of regional economies in the 'Japanese productive system' encouraged an 'evolution towards higher value-added activities in the NIEs [and] direct transfers of evolved technologies towards the ASEAN 4 and China', the latter becoming a major area of Japanese investment after 1991.[61]

Regional economic integration under Japanese auspices was not an outcome that the US had desired or foreseen. During the first few decades of the Cold War the US structured its regional relations around bilateral trade links that were characterised by deep single-market dependencies. As long as it did not challenge American economic predominance, the east Asian developmental state was tolerated, indeed encouraged, as part of a Cold War compact in which the United States' allies in northeast Asia traded their political sovereignty for unrestricted access to the US market. The northeast Asian developmental states were brought into the American system on the understanding that 'Japan's sun was to rise high but not too high; high enough to cause trade problems for the [western] allies in declining industries'[62] but certainly not so high as to become a competing centre of the world capitalist economy. There was hence a perceptible relief in the United States when Japan plunged in 1990 into a long period of economic stagnation after the bubble in the FIRE (Finance, Insurance, Real Estate) sector burst – another unintended effect of the 1985 appreciation of the

JPY. The crisis proved, in the condescending words of a US author, that the 'Japanese model was not a different type of capitalism but a holdover from an earlier stage of capitalism'.[63] The subtext was that the east Asian latecomers to modern capitalism had been put back in their rightful place.

The same imperial mentality was evidenced during the acute 1997–1998 regional crisis which the US sought to exploit to 'secure ownership of the region's domestic economies' and to maintain east Asia's 'dependence on external demand and foreign-owned or foreign financed production capacity'.[64] US management of the crisis confirms Immanuel Wallerstein's judgment that aggressive efforts to gain access to local financial markets and corporate assets, during and after the crisis, were part of an effort to dismantle 'developmentalist policies throughout the world'.[65] In contrast to the US Treasury's rapid and decisive bailout of Mexico in 1994, the US and its transatlantic partners sat back for months while the crisis spread through east Asia. The US Treasury vetoed the Japanese proposal to set up an Asian Monetary Fund (AMF) which would have pooled Asian resources and provided much needed liquidity, with few or no conditions attached, to countries facing massive time-compressed capital outflows. An IMF bailout with restrictive conditions was arranged only when it became clear that the crisis was spreading contagiously to global markets.[66] This opportunistic and coercive behaviour generated nationalist backlashes and stimulated intense efforts to develop regional mechanisms of protection. As Heribert Dieter and Richard Higgott put it, US and IMF actions and non-actions pushed the east Asian policy elites to consider 'the benefits of regionalism without the Caucasians'.[67]

The most outspoken proposals came in 1998 from Malaysia which, under then Prime Minister Mohamad Mahatir's leadership, called for regional capital controls and advocated the replacement of the dollar as a settlement instrument in regional trade. For lack of appropriate mechanisms and institutions making this possible, this did not occur (although the idea resurfaced a few years later). However, as seen in subsequent initiatives, there has been strong regional convergence around the more general aim of creating a common market and finding ways to shield local economies from global market turbulences and external pressures. In 1999, the Association of South East Asian Nations (ASEAN) invited China, Japan and the Republic of Korea (ROK) to create a common market. At the subsequent ASEAN+3 summit that year, regional leaders discussed the long-term aim of future monetary union along the

European model. In 2000, the Chiang Mai initiative led to bilateral swap arrangements among central banks and was understood as a first step towards the creation of a regional financial institution to pool currency reserves. In 2003, ASEAN+3 announced the establishment of the Asian Bond Fund (ABF), initially capitalised at $1 billion. Designed to channel reserves held by Asian central banks back into the region, the ABF would, as regional leaders insisted, redirect a share of Asian financial flows away from western markets and should gradually allow the region to replace the dollar as an intra-regional settlement instrument.[68] In 2005–2006, senior officials at the Asian Development Bank began pushing for the creation of an Asian Currency Unit (ACU) as a step towards monetary union.[69] The latest initiative, in May 2008, was the announcement by Finance ministers from 13 east Asian countries to create an $80 billion pool to protect regional currencies, replacing the bilateral currency swap arrangements under the earlier Chiang Mai initiative.[70]

CHINA'S EMERGING ROLE

Though still incomplete, these incremental steps towards protective monetary regionalism have set basic frameworks for the future institutionalisation of a regional system of monetary coordination and integration. Again, there is no direct causal relation between the Bush administration's expansionism and the above. But while the United States has been busily building and deploying its military power and accumulating large deficits, east Asia has been reinforcing regional cooperation and, in the case of China, accumulating wealth and financial power. China has in fact emerged as the main beneficiary of the multiple crises of the past decade, both on a regional and global level. It was protected by capital controls from financial contagion during the 1997–1998 crisis and played a crucial in role in regional recovery. In contrast to the Japanese economy, which stalled during the decade, China remained on a strong growth trajectory: Chinese annual GDP growth averaged 9.3 per cent between 1997 and 2007 against Japan's 1.2 per cent. China played an important supportive role in reviving economic activity in the region by absorbing a growing share of regional exports. The choice not to depreciate the renminbi (RMB) in 1998, despite the wave of regional currency devaluations, proved a crucial decision, avoiding a cascade of further competitive depreciations in the region. While the US short-sightedly squashed Japanese efforts of regional leadership, China was able to demonstrate 'responsibility and leadership through its policy choices'.[71]

In the aftermath of the crisis, trade and investment flows between China and the rest of Asia grew significantly, proving an important factor in regional recovery. The share of NIE and ASEAN exports to China rose respectively from 17.5 per cent and 8.9 per cent in 1990, to 25.4 and 11.1 per cent in 2006. Since the late 1990s, regional Asian trade with China has been growing faster than Asian trade with the US: Japan's imports from China already exceed those from the US and Japanese exports to China have been steadily rising. This same trend is also apparent in South Korean, Thai, Malaysian and Singaporean trade flows.[72] 'China', notes a 2007 IMF study:

> ...has displaced the United States as the largest export market for an increasing number of Asian countries. It has also been pivotal in boosting intraregional trade and Foreign Direct Investment (FDI), particularly in the form of intermediate goods channelled through multinationals as part of cross-border chains...The potential expansion of China's domestic market creates opportunities for the regional economies, for example, to produce higher-tech goods that China is unlikely to be able to produce domestically in the near future.[73]

Hence the self-congratulatory assessment of senior Chinese leaders that the 'launch of East Asian cooperation can be directly attributed to the Asian Financial Crisis of 1997. The process of the East Asian cooperation has been consolidated day by day since then [and is now] based on a multi-layered, multi-faceted structure'.[74] Given important development differentials between countries, as well as a complex set of interstate problems, a truly cohesive east Asian regional system is still quite a long way off. Chinese–Japanese relations in particular remain an unstable mix of cooperation and rivalry. Yet we may well be witnessing the first steps of the construction of a China-centred regional political economy.

China, along with a few other emerging economies, has also come out of the past decade in a much-enhanced global financial position. Prior to the outbreak of the 2008 crisis, observers had noted a 'global financial power shift' highlighted by constantly rising US deficits and corresponding surpluses in emerging states, China in particular.[75] Net US external debt rose from $360 billion or 5 per cent of GDP in 1997 to $3.7 trillion, or 27 per cent of GDP in 2007. During the same time frame, China's foreign currency reserves resulting from trade surpluses rose from $170 billion to over $1 trillion, more than a third of Asian reserves and nearly one-fifth of total international reserves.[76]

Table 7.1   Major Foreign Holders of US Treasury Securities (end July 2008)

	Asia	Japan	China	UK	Oil Ex**	Brazil	Carib*	Lux	Russia
$billions	1,256	593	518.7	290.8	173.9	148.4	133.5	75.8	74.1

Source: Treasury Department, Washington, D.C.[77]
* Caribbean countries, including offshore centres
**Oil exporting countries

China has thus become an increasingly important source of financing of US deficits and presently owns a significant share of sovereign US debt – around $500 billion out of a total $2.676 trillion of the Treasury securities owned by foreign holders are held by China, placing it in a position just behind Japan and far ahead of the oil exporting states. Total Chinese holdings in the US are estimated above $1 trillion.[78] This configuration has generated a complex and uneasy relationship of co-dependence between the United States and China in which the US' dependence on external capital flows, and hence its vulnerability to exogenously dictated adjustments, is matched by China's and other surplus countries' continuing dependence on the American domestic market to maintain export-dependent growth trajectories. Co-dependency also applies with respect to the dollar, the value of which depends on continued and rising inflows of capital and which surplus countries cannot suddenly divest themselves from without incurring major losses.

Balance of Financial Terror

This configuration of co-dependence is perilous for both parties and its sustainability over time is questionable. The threshold at which equilibrium is broken, that is when one or another player chooses to defect or is forced to defect from the game, cannot be known in advance. Commenting on these financial asymmetries a few years ago, Lawrence Summers noted that the US' 'substantial dependence on foreign capital and a substantial current account and trade deficit' had generated a 'balance of financial terror' that was fraught with dangers for the United States. One of the 'troubling aspect[s] of this dependence', he wrote, 'is its geopolitical significance':

There is surely something odd about the world's greatest power being the world's greatest debtor. In order to finance prevailing levels of consumption and investment, must the United States be as dependent as it is on the discretionary acts of what are inevitably political entities in other countries? It is true and can be argued forcefully that the incentive for Japan or China to dump treasury bills at a rapid rate is not very strong, given the consequences that it would have for their own economies. That is a powerful argument, and it is a reason a prudent person would avoid immediate concern. But it surely cannot be prudent for us as a country to rely on a kind of balance of financial terror to hold back reserve sales that would threaten our stability.[79]

If the unwinding of global imbalances 'happens suddenly and without control', he added, 'the consequences are likely to be very serious for the cyclical performance of the United States and the global economy. Ultimately, the consequences of these adjustments being mismanaged are likely to be profound for the global integration process that we all regard as so very important'.[80] It so happens that the adjustment, if one can call it that, has not come from an abrupt unwinding of global imbalances and withdrawals from the dollar but rather from an extraordinary crash of the American financial system. It is too early to tell how the crisis, which has rapidly spread to the global economy, will ultimately affect the world system and the relative positions of states. But one can conjecture that the expected sharp and durable contraction of economic activity and consumption in the most developed areas of the world economy over the next few years will make imperative for those emerging countries and world regions in a position to do so to rely increasingly on domestic demand and on autonomous sources of financing and investment to maintain growth momentum. However difficult this may prove in the short run, refocusing on endogenous national or regional growth factors appears an unavoidable step that, of all emerging regions, east Asia is in the best position to effect. Greater reliance on endogenous development would weaken the gravitational pull of dominant markets.

CHALLENGE TO US DOMINANCE

Over the past two decades, the United States has sought to enmesh China in the disciplines of the world economy, set until now by the multilateral institutions and the dominant western states. The assumption was that this would shape China's economic model and its political path, in other words that the disciplines would tame Chinese power, provoke an evolution of the political system and pattern the Chinese economy to meet the needs of dominant markets. However, the Chinese leadership's decision in the late 1970s gradually to integrate the world capitalist economy, leading to China's accession to the World Trade Organization in 2001, is now proving a challenge to American predominance. Like the United States or Japan in the late nineteenth century (see Chapter 2), China has successfully harnessed global capital and trade flows and channelled them into national economic expansion. The state has controlled liberalisation, at times accelerating the process or slowing it according to conjunctural needs.[81] Initial Chinese reactions to the global 2008 financial crisis suggest a renewed emphasis on state control: 'The Western consensus on the relation between the market and the government should be reviewed.'[82] It is noteworthy that Chinese scholars read their country's growth trajectory in historic terms, comparing it to that of the United States in the latter part of the nineteenth century. 'China's rise in the twenty-first century', writes Hu Angang 'is similar to the rise of the United States in the nineteenth and twentieth centuries'.[83] The comparison is indeed relevant and points to a paradox of global capitalist expansion. By selectively investing some social spaces rather than others, global capital flows do not uniformly generate dependency, underdevelopment and constraints. In some circumstances, they concur to the historical construction of those nation-states that are able to harness them to endogenous development objectives.

China has made no claim to global leadership. In fact, the PRC has taken great pains to avoid tensions with the United States, as seen in its cautious voting record at the United Nations Security Council in recent years.[84] Yet China's emerging position as a new centre of world capitalism is a far more problematic outcome for American power than the Japan-centric 'regional bloc' that Summers decried in 1989. Along with other emerging world regions, China will in future gain an increasingly important say in world politics and the management of the world economy. Hu Angang stresses that 'China is transforming the international system and its 'rise will inevitably lead to multi-polarization of the world. In the twenty-first century, no country, not even the United States can rule the world'.[85]

8
Conclusion
Order, Hierarchy and Pluralism

One thought alone preoccupies the submerged mind of Empire: how not to end, how not to die, how to prolong its era.

J.M. Coetzee[1]

'The imperial self', writes the American studies scholar Stephen Whitfield, 'does not know how to stop, indeed, does not see the *point* of stopping in struggling to gratify its desires even at the expense of others'. He adds: 'The attributes associated with 'the imperial self' have been, I suspect, more pronounced in America [than in Europe]'.[2] Indeed, unlike the western European imperial states whose world ambitions have been mostly if not entirely extinguished by two world wars and decolonisation, resurfacing intermittently in the UK and France as a nostalgia for lost 'grandeur', empire is a reality of the present as far as the US is concerned. Apart from the Civil War (1861–1865), which despite its human cost helped propel the country towards industrial modernity, the US never suffered the kinds of historical catastrophes experienced by western Europe, Russia or Japan. To the contrary, the two world wars proved to be stepping-stones in the US' long ascending movement from the confines to the centre of the world system, a movement that nurtured and was nurtured by an imagination of world empire as destiny. In the nineteenth and early twentieth centuries, the sense of limitlessness generated by continuous expansion was compounded by a feeling of immunity due to the absence of historical tragedy. Repeated failures and defeats after 1945 in the post-colonial world have dented but not erased these features of American imperial identity. The imperialist urge of the late twentieth century shows just how lively the American imperial imagination continues to be.

IMPERIAL COSMOLOGIES

This book has brought to light broad continuities in American expansionism over long periods. It has evidenced the self-conscious way in which US leaders participated and competed in the nineteenth-century inter-imperialist system, the likeness of late nineteenth-century and late twentieth-century visions of American world purpose and the constancy of core American assumptions about world order and international hierarchy. Just as the late nineteenth-century imperialists looked to existing or previous world empires as mirrors in which the US' destiny as the future centre of the world was reflected, American leaders since the Second World War have conceived of *Pax Americana* as the natural and hence necessary outcome of a historical process of imperial selection and succession. The explicit assertion of racial superiority of the late nineteenth-century empire-builders is outside the bounds of permissible political discourse today. But basic assumptions regarding the US' world historical role and international hierarchy have persisted, varying only slightly from one period and one administration to another. Like the 'vigorous empire men' of the 1890s who envisioned the US as the coming 'heart of the world',[3] post-1945 American leaders have with few exceptions perceived the US as an 'imperial state…primarily responsible for shaping and maintaining a necessary modicum of world order',[4] indeed as 'the center of the cosmos with other nations in orbit around it'.[5]

This cosmological scheme is ultimately derived from the western experience of domination that led the Europeans and Americans to believe that they were the sole subject of international history. It is at the root of the postulate, shared by historical actors and many mainstream contemporary American international relations theorists that the world needs a 'benevolent despot' to guarantee international order. Failing that, the mechanisms of interstate anarchy generate instability and conflict. The assumption, formalised in 'hegemonic stability theory', that concentration of power in the hands of a predominant state engenders order logically implies that pluralism is risk-laden. In the absence of a centre setting the rules, putting into place regimes of international governance and imposing the disciplines of world order, the international system tends to decay, leading to 'chaos and an interim of troubles' until a new order is established.[6] The corollary is that the perpetuation of hegemony is in the universal interest since, as George Liska wrote in 1967, the 'globally paramount state [establishes an order that harmonises] the particular interests of the imperial state with the interests of the commonweal'.[7] Habituated since 1945 to US world predominance, American policy-makers and mainstream theorists appear incapable of thinking outside of this conceptual box.

Contemporary American authors assume that 'a world without US primacy will be a world with more violence and disorder'[8] or that 'the benevolent hegemony exercised by the United States is good for a vast portion of the world's population'.[9] There are variations on these themes. 'Benevolent despotism', writes Charles Kindleberger, 'is the most efficient system' even if 'like a pluralist system of cooperation among equals or the balance of power' it is 'subject to entropy'. Sooner or later, the despot tires, loses control, ceases to be benevolent and stops working in 'the overall interest of the totality'.[10] According to John Ikenberry the problem facing 'leading or hegemonic states' that have acquired a 'preponderance of material power capabilities', such as the US in the post-Cold War, is to choose between dominating, abandoning or transforming the international system. Since states having acquired such a position rarely abandon them voluntarily, the real choice is to dominate or to 'transform [the] favourable postwar position into a durable order that commands the allegiance of the other states within the order'.[11] Or, as Stephen Walt framed the issue recently, the problem is how to get the 'rest of the world to welcome US primacy', rather than trying to tame US power, by encouraging other 'states to see its dominant position as beneficial (or at least bearable)' and by convincing them that 'American power...will be used judiciously and for the broader benefit of mankind'.[12] The US, he believes, does not have terribly much convincing to do since 'America's Asian and Persian Gulf allies...leap to offer Washington new facilities and access agreements and go to great lengths to conform their foreign policy to ours' whenever they 'begin to fear that the US role might decline'.[13] This statement reproduces the imperial conceit that the US was invited to acquire world-empire and, like Athens, simply accepted it 'when it was offered'.[14]

Theory and Policy

Social theory is reflexive. The knowing subject cannot achieve the 'objectivism of the distant gaze of an observer who remains as remote from himself as from his object'.[15] She/he speaks from a specific location in social space-time, emitting judgments and interpretations that 'modify the facts on which [they are] passed'.[16] While less so than during the Cold War, the American academic milieus specialising in international relations and security remain interlaced with policy-making elites. This proximity of scholars and policy-makers helps to account for their coincidence of visions and shared normative concerns regarding the perpetuation of American power and authority. Prominent scholars go in and out of government, sometimes occupying senior policy making or advisory positions.[17] Many former government officials likewise find positions in the constellation of 'think tanks' or university centres dealing with international security affairs (this flow process is even more pronounced between government and the corporate sector). Influences are reciprocal. Policy is theory laden and theory often becomes geared to solving practical issues of statecraft and policy. Keynes famously pointed out that the 'practical men' of power 'who believe themselves to be quite exempt from any intellectual influences, are usually the slaves of some defunct economist. Madmen in authority, who hear voices in the air, are distilling their frenzy from some academic scribbler of a few years back'.[18] Conversely, some scholars derive satisfactions from being in or close to power, not least the sense that they are themselves historical actors or at least influences in the making of policy.

LOGIC OF WORLD POWER

Keeping in mind what has just been said, I want to conclude by addressing the problem of change. We have seen in previous chapters how the United States used its position in the international system to inhibit centrifugal movements during the Cold War. I argued that the persistence of imperial politics in the post-Cold War evidenced expansionist motives independent of any specific external challenge or security threat. In his post mortem of the Cold War John Lewis Gaddis writes that had the US known what is now known about Soviet weaknesses, it could have spared itself the effort and trouble of intervening 'hyperactively' in post-colonial societies: 'It is clear in retrospect that Western anxieties about Soviet advances [in the Middle East] were quite exaggerated. Anti-colonialism endangered British and French interests, to be sure, but it did not ensure gains for the Soviet Union'.[19]

Yet, despite what we now know and in the absence of an overriding strategic challenge after the fall of the Berlin Wall, US interventionism not only continued but was intensified in the Gulf in the aftermath of the Cold War. The 1990–1991 Gulf crisis was a 'gift of the gods' for an imperial establishment that did not really know what to do with its ambiguous Cold War 'victory'. Saddam Hussein's miscalculation allowed the US to reassert its authority and to 'use the center to order the periphery, while using the periphery to maintain its influence over the center',[20] i.e. Europe and Japan. The war led to escalating commitments, notably the deployment of forces from the Central Command (the Central Command is one of the five combattant commands of the US armed forces) in Saudi Arabia,[21] exacerbating local political and cultural tensions that became fully apparent on September 11. Under an administration committed to an agenda of limitless power expansion, US interventionism culminated in the invasions of Afghanistan and Iraq and the spatially and temporally unbounded 'Global War on Terror' (GWOT). While the George W. Bush administration's extraordinary ambition was at variance with more cautious earlier exercises of power it nonetheless falls within a wider historical pattern.

Can this pattern be broken? There is a new and far more hopeful political configuration in the United States. Elected on a wave of rejection of the domestic and international policies of the Bush administration, President Barack Obama has pledged to withdraw US forces from Iraq. More generally, he has shifted the tone and emphasis of American foreign policy, stressing the need for cooperation on global issues, such as climate change. He has also begun to reverse some of the more egregious abuses of power of the previous administration, by announcing the closing of the Guantanamo prison facility and giving detainees a hearing in civilian courts, and has made important early symbolic gestures towards the Muslim world, stressing the need for dialogue and mutual respect. The administration is moving away from confrontation towards dialogue with Iran and Syria. In like manner, he has made initial gestures to repair deeply strained relations with Russia. All of this suggests a capacity of renewal and points to a new direction in US foreign policy. Yet, at the same time, President Obama continues to use the traditional idiom of American power and world destiny, framing his agenda as a way to 'make this century another American century'.[22]

Structural Constraints

The greater difficulty lies in deeper structural constraints. The United States' logic of world power limits the possibility of translating democratic transformations at domestic level into transformations of policy at world level. Individual leaders inherit and briefly preside over what Michael Cox defines as a 'very special state with an enormous amount of power'[23] and an imperial system of which they are caretakers. With the possible exception of Bill Clinton, 'all US presidents from Franklin Roosevelt' to George W. Bush 'have been war presidents'.[24] The emphasis of policy may vary from one administration to another, according to the composition of social forces making up the presidency and changing international circumstances, resulting in policies that are more or less cooperative or more or less attuned to global interests. These variations are not insignificant, of course. The George W. Bush administration shows that variations of degree matter a great deal in terms of their impact and outcomes. But new leaders, however liberal and democratic in outlook, cannot erase the past or simply decide to liquidate the imperial system itself. They are caught in the same bind as British Liberal and Labour leaders in the late nineteenth and twentieth centuries who found once in power, in Elizabeth Monroe's words, that 'a worldwide Empire…cannot change direction overnight'. Successive British governments, she writes, found 'that more has gone before than [they] imagined – too much to alter quickly'.[25]

The Carter administration provides a good illustration of this point. Elected in the aftermath of Vietnam and Watergate on the back of powerful movements of social change, it represented currents of opinion within the more internationalised components of business and the policy establishment, which recognised that world transformations of the late 1960s and the early 1970s demanded 'a new approach to empire'.[26] Regrouped in the Trilateral Commission, a private elite club whose multinational composition and aims reflected the new approach, these 'managerial' currents favoured 'world order bargains', more inclusive global forums and 'practical patterns of accommodation' with the Soviet Union, the People's Republic of China and post-colonial states.[27] They were aware that the US should 'factor in the views of our allies into common decisions'[28] rather than overtly affirming American supremacy. Some of the more liberal partisans of the 'management of inter-dependence' were 'enthusiastic about the possibility of entrusting international institutions with expanded roles, especially in relation to the new agenda of environmental, economic, and social issues'.[29] However, a major concern of the Commission's leading American members was to reconfigure US policy in such a way as to restore the US' power and authority.[30] Zbigniew Brzezinski, co-founder and director of the Commission, wrote in 1975: 'The United States, though no longer in as decisively favored a position as in the early 1950s, still remains a crucial force in world affairs. In fact, the present crisis has made its role more important than at any point in the last 10 years. Thus, the time has come to bury the cliché about the retraction of American power.'[31]

The new approach found concrete application during the first years of the Carter presidency. Carter rejected the 'intellectual and moral poverty' of the course of policy that had led the US into Vietnam.[32] The administration initially reduced defence spending and placed human rights at the centre of foreign policy, putting pressure on South Africa to end apartheid and on the Shah of Iran to relax the police state (human rights policy was also used to stimulate challenges to Soviet authority in Central and Eastern Europe). In an important symbolic gesture, Carter signed the 1977 Panama Canal Treaty that ceded sovereignty of the canal back to Panama. As Gerry Sanders demonstrates in his detailed study of the 1970s divide in the power elite, the imperialists that wanted to continue the 'contest for power'[33] and restore the 'will to victory',[34] and who steadfastly supported authoritarian anti-communist states,[35] virulently contested these policies. By early 1979, at the latest, a new consensus emerged in favour of a return to containment, the modernisation of nuclear forces and renewed clandestine interventionism in the 'Third World', notably but not only in Afghanistan. According to Robert Gates, the present Secretary of Defense and former CIA Director who worked at the National Security Council under Zbigniew Brzezinski, President Carter authorised clandestine interventions in Africa, Grenada, Nicaragua and El Salvador soon after entering the White House and 'sustained virtually every major strategic modernization program', paving the way for the more expansive operations and build up under Ronald Reagan.[36]

In other words, the crisis of the late 1960s and early 1970s, which had generated favourable domestic circumstances for a reorientation of US foreign and security policy, proved insufficient to produce lasting transformational effects. The Clinton administration's post-Cold War 'econocentric'[37] or informal imperial approach, even if it was far from benign for societies on the receiving end, represented a break from power politics. It too gave way in the late 1990s to a renewed emphasis on military power and then, in 2000–2001 to predatory expansionism. The imperial system is a historical structure that inhibits pluralism and constrains the ability of domestic and international actors to effectuate democratic change.[38]

PATHWAYS OF CHANGE

Under what conditions then would post-imperial transformation be possible? The answer given by some neo-realists is that systemic or world order change is induced by recurrent 'hegemonic wars' resulting from 'an increasing disequilibrium between the burden of maintaining an empire or hegemonic position and the resources available to the dominant power to carry out this task'.[39] One imperial world order succeeds another: 'disequilibrium replaces equilibrium and the world moves toward a new round of hegemonic conflict. It has always been thus and always will be, until men either destroy themselves or learn to develop an effective mechanism of peaceful change.'[40] Yet it has not always been thus. The assumption is based on less than 200 years of international history. There was no 'hegemonic' world order prior to 1820. Cause and consequence of the deepening economic and technological divergence between the Euro–Atlantic area and the rest of the world, global western expansion created durable structures of inequality that are coterminous with 'hegemony'. International hierarchy has been relatively stable since the nineteenth century, with power and wealth concentrated in a handful of states accounting for a small fraction of the world population.[41] While the centre of gravity of world capitalism shifted during that historical period from Europe to the United States, the international system remained centred in the Atlantic and ordered by the west.

Looking at world order in this way shifts the Archimedean vantage point. Janet Abu-Lughod does precisely that when she writes that American hegemony 'rather than marking the beginning of a new phase...appears to represent the end of an old one'.[42] Nearly two decades ago, when most observers were focused on the diffusion of power within the western core (Japan included), she anticipated an end of the era of 'European/Western hegemony' and a 'return to the relative balance of multiple centers [of the pre-western era]' which would lead to 'a shift to different rules of the game'.[43] Indeed, the recent economic emergence or re-emergence of previously peripheral world regions points to one of the possible pathways of systemic change: the coming into being of a plural and polycentric world system. Given still important development differentials with the most technologically advanced areas of the world economy, it is likely to take a few decades for that movement to be accomplished. China, India, Brazil, South Africa and other emerging or re-emerging states face significant international and domestic constraints: global market exposure, uneven domestic social and economic development and infrastructural and environmental bottlenecks. Nonetheless, the duration and intensity of China's economic growth in particular has irreversibly transformed both China and the world, making the most populous country of the world into an active unit of the international system. Because China and some of the other emerging actors of the twenty-first century were not part of *Pax Americana* and are therefore not subject to the mechanisms of control generated by hegemonic alliance systems, they enjoy far greater autonomy than Germany or Japan did in the 1970s or still do today. At the same time, the US' relative autonomy has declined and it cannot set the global agenda alone.

LONG EXIT FROM EMPIRE

For reasons sketched at the outset of this conclusion, the United States finds it difficult to accept a plural world. Since 1945, American leaders have been habituated to being at the centre and the apex. They have assumed that without the US to guarantee world order, the balance of power in Europe, Asia and the Middle East would simply fall apart. In the aftermath of the Cold War, Henry Kissinger cautioned that Europe would prove incapable of managing the transition alone: 'Without America, Great Britain and France cannot sustain the political balance in Western Europe; Germany would be tempted by nationalism; Russia would lack a global interlocutor'. Russia and Germany would end up '[fixating] on each other as either principal partner or principal adversary', leading to condominium or crisis.[44] John Mearsheimer contemporaneously predicted that the departure of the two superpowers from their respective spheres of influence would generate insecurity, driving newly unified Germany to rearm and generating a drift towards continental conflict.[45] This same logic applied *a fortiori* to other world regions such as east Asia, where a US military withdrawal was/is considered a recipe for regional conflict.[46] These assumptions were almost immediately invalidated by Europe's move towards monetary unification, the relaxation of tensions in the Korean peninsula and enhanced east Asian regional monetary cooperation. The underlying concern of policy-makers, expressed by Kissinger, was that a retrenchment of American commitments would lessen US influence and lead to the emergence of a 'grouping that would have the capacity to outstrip America economically and, in the end, militarily'.[47] This would turn 'America...into an island off the shores of Eurasia' with a 'grossly diminished capacity for effective resistance and a growing inability to shape events'.[48]

'Spokesmen of leading powers', write Peter Cain and Anthony Hopkins, 'do not take readily to the idea that the end of their period of dominance is not necessarily the end of the world. Accordingly, they find it hard to envisage pluralistic alternatives to the rule of a single power'.[49] If Great Britain's long exit from empire is anything to go by, transformation of the way the US sees and deals with the world will be a difficult and drawn-out process. Late nineteenth-century imperialists believed that Britain had received from the 'Almighty a gift of a lease on the universe for ever'.[50] Economically weakened by the First World War, Britain nonetheless maintained her world position. The war's impact 'was not great enough to ensure American dominance of the world economy after 1918... her empire, her enormous accumulation of financial assets spread across the globe, and the banking and commercial skills of the City would be critical in keeping her at the centre of the world economic stage well into the twentieth century'.[51] Indeed, Britain's 'continuing ambition and success as an imperialist power'[52] was evidenced in the expansion of the empire after the war through the mandates system in the Middle East and the continuing control she exercised over the already constituted empire.

The decisive turn came with the Second World War that led to Britain's financial and economic exhaustion and the definitive re-centring of the world capitalist economy from Europe to the United States. But even then, despite the urgent need to restore the war-torn domestic economy, post-war 'Labour leaders sought energetically to maintain and in some cases to expand Britain's imperial role, and in so doing they used up resources that might otherwise have been allocated to domestic expenditures'.[53] So did the Conservatives, of course, leading to Britain's ill-fated adventure in Egypt in 1956. Like France's colonial wars, these were rearguard efforts 'to play a role in world affairs which in fact was beyond [Britain's] real powers'.[54] The afterglow of empire is not entirely gone. The revival of liberal-imperialist discourse during Tony Blair's tenure shows that Empire still stirs the official mind.

The United States' present position is hardly comparable to Britain's in 1945. To be sure, its monopoly-seeking behaviour and the systemic crisis of the US financial system that came on top of this have undermined the country's strength and its international legitimacy, accentuating the deeper movement towards polycentrism in the world political economy. But the US still accounts for over a fifth of world gross domestic product, remains the dominant world military power and is the primary source of scientific innovation. Though it faces growing financial constraints, it is not about to become a secondary power. Unless forced to do so, the US will not suddenly dismantle the security structure that gives it international political leverage. However, looking ahead, as the historical rebalancing towards non-western world regions unfolds, the US will be faced with a new plural and non-hierarchical configuration of world politics.

PLURALIST COOPERATION

The end of the Cold War created 'the best opportunity the world has yet seen to construct an international system based on the rule of law and on rules of conduct agreed by all'.[55] Under George W. Bush, the United States ruined that prospect, choosing instead to deconstruct the international institutional system and to abandon international law in a disastrous effort to expand and establish unique authority. The effort has spectacularly failed and caused great damage. The challenge henceforth is to reinvent the institutions and mechanisms of cooperation fitting to a plural and interdependent world system. In particular this implies democratising and expanding the competencies of international institutions responsible for global governance. Though its outcomes remain open, the present world economic crisis has already demonstrated that global cooperation or at very least coordination has been required to avoid a complete breakdown of the world financial system and the world economy.

Cooperation is both normatively desirable and objectively necessary to deal with global problems such as climate change or pandemics that are inherently insoluble at the national level. There is a growing common understanding, reflecting an incipient global consensus, that the human future is bound to finding solutions to these and other transnational issues. This new awareness is translating, though with difficulty, into political will (the Kyoto Accords). A similar effort of imagination and political will can and should be applied to reduce international socio-economic disparities. The alternative is further fragmentation and the perpetuation and/or escalation of conflicts.

Given the historic record, it is reasonable to remain agnostic about the future trajectory of world politics. The international system remains segmented along national lines. Rivalries might overcome cooperation. The fading of the structures of international hierarchy created in the nineteenth century might lead, if the transition is not properly managed, to a self-fulfilling prophecy of a 'clash of civilisations'. It could also conceivably lead to a Sino-American duopoly, which might or might not be stable but would certainly not be in the universal interest. But it also generates the possibility for what the French legal scholar Mireille Delmas-Marty has called a 'pluralist multilateral type of harmonisation' of law in which universal concepts such as human rights are applied in differentiated fashion, that is 'put into relation with temporally and spatially localised realities'.[56] An alternative to the imposition of hegemonic norms, this remark can be applied more broadly to world politics through the notion of 'an ordered pluralism that is the only way to avoid the dual menace of hegemonic order or impotent disorder'.[57] The choice then is not between empire or hegemony and chaos, but between the latter and systems of inclusive institutionalised cooperation in which convergence around common objectives is dictated by the congruence over different areas of national interests and the wider global interest.

That choice is of course not the United States' alone. But an ordered pluralism cannot emerge if the US does not disengage from empire or if it attempts, against the tides of current history, to retain global 'primacy'. Disengagement from empire doesn't mean the US would become 'an island off the shores of Eurasia'. Rather it means moving away from efforts to maintain military supremacy and economic disparity towards a more democratic pattern of relations with the rest of the world to which the US is inescapably intertwined. The problem today is not to make American hegemony attractive or 'bearable' for the rest of the world, but for the United States to come to terms with emerging and novel conditions of equality. Certainly, that is the major lesson of the failure of the Bush administration's imperial campaign. The conjunction of new political leadership and system-wide crisis has generated the conditions of possibility for a transformation of the international system. Yet it remains to be seen whether these new political and social circumstances can lessen the hold of imperial structures, habits and worldviews that until now have inhibited democratic change.

Notes

CHAPTER 1

1. David Harvey (2003) *The New Imperialism* New York: Oxford University Press, p.29
2. Susan Strange (1989) 'Towards a Theory of Transnational Empire', in Ernst-Otto Czempiel and James N. Rosenau (eds) (1989) *Global Changes and Theoretical Challenges: Approaches to World Politics for the 1990s* Lanham, Md.: Lexington Books, pp.161–76
3. Alan Greenspan (1998) 'The Ascendance of Market Capitalism', remarks by Chairman Alan Greenspan before the *Annual Convention of the American Society of Newspaper Editors* (Washington, D.C.: The Federal Reserve Board, April 2, 1998)
4. Stephen M. Walt (2006) *Taming American Power: The Global Response to U.S. Primacy* New York: W.W. Norton, p.30
5. Robert W. Cox (with Michael G. Schechter) (2002) *The Political Economy of a Plural World: Critical Reflections on Power, Morals and Civilization* London: Routledge, p.41
6. There is a vast literature on the subject of asymmetric economic relationships and structures of dependency. For a critical synthesis see Ronald H. Chilcote (2000) *Theories of Comparative Political Economy* Boulder, Co.: Westview Press
7. Strange, *Towards a Theory*, p.167
8. Robert Wade (2002b) 'The American Empire and its Limits', *DESTIN Working Papers Series*, No. 02–22, London: London School of Economics
9. Internationalisation since the mid 1980s has generated a significant degree of social and spatial unevenness within China, but the state never lost control in the way that smaller and more vulnerable emerging countries did. This issue is discussed in Chapter 7
10. Stanley Hoffmann (2003) 'America Goes Backward', *New York Review of Books*, 50: 10 (June 12)
11. Condoleezza Rice (2000) 'Promoting the National Interest', *Foreign Affairs*, 79: 1 (January–February)
12. Charles Krauthammer, 'The Unipolar Moment', *Foreign Affairs*, 70: 1 (Winter 1990–91), pp.23–33
13. Edward Hallett Carr (2001[1939]) *The Twenty Years' Crisis, 1919–1939: An Introduction to the Study of International Relations* New York: Palgrave, p.215
14. Martin Wolf (2009) 'Seeds of its Own Destruction', *Financial Times,* March 8
15. Peter J. Katzenstein (2006) 'Introduction', in Peter J. Katzenstein (ed.) (2006) *The Culture of National Security: Norms and Identity in World Politics* Princeton, N.J.: Princeton University Press, p.2
16. Kenneth Waltz (1993) 'Neorealism: Confusions and Criticisms', *Journal of Politics and Society*, 15: 1, pp.2–6

17. Peter J. Katzenstein (1993) 'Taming of Power: German Unification, 1989–1990', in Meredith Woo-Cumings and Michel Loriaux (eds) (1993) *The Past as Prelude, History in the Making of a New World Order* Boulder, Co.: Westview Press, pp.59–81

18. Ibid., p.380

19. C. Wright Mills (2000[1956]) *The Power Elite* New York: Oxford University Press

20. Joseph A. Schumpeter (1966) *Imperialism and Social Classes: Two Essays by Joseph Schumpeter*, New York: Meridian Books, p.25

21. Andrew Bacevich (2005) *The New American Militarism* New York: Oxford University Press. See also Michael Mann (2003) *Incoherent Empire* London: Verso; Chalmers Johnson (2004) *The Sorrows of Empire: Militarism, Secrecy, and the End of the Republic* New York: Metropolitan Books

22. Immanuel Wallerstein (2000) 'The Three Instances of Hegemony', in *The Essential Wallerstein*, New York: The New Press, p.263

23. Giovanni Arrighi (1994) *The Long Twentieth Century: Money, Power and the Origins of Our Times* London: Verso

24. Giovanni Arrighi (2005) 'Hegemony Unravelling', *New Left Review*, 32 (March–April), pp.50–80

25. I am using the expression in the sense defined by Aníbal Quijano when he speaks of the systems of domination and control and the representations of otherness of the modern era. See Aníbal Quijano (2000) 'Coloniality of Power and Eurocentrism in Latin America', *International Sociology*, 15: 2, pp.215–32

26. For a synthesis of the various perspectives in this growing field of international relations see Stephen Hobden and John M. Hobson (eds) (2002) *Historical Sociology of International Relations* Cambridge, UK: Cambridge University Press

27. Fernand Braudel (1977) *Afterthoughts on Material Civilization and Capitalism* Baltimore, Md.: Johns Hopkins University Press

28. I am borrowing the expression 'culture of force' from Christopher Newfield (2006) 'The Culture of Force', *The South Atlantic Quarterly*, 105: 1 (Winter), pp.241–63

29. Robert W. Cox (1981) 'Social Forces, States and World Orders: Beyond International Relations Theory', *Millennium: Journal of International Studies*, 10: 2, p.129

30. Franz Schurmann (1974) *The Logic of World Power: An Enquiry into the Origins, Currents and Contradictions of World Politics* New York: Pantheon Books

31. William Appleman Williams (1969[1959]) *The Tragedy of American Diplomacy* New York, Delta Books

32. Mann, *Incoherent Empire*

33. Michael Ignatieff (2003) 'The Burden', *The New York Times Magazine* (January 5)

34. Charles Maier (2006) *Among Empires: American Ascendancy and Its Predecessors* Cambridge, Mass.: Harvard University Press

35. Maier, *Among Empires*. See also, for instance, Andrew J. Bacevich (2008) *The Limits of Power: the End of American Exceptionalism* New York: Metropolitan Books

36. Sebastian Mallaby (2002) 'The Reluctant Imperialist: Terrorism, Failed States, and the Case for American Empire', *Foreign Affairs*, 81: 2 (March–April), pp.2–7

37. William E. Odom and Robert Dujarric (2004) *The Accidental Empire: America's Inadvertent Empire* New Haven, Conn.: Yale University Press

38. Robert Kagan (1998) 'The Benevolent Empire', *Foreign Policy*, 111 (Summer), pp.24–35

39. Moses I. Finley, *Ancient History, Evidence and Models* London: Chatto and Windus, p.79

40. Stephen Howe (2003) 'American Empire: the history and future of an idea', available at www.opendemocracy.net/conflict-americanpower/article_1279.jsp

41. John Gallagher and Ronald Robinson (1953) 'The Imperialism of Free Trade', *The Economic History Review*, New Series, 6: 1, pp.1–15

42. Ibid.

43. Herbert Feis (1973[1920]) *Europe: The World's Banker, 1870–1914* Clifton, N.J.: Augustus M. Kelley Publishers, p.5

44. Karl Polanyi (1972[1944]) *The Great Transformation* Boston, Beacon Press, p.14

45. Peter J. Cain and Anthony B. Hopkins (2002) *British Imperialism, 1688–2000* London: Longman-Pearson

46. Braudel, *Afterthoughts*

47. Arrighi, *The Long Twentieth Century*

48. Robert Gilpin (1981) *War and Change in World Politics* New York: Cambridge University Press

49. Richard A. Falk (2004) *The Declining World Order, America's Imperial Geopolitics* New York: Routledge, p.26

50. Polanyi, *The Great Transformation*, p.6

51. David Calleo (1987) *Beyond American Hegemony, the Future of the Western Alliance* New York: Basic Books, p.31

52. John R. Seeley (1971[1883]) *The Expansion of England* Chicago, Ill.: University of Chicago Press, p.141

53. Nicholas Lemann (2002) 'The Next World Order: The Bush Administration may have a brand-new doctrine of power', *The New Yorker* (April 1)

54. Mark Turner and Quentin Peel (2003) 'Is the Post-1945 World Order Falling Apart?', *Financial Times* (March 10)

CHAPTER 2

1. Hannah Arendt (1994) *The Origins of Totalitarianism* New York: Harcourt, p.125

2. The prominent works used in this study are: Paul Bairoch (1977) *Victoires et déboires. Histoire économique et sociale du monde du XVIᵉ siècle jusqu'à nos jours* (3 Vols) Paris: Gallimard; Christopher A. Bayly (2004) *The Birth of the Modern World, 1780–1914: Global Connections and Comparisons* London: Blackwell; Fernand Braudel (1985) *La dynamique du capitalisme* Paris: Arthaud; K.N. Chaudhuri (1991) *Asia Before Europe: Economy and Civilization of the Indian Ocean From the Rise of Islam to 1750* New York: Cambridge University Press; Jack Goody (1996) *The East in the West* New York: Cambridge University Press; Andre Gunder Frank (2001) *Re-Orient:*

Global Economy in the Asian Age Berkeley, Cal.: University of California Press; Joseph E. Inikori (2002) *Africans and the Industrial Revolution in England: A Study in International Trade and Economic Development* Cambridge, UK: Cambridge University Press; Janet L. Abu-Lughod (1991) *Before European Hegemony: The World System A.D. 1250–1350* New York: Oxford University Press; Kenneth Pomeranz (2000) *The Great Divergence* Princeton, N.J.: Princeton University Press

3. Pomeranz, *The Great Divergence*, p.8
4. Term coined by Jan de Vries in 1994; see Jan de Vries (1994) 'The Industrious Revolution and the Industrial Revolution', *Journal of Economic History*, 54, pp.249–70
5. Pomeranz, *The Great Divergence*, pp.45–6
6. Bayly, *The Birth of the Modern World*, pp.56–7
7. Goody, *The East in the West*, p.89
8. Gunder, *Re-Orient*, p.127
9. Available at www.un.org/esa/population/publications/sixbillion/sixbillion.htm
10. Paul Bairoch, 'International Industrialisation Levels from 1750 to 1980', *The Journal of European Economic History,* 11: 1 (Spring 1982), pp.269–333
11. Adam Smith (1991) *The Wealth of Nations* New York: Prometheus Books, p.76
12. Bairoch, *Victoires et déboires*, Vol. 1, p.111
13. Phyllis Deane (1979) *The First Industrial Revolution* Cambridge, UK: Cambridge University Press, p.88. Deane emphasises that in the 1760s total British cotton textiles sales amounted to a mere £600,000, with exports averaging £200,000, compared to the £5.5 millions for woollen goods
14. Pomeranz, *The Great Divergence*, p.283
15. Wolfgang J. Mommsen (1982) *Theories of Imperialism* Chicago, Ill.: University of Chicago Press, p.75
16. First theorised by Raúl Prebisch, Theotonio dos Santos and other dependency theorists, this core–periphery tension was given systematic theoretic formulation by Immanuel Wallerstein's critical historical sociology. In Fernand Braudel's simple and elegant formulation, 'The centre is nothing other than the dominant point, the capitalist superstructure of the whole construction. Since there is a reciprocity of perspectives, if the centre depends on the supplies of the periphery, the latter depends on the needs of the centre which dictates its law (to the periphery)' (Braudel, *La dynamique*)
17. Eric J. Hobsbawm (1990[1968]) *Industry and Empire: From 1750 to the Present Day* London–New York: Penguin Books, p.134
18. Arrighi, *The Long Twentieth Century*, p.161
19. Bairoch calculates that in 1860 the opium produced in India accounted for 8 per cent of total 'Third World' exports, in value terms. Bairoch, *Victoires et déboires*, Vol. 2, pp.632–3. 'It is to be observed with regard to India', Marx wrote in 1853, 'that the British Government of that country depends for full one-seventh of its revenue on the sale of opium to the Chinese while a considerable proportion of the Indian demand for British manufactures depends on the production of that opium in India.' Karl Marx (1853) 'Revolution in China and In Europe', *The New York Daily Tribune* (June 14)
20. Herbert Feis (1973[1930]) *Europe: The World's Banker, 1870–1914* Clifton, N.J.: Augustus M. Kelley Publishers, p.5

21. Paul Bairoch and Richard Kozul-Wright (1996) 'Globalization Myths: Some Historical Reflections on Integration, Industrialization and Growth in the World Economy', *UNCTAD Discussion Paper No. 113*, (Geneva, March), p.16

22. Robert Bellah (1985[1957]) *Tokugawa Religion, the Cultural Roots of Modern Japan* New York: Free Press

23. Niall Ferguson (2004) *Colossus, the Price of America's Empire* New York: Penguin Press, p.198

24. Gilpin, *Political Economy*, p.183

25. Edward Said (2003[1979]) *Orientalism* New York: Vintage Books, p.5

26. Hendrik L. Wesseling (1997) 'Imperialism and Colonialism, Essays on the History of European Expansion', in *Contributions in Comparative Colonial Studies No. 32* Westport, Conn.: Greenwood Press, pp.3–26

27. Polanyi, *The Great Transformation*, p.6

28. John Stuart Mill (1984[1859]) 'A Few Words on Non-Intervention', in *The Collected Works of John Stuart Mill*, Vol. 21, Toronto: University of Toronto Press (originally published in London), pp.118–19

29. See Olivier Le Cour Grandmaison (2005) *Coloniser, exterminer. Sur la guerre et l'Etat Colonial* Paris: Fayard. For a detailed and subtle discussion of the shift from liberal anti-imperialism in the eighteenth century and the turn to liberal imperialism in the nineteenth, see Jennifer Pitts (2005) *A Turn to Empire, The Rise of Imperial Liberalism in Britain and France* Princeton, N.J.: Princeton University Press

30. Pitts, *A Turn to Empire*, p.238

31. Japanese and Russian imperialism are not included here

32. Arendt, *The Origins of Totalitarism*, p.185. Estimates of the death toll vary, but it is certainly in the millions. See Adam Hochschild (2006) *King Leopold's Ghost: A Story of Greed, Terror and Heroism in Colonial Africa* London: Pan Books

33. On Algeria, see Le Cour Grandmaison, *Coloniser, exterminer*. Ecological collapses due to colonisation include major famines in a number of colonial areas. Bairoch estimates the number of deaths caused by famines in India between 1875 and 1900, due in large part to the conversion of arable land previously used for agricultural production and local consumption to export-oriented production to meet metropolitan needs, at 26 million people. The total population of India in 1870 was 250 million. See Bairoch, *Victoires et déboires*, Vol. 2, p.864. Likewise, it has been argued that the large famines in China in the early part of the twentieth century were caused by the conversion of arable land into poppy production. See Carl A. Trocki (1999) *Opium, Empire and the Global Political Economy: A Study of the Asian Opium Trade, 1750–1950* New York: Routledge

34. A. Dirk Moses (ed.) (2005) *Genocide and Settler Society: Frontier Violence and Stolen Indigenous Children in Australian History* New York: Berghahn, p.4

35. Caroline Elkins (2005) *Imperial Reckoning: The Untold Story of Britain's Gulag in Kenya* New York: Owl Books, p.90. Elkins points out that while the 'detention camps in Kenya would never systematically aim to eliminate a whole population as did the Nazi death camps, the conditions were in place by 1953 to transform a fledgling camp system into a far broader locus of torture, hard labor and killing' (ibid.)

36. Jürgen Zimmerer, 'Colonial Genocide and the Holocaust. Towards an Archaeology of Genocide' in Moses, *Genocide and Settler Society*, pp.49–76. Expanding on and critiquing Arendt's remarks in *The Origins of Totalitarianism* regarding German and Belgian colonial genocide, Zimmerer suggests that there are structural similarities, though not identity, between colonial genocide, including by liberal western states, and the later 'extremely radicalized variant' of biological interpretations of history and racial hierarchy that took hold under National Socialism in Germany. There were genocidal tendencies and moments in colonial expansion, whereas 'genocide is one if not the main characteristic of national socialism'. In the same volume, editor A. Dirk Moses notes that 'vastly more scholarly and popular attention has been devoted to the Holocaust...and to state sponsored killing in the twentieth century in general' than to colonial genocide. The paradox, he writes, is that 'the largest of the modern empires, Great Britain, was at once an implacable opponent of totalitarianism and the source of those settlers who swept aside millions of indigenous peoples to establish progressive democracies in North America, New Zealand and Australia. Bulwarks of liberty, Britain and its former colonies also have blood on their hands'. Moses, *Genocide and Settler Society*, pp.4–5

37. Ira Katznelson (2002) 'Flexible Capacity: the Military and Early American Statebuilding', in Ira Katznelson and Martin Shefter (eds) (2002) *Shaped by War and Trade, International Influences on American Political Development* Princeton, N.J.: Princeton University Press, p.89

38. Ibid., pp.98–9, 101

39. Williams, *The Tragedy*, p.19

40. Inikori, *Africans and the Industrial Revolution,* p.214

41. The estimates, based on Inikori, include the Caribbean and Mainland British America, but exclude Canada (Inikori, *Africans and the Industrial Revolution*)

42. Cain and Hopkins, *British Imperialism,* pp.89–90

43. David Richardson (1987) 'The Slave Trade, Sugar, and British Economic Growth, 1748–1776', in 'Caribbean Slavery and British Capitalism', *The Journal of Interdisciplinary History*, 17: 4 (Spring), p.741

44. Cain and Hopkins, *British Imperialism,* p.63

45. These ratios are my own computations based on two different sets of figures in Inikori's study, *Africans and the Industrial Revolution*, pp.197–214. Since those sets use different timelines, I smoothed out irregularities to arrive at the results. They are therefore approximate but nonetheless sufficiently close to the original sets to be considered accurate representations of the relative trade ratios under discussion

46. Hobsbawm, *Industry and Empire*, p.56

47. Ibid., p.69

48. Ibid., p.58

49. Morton Rothstein (1970) 'The Cotton Frontier of the Antebellum South: A Methodological Battleground', *Agricultural History*, 44: 1 (January), p.157

50. Adam Rothman (2005) *Slave Country: American Expansion and the Origins of the Deep South* Cambridge, Mass.: Harvard University Press, p.xi

51. The original Constitution of the United States of America distinguished between 'the people', 'Indians', and 'other persons' (slaves) and contained three clauses that enshrined and consolidated the institution of slavery: a) Article I, Section 2, Clause 3, or the 'three-fifths clause' gave the Southern

slave states disproportionate power by authorising them to count three-fifths
of 'other persons' in apportioning their Representatives in Congress and their
weight in the Electoral College. As a result, the Southern states controlled the
lower House of Congress nearly uninterrupted until the Civil War. For the
same reason, of the first 12 Presidents until 1850, ten had been slave owners
or were slave owners at the time of their presidency. As a result, the Southern
states also had disproportionate power in the Supreme Court. The 'three-fifths
clause' states: 'Representatives and direct Taxes shall be apportioned among
the several States which may be included within this Union, according to
their respective Numbers, which shall be determined by adding to the whole
Number of free Persons, including those bound to Service for a Term of Years,
and excluding Indians not taxed, three-fifths of all other Persons'. The other
two clauses are: b) Article I, Section 9, Clause 1, which prohibited Congress
from ending the slave trade before 1808: 'The migration or importation of
such persons as any of the States now existing shall think proper to admit shall
not be prohibited by the Congress prior to the year 1808'; and c) Article IV,
Section 2, Clause 3, the fugitive-slave clause which mandated the forcible
return of fugitive slaves from free states to the South: 'No Person held to
Service or Labour in one State, under the Laws thereof, escaping into another,
shall, in Consequence of any Law or Regulation therein, be discharged from
such Service or Labour, but shall be delivered up on Claim of the Party to
whom such Service or Labour may be due'. See Paul Finkleman (2001) *Slavery
and the Founders, Race and Liberty in the Age of Jefferson* New York: M.E.
Sharpe; Sanford Levinson (2006) *Our Undemocratic Constitution* New York:
Oxford University Press; Rothman, *Slave Country*. For a concise critique see
Thurgood Marshall (1987) 'Reflections on the Bicentennial of the United
States Constitution', *Harvard Law Review*, 101: 1 (November)

52. See James A. McMillin (2004) *The Final Victims: Foreign Slave Trade to North
America, 1783–1810 (The Carolina Low Country and the Atlantic World)*
Columbia, S. Car.: University of South Carolina Press. McMillin estimates
the total number of slaves brought into the US from 1783 to 1810 at 170,000
(ibid., p.118)

53. Inikori calculates that the share, in value terms, of export commodities
produced by African slaves in all the Americas was 80 per cent in the last
two decades of the eighteenth century and 68.8 per cent in 1848–1850. Inikori,
Africans and the Industrial Revolution, p.197

54. Prior to 1812, writes Bradford Perkins, international trade was 'an extremely
important factor in the economy' and played a vital role in the country's
prosperity. Bradford Perkins (2002) *The Creation of a Republican Empire,
1776–1865* New York: Cambridge University Press, pp.7, 201. Average per
capita GNP of *free* Americans in the late eighteenth century was close or
equivalent to that of Britons and median income was one of the highest in
the world. According to Paul Bairoch's computations, US GNP per capita in
1800 equalled that of Great Britain (Bairoch, *Victoires et déboires*, Vol. 2).
Angus Maddison comes to different results, with US GDP, rather than GNP,
per capita representing two-thirds of Britain's average per capita GDP in
1820. Angus Maddison (2001) *The World Economy: A Millennial Perspective*
Paris: OECD Development Centre. However, as Peter A. Coclanis shows, by
most estimates median per capita income of *free* individuals in the United
States on the eve of Independence was one of the highest in the world: 'British

America's free population was extremely wealthy on the eve of the Revolution. A generation of scholarship has made that fact clear. Moreover, as work on wealth-holding patterns in the early modern period proceeds, it is becoming increasingly apparent that nowhere else in the world did a population of comparative size live so well...the free population of British North America... enjoyed higher incomes and living standards in 1774 than roughly 70% of the world's inhabitants in the 1980's'. Peter A. Coclanis (1990) 'The Wealth of British America on the Eve of the Revolution', *Journal of Interdisciplinary History*, 21: 2 (Autumn), p.245. Coclanis also points out in a study of South Carolina that the factor that mattered most in the wealth of the southern states was 'the area's integration into the Atlantic economy, that is, into a network of factor and product markets of intercontinental scope'. Peter A. Coclanis (1991) *The Shadow of a Dream: Economic Life and Death in the South Carolina Low Country, 1670–1920* New York: Oxford University Press, p.91

55. Martin Shefter, 'War, Trade and U.S. Party Politics', in Katznelson and Shefter, *Shaped by War and Trade*, p.115

56. Originally used by John O'Sullivan in 1845, the expression 'Manifest Destiny' was later mobilised by the editor of the *Democratic Review*, and other expansionists close to the *Review*, to justify slavery, the annexation of Texas (which became a slave state in 1845) and the war with Mexico. It was also used in the post-civil war context to legitimise international territorial expansion of the late 1890s. See Julius W. Pratt (1927) 'The Origins of Manifest Destiny', *American Historical Review*, 32: 4 (July), pp.795–8. On the racialist outlooks that fuelled territorial expansion see Reginald Horsman (1999) *Race and Manifest Destiny: The Origins of American Racial Anglo-Saxonism* Cambridge, Mass.: Harvard University Press. On the *Democratic Review*, see Robert J. Scholnick (2005) 'Extermination and Democracy: O'Sullivan, the *Democratic Review*, and Empire 1837–1840', *American Periodicals*, 15: 2, pp.123–41

57. Lance E. Davis and Robert J. Cull (1994) *International Capital Markets and American Economic Growth (1820–1914)* New York: Cambridge University Press, pp.2, 11 and 112

58. Ibid., p.111

59. Ibid.

60. Cain and Hopkins, *British Imperialism*, p.91

61. Feis, *Europe: The World's Banker*, p.25

62. Ibid.

63. Davis and Cull, *International Capital Markets,* pp.38–9

64. United States Census, available at www.census.gov/population/censusdata/table-2.pdf

65. Walter T.K. Nugent (1995) *Crossings: The Great Transatlantic Migrations, 1870–1914* Bloomington, Ind.: Indiana University Press

66. Charles Hirschman (2005) 'Immigration and the American Century', *Demography*, 42: 4 (November), pp.595–620

67. See Barry Edmonston and Jeffrey Passel (eds) (1994) *Immigration and Ethnicity: The Integration of America's Newest Arrivals* Washington, D.C.: Urban Institute Press, referenced in Hirshman, 'Immigration'

68. In the late nineteenth century social imperialists in Britain and France saw external expansion as an answer to domestic social challenges. In 1871, Ernest

Renan wrote 'large-scale colonisation is a first order political necessity. A nation which does not colonise is irremediably destined to socialism and to a war between rich and poor'. Ernest Renan (1990[1871]) *La réforme intellectuelle et morale de la France* Brussels: Complexe. In a statement made famous by V.I. Lenin, Cecil Rhodes said: 'My cherished idea is a solution for the social problem, i.e., in order to save the 40,000,000 inhabitants of the United Kingdom from a bloody civil war, we colonial statesmen must acquire new lands to settle the surplus population, to provide new markets for the goods produced by them in the factories and mines. The Empire, as I have always said, is a bread and butter question. If you want to avoid civil war, you must become imperialists.' For a discussion of British social imperialism see Bernard Semmel (1960) *Imperialism and Social Reform: English Social-Imperial Thought, 1895–1914* London: George Allen and Unwin

69. Bairoch and Kozul-Wright, 'Globalization Myths', p.12
70. Herbert Feis points out that 'foreign capital rendered vital aid' in Japan's industrial and military modernisation efforts. 'By virtue of that capital no less than through its political allegiance, Great Britain may be said to have made a great power of Japan'. Though this certainly understates the endogenous factors of Japan's accelerated development, it points usefully to the differentiated spatial effects of globalised capital flows. See Feis, *Europe: The World's Banker*, pp.423–9
71. After 1850, the British economy relied increasingly on invisible earnings, notably high rates of return on international investment. Cain and Hopkins note that the 'service sector generated an increasingly large invisible income which filled the visible trade gap' that was complemented by 'income from foreign assets' on which Britain became more and more dependent. Foreign assets 'had reached the equivalent of almost 7 per cent of GDP in the 20 years' before the First World War. Cain and Hopkins, *British Imperialism*, p.164. See also Hobsbawm, *Industry and Empire*

CHAPTER 3

1. Cited in Williams, *The Tragedy*, p.34
2. H.H. Powers (1898) 'The War as a Suggestion of Manifest Destiny', *The Annals of the American Academy of Political and Social Science*, 12: 2, p.8
3. William Earl Weeks, 'American Nationalism, American Imperialism: An Interpretation of U.S. Political Economy, 1781–1861', *Journal of the Early Republic*, 14: 4 (Winter), p.489
4. Katznelson, 'Flexible Capacity', p.99
5. See James W. Cummings (2008) *Towards Modern Public Finance: The American War with Mexico, 1846–1848* Pickering and Chatto, London
6. Bradford Perkins cites the Russian negotiator as follows: 'It was a question of our selling…or our seeing them seize it'. See Perkins, *The Creation of a Republican Empire*, p.198
7. The Treaty of Wanghia signed on July 3, 1844, gave the United States the same extraterritorial rights as Britain was awarded in the Treaty of Nanking. Article XXI of the Treaty asserted: 'Subjects of China who may be guilty of any criminal act towards citizens of the United States shall be arrested and punished by the Chinese authorities according to the laws of China, and citizens of the United States who may commit any crime in China shall be

subject to be tried and punished only by the Consul or other public functionary of the United States thereto authorized according to the laws of the United States'. The new Treaty, negotiated under Franklin D. Roosevelt, abrogated all of the provisions of previous treaties and agreements that gave the United States jurisdiction over its citizens in China, its rights in the International Settlements and its rights of navigation and police in the coastal and inland waters of China

8. John Paton Davies (1977) 'Two Hundred Years of American Foreign Policy: the U.S. and East Asia', *Foreign Affairs*, 55: 2 (January), p.369

9. My count by region is based on the list of American military interventions compiled by Richard F. Grimmett (2008) 'Instances of Use of United States Armed Forces Abroad, 1798–2007', *CRS Report for Congress* Washington, D.C., Congressional Research Service

10. A 'unit is said to be active if through its own action and in its own interest it is capable of modifying its environment, that is the behaviour of the units with which it is in relation'. See: Perroux, *Pouvoir et économie généralisée*, p.236

11. 'Foreign Trade of Japan', *The New York Times* (May 18, 1901)

12. Exports of engineering equipment to Britain rose from £131,562 in 1879 to £3,595,496 (in constant pounds) in 1900. See R.C. Floud (1974) 'The Adolescence of American Engineering Competition, 1860–1900', *The Economic History Review*, New Series, 27: 1 (February), pp.57–71

13. Davis and Cull, *International Capital Markets*, pp.81–6. American foreign investment was primarily concentrated in railroads, mines and raw materials in the western hemisphere, or in agricultural staples such as sugar and tropical fruits in the Caribbean. Cuba and the West Indies thus accounted for 10.6 per cent of US direct investment in 1914. In Europe, American foreign investment was concentrated in manufacturing and transport

14. See Charles Kindleberger (1977) 'Two Hundred Years of American Foreign Policy: U.S. Foreign Economic Policy, 1776–1976', *Foreign Affairs*, 55: 2 (January)

15. I am borrowing the subtitle of Healy, *U.S. Expansionism*

16. Walter LaFeber (1998[1968]) *The New Empire: An Interpretation of American Expansion, 1860–1898* Ithaca, NY: Cornell University Press, p.xvii

17. See Horsman, *Race and Manifest Destiny*, pp.272–97

18. Amy Kaplan points out insightfully that the 1898 war and international empire helped to channel domestic energies outward and heal the still open wounds of the Civil War and Reconstruction. The 1898 war helped to reconcile and reunify the south and the north of the United States, 'by bringing them together against a common external enemy', thereby re-establishing narrative continuity to the American expansionary experience. Amy Kaplan and Donald E. Paese (eds) (1993) *Cultures of United States Imperialism* Durham, N.C.: Duke University Press, p.219

19. William Appleman Williams' expression. The most prominent figures of the 'little imperialist elite' which functioned as a network were Theodore Roosevelt, Henry Cabot Lodge, Brooks Adams, Alfred Thayer Mahan, Elihu Root and John Hay. See Williams, *The Tragedy*

20. See 'American Supremacy', *The New York Times* (September 22, 1900)

21. Cited in Howard K. Beale (1989[1956]) *Theodore Roosevelt and the Rise of America to World Power* London: Johns Hopkins University Press, p.76

22. Cited in Healy, *U.S. Expansionism*, p.46

23. H.H. Powers, 'The War as a Suggestion'

24. Cited in John P. Mallan (1956) 'Roosevelt, Brooks Adams and Lea: The Warrior Critique of Business Civilization', *The American Quarterly*, 8: 3 (Autumn), pp.213–30

25. *New York Times*, 'Supremacy'

26. Editorial of the *Washington Post*, cited in Howard Zinn (2003) *People's History of the United States: 1492–Present* New York: Harper Collins Publishers

27. George F. Kennan (1951) *American Diplomacy, 1900–1950* Chicago: University of Chicago Press, pp.14–17. Kennan's account neglects the powerful economic forces underlying expansionism. Nonetheless, he points usefully to the preponderant influence of elite power groups in the initiation of imperialist policy. Howard K. Beale likewise stresses the role of 'strategically placed expansionists' inside and outside government: 'Collectively, these men were a potent influence in giving American participation in world affairs a nationalist and imperialist cast'. See Beale, *Theodore Roosevelt*, p.23. Walter LaFeber reports a meeting held in 1897 between Brooks Adams, Theodore Roosevelt and Henry Cabot Lodge 'to plot strategy': 'By the end of the year they reached a consensus on policy... Roosevelt carried that consensus to (President) McKinley'. LaFeber, *The New Empire*, p.671

28. The founding formulation is found in Alexis de Tocqueville's *Democracy in America*. The major twentieth-century formulation is Louis Hartz (1991[1956]) *The Liberal Tradition in America* Fort Washington, PA: Harvest Books. Arthur Schlesinger Jr reprises the idea with his notion of 'pervasive liberalism'. See Arthur Schlesinger Jr (1963) 'Liberalism in America: A note to Europeans', in *The Politics of Hope* Boston: Houghton Mifflin

29. Judith N. Shklar (1998) *Redeeming American Political Thought*, Stanley Hoffmann and Dennis F. Thompson (eds), New York: The University of Chicago Press, p.92

30. Robert O. Paxton (2004) *The Anatomy of Fascism* New York: Alfred A. Knopf, p.49

31. Russell F. Weigley (1973) *The American Way of War: a History of United States Military Strategy and Policy* New York: Macmillan, pp.158–9

32. Ibid.

33. Ibid., p.158

34. Ibid., pp.156–60

35. See Walter L. Williams (1980) 'United States Indian Policy and the Debate over Philippine Annexation: Implications for the Origins of American Imperialism', *The Journal of American History*, 66: 4 (March), pp.810–31

36. Alfred Beveridge (1900) 'In Support of an American Empire', in United States, Congress, Joint Committee on Printing, *Congressional Record*, 56 Cong., I Sess., Washington, D.C.: US Government Printing Office, January 9, pp.704–12

37. Ibid.

38. On the use of torture during the Filipino campaign see Paul Kramer (2008) 'The Water Cure: Debating Torture and Counterinsurgency – A Century Ago', *The New Yorker* (February 25). Anti-imperialists denounced the use of torture, notably the American 'water cure which exploded Filipino bellies but left no outward evidence of torture' (ibid.)

39. Beveridge, 'In Support of an American Empire'
40. Cited in Beale, *Theodore Roosevelt*, p.161. *The New York Times* selected this passage in its book review of December 30, 1894. See 'Theodore Roosevelt's New Volume', *The New York Times* (December 30, 1894)
41. Ibid.
42. Beale, *Theodore Roosevelt*, p.161
43. Cited in Michael H. Hunt (1987) *Ideology and U.S Foreign Policy* New Haven, Conn.: Yale University Press, p.127
44. Cited in Williams, 'United States Indian Policy', p.825
45. Cited in Robert Seager II (1997) *Alfred Thayer Mahan: The Man and his Letters* Annapolis, Md.: Naval Institute Press, p.421
46. Walter L. Williams writes: 'Because of their experience fighting Indians, United States Army leaders in 1900 were probably better equipped to fight a guerrilla war than at any subsequent time in the twentieth century. By compiling biographical data on the thirty generals in service in the Philippines between 1898 and 1902, it was found that twenty six (87 per cent) had experience with Indians in the West. Moreover, of the remaining four generals, three were Westerners and the fourth had some experience in the West. In general, there was a remarkably high exposure to the military ramifications of United States Indian policy among the army leadership in the Philippines.' Williams, 'United States Indian Policy', p.828
47. The Supreme Court ruling in *Cherokee Nation v. Georgia* defined the Cherokee people, and by extension all Native American cultures, as 'domestic dependent nations'. See US Supreme Court, *Cherokee Nation v. Georgia,* 30 U.S. (5 Pet.) 1 (1831), available at http://supreme.justia.com/ us/30/1/case.html. The later 1886 *United States v. Kagama* substituted the word communities for the word nations: 'communities dependent upon the United States'. See US Supreme Court, *United States v. Kagama*, 118 U.S. 375 (1886), available at http://supreme.justia.com/us/118/375/case.html
48. E.W. Huffcut (1899) 'Constitutional Aspects of the Government of Dependencies', in 'The Foreign Policy of the United States: Political and Commercial', Proceedings of the Annual Meeting of the American Academy of Political and Social Science, April 7–8, 1899, *The Annals of the American Academy of Political and Social Science*, 13: 12 Supplement (May 1899), Newbury Park, Calif.: Sage, p.37
49. A. Lawrence Lowell (1899) 'The Government of Dependencies', in *The Annals of the American Academy of Political and Social Science*, 13: 12 Supplement (May 1899), p.51
50. Theodore S. Woolsey (1899) 'The Government of Dependencies', in *The Annals of the American Academy of Political and Social Science*, 13: 12 Supplement (May 1899), p.9. See Earl S. Pomeroy (1944) 'The American Colonial Office', *The Mississippi Valley Historical Review*, 30: 4 (March), pp.521–32
51. Anthony Anghie (2005) *Imperialism, Sovereignty and the Making of International Law*, Cambridge Studies in International and Comparative Law No. 37, Cambridge, UK: Cambridge University Press, p.283
52. Cited in Paul Kramer (2002) 'Empires, Exceptions, and Anglo-Saxons: Race and Rule Between the British and United States Empires, 1880–1910', *The Journal of American History* (March), p.1315
53. Seager, *Alfred Thayer Mahan*, p.419

54. Frank Schumacher (2002) 'The American Way of Empire: National Tradition and Transatlantic Adaptation in America's Search for Imperial Identity, 1898–1910', German Historical Institute *Bulletin*, 31 (Fall), pp.35–50

55. Cited in Healy, *U.S. Expansionism*, p.21. Root was the architect of US colonial policy

56. 'The Foreign Policy of the United States: Political and Commercial', *Annals of the Academy of Political and Social Science*, 13: 12 Supplement (May 1899)

57. See 'The New Haven Meeting of the American Historical Association', *The American Historical Review*, 4: 3 (April 1899), pp.409–22

58. Charles M. Andrews (1900) 'The Boston Meeting of the American Historical Association', *The American Historical Review*, 5: 3 (April), pp.423–39

59. A. Lawrence Lowell (1900) *Colonial Civil Service: The Selection and Training of Colonial Officials in England, Holland and France* New York: The Macmillan Company

60. Editorial of *The New York Times*, December 14, 1898

61. Woolsey, 'The Government of Dependencies', p.8

62. See Earl S. Pomeroy, 'The American Colonial Office', pp.521–32

63. The most notable instances in the latter part of the nineteenth century were the United States' sharp reaction to French plans to build an inter-oceanic canal through Panama in 1879 (memories of Louis Napoleon Bonaparte's short-lived attempt to install a monarchy in Mexico during the American Civil War were still fresh) and its even more categorical rejection of Britain's right to meddle in hemispheric affairs during the 1895 Venezuelan crisis. See Beale, *Theodore Roosevelt* and Healy, *U.S. Expansionism*

64. Lindley M. Keasbey (1896) 'The Nicaraguan Canal and the Monroe Doctrine', *The Annals of the American Academy of Political and Social Science*, 7 (January), pp.1–31

65. Beale, *Theodore Roosevelt*, p.149

66. See 'Americans to Benefit by Cecil Rhodes' Will', *The New York Times*, April 5, 1902

67. General Butterfield, cited in 'Capt. Mahan on Expansion', *The New York Times*, December 1, 1898

68. 'Article by Mr. Olney', *The New York Times*, February 25, 1900

69. Beveridge, 'In Support of an American Empire'

70. Kramer, 'Empires, Exceptions', pp.1313–53. Reginald Horsman points out that 'the Anglo Saxonism of the last half of the century was no benign expansionism…It assumed that one race was destined to lead, others to service, one race to flourish, many to die. The world was to be transformed…by the power of a superior race'. Horsman, *Race and Manifest Destiny*, p.303

71. Kramer, 'Empires, Exceptions', p.1318

72. Kees Van der Pijl, *The Making of an Atlantic Ruling Class*, p.33

73. Cited in Seager, *Alfred Thayer Mahan*, p.421

74. Cited in Beale, *Theodore Roosevelt*, p. 95

75. Christopher Saunders and Iain R. Smith (2001) 'Southern Africa, 1795–1901', in Andrew Porter (ed.) (2001) *The Oxford History of the British Empire* (*OHBE*): Vol. 3: *The Nineteenth Century* Oxford: Oxford University Press, p.617

76. Monroe, *Britain's Moment*, p.131. On international reactions to the war see Keith Wilson (ed.) (2001)*The International Impact of the Boer War* London:

Acumen. On the financial dimension see Kathleen Burk (1992) 'Money and Power: the Shift from Great Britain to the United States', in Joussef Cassis (ed.) (1992) *Finance and Financiers in European History, 1880–1960* New York: Cambridge University Press

77. As Victor G. Kiernan puts it, 'It was the favourite text of the Manifest Destiny men that the U.S., outstripping Britain in the Anglo-Saxon fold, must soon move to the front'. See V.G. Kiernan (2005[1978]) *America: The New Imperialism – From White Settlement to World Hegemony* London: Verso, p.130

78. Cited in Beale, *Theodore Roosevelt*, p.98

79. Ibid., p.101

80. In 1910, Roosevelt made a series of public appearances in Egypt and London in which, to the disgust of British liberals who wanted to soften the iron hand of imperial rule, he urged British leaders to re-establish their authority forcefully. See Beale, *Theodore Roosevelt*, pp.165–8. V.G. Kiernan quotes the British liberal anti-imperialist W.S. Blunt as writing of Roosevelt in his diary: 'he is a buffoon of the lowest American type...That swine has made another speech about Egypt, worse than before', Kiernan, *America*, p.198

81. See William Appleman Williams (1952) 'Brooks Adams and American Expansion', *The New England Quarterly*, 25: 2 (June), p.219

82. Cited in David P. Calleo and Benjamin M. Rowland (1973) *America and the World Political Economy: Atlantic Dreams and National Realities* Bloomington: Indiana University Press, p.50

83. Adams, like Theodore Roosevelt and Mahan, believed that a strong state was required to secure American success in inter-imperialist competition. State building and empire building went hand in hand: overseas expansion laid the groundwork for the modern American armed forces and the modern state

84. Brooks Adams (1900) *America's Economic Supremacy* New York and London: The Macmillan Company, p.51

85. I am borrowing the title of Akira Iriye's monograph. See Akira Iriye (1995[1993]) *The Cambridge History of American Foreign Relations*, Vol. 3: *The Globalizing of America 1913–1945* London: Cambridge University Press

86. Warren Zimmerman (2002) 'First Great Triumph: How Five Americans made Their Country a World Power', Carnegie Council Transcript, Washington, D.C.: October 9, available at www.cceia.org/resources/transcripts/142.html. See also Warren Zimmerman (2002) *First Great Triumph: How Five Americans made Their Country a World Power* New York: Farrar, Straus and Giroux

87. Gabriel Kolko (1969) *The Roots of American Foreign Policy* Boston: Beacon Press, p.40

88. Walter Lippmann, *U.S. Foreign Policy* New York: Overseas Publishers, pp.18–26

89. The standing Armed Forces grew from 27,500 in 1897 to over 250,000 in 1901, 120,000 deployed in the Philippines. Significant outlays were made available to the navy, with the General Board of the navy being 'charged with preparing plans for the defense of the nation and its dependencies'. Russell Weigley points out that President Roosevelt easily obtained authorisation from Congress for a new fleet that made the US navy the 'second in battleship

strength among the fleets of the world'. Weigley, *The American Way of War*, pp.186–7. After the war in the Philippines, the US armed forces were drawn down to just under 100,000. War and international expansion also played a decisive role in the build-up of presidential power. Woodrow Wilson noted the trend when still an academic, writing in 1907 that the presidency was 'now at the front of affairs, as no President, except Lincoln, has been since the first quarter of the nineteenth century'. See James T. Patterson (1976) 'The Rise of Presidential Power before World War II', *Law and Contemporary Problems*, 40: 2, Presidential Power: Part 1 (Spring), pp.39–57

90. Bairoch, *Victoires et déboires*, Vol. 2; Cain and Hopkins, *British Imperialism*, p.450

91. Cited in Robert Buzzanco (1999) 'What Happened to the New Left: Toward a Radical Reading of American Foreign Relations', Bernath Lecture, *Diplomatic History*, 23: 4 (Fall), p.591

92. Cain and Hopkins, *British Imperialism*, p.450

93. See Robert J.C. Young (2001) *Postcolonialism: An Historical Introduction* Oxford: Blackwell

94. Cited in Robert Holland (1999) 'The British Empire and the Great War, 1914–1918', in Judith M. Brown and William Roger Louis (eds) (1999) *OHBE*: Vol. 4: *The Twentieth Century* Oxford: Oxford University Press, p.124

95. Erez Manela (2007) *The Wilsonian Moment: Self-Determination and the International Origins of Anticolonial Nationalism* New York: Oxford University Press

96. See Telegram from 'The Chargé in Great Britain (Laughlin) to the Secretary of State', in *FRUS*, *Foreign Relations*, Supplement 1, 1918, FRUS, p.366, available at http://digital.library.wisc.edu/1711.dl/ FRUS

97. Carr, *The Twenty Years' Crisis*, p.215

98. Cited in LaFeber, *The New Empire*, p.415

99. The United States dispatched expeditionary forces on more than 20 occasions in the Caribbean alone between 1898 and 1920. Louis A. Pérez Jr argues that the United States intervened in Cuba in 1898 to forestall a social revolution that would have threatened American economic interests in the Caribbean and Latin America. See Louis A. Pérez (1990) *Cuba and the United States: Ties of Singular Intimacy* Athens, Ga.: University of Georgia Press

100. Hunt, *Ideology and U.S. Foreign Policy*, p.137

101. Van der Pijl, *The Making of an Atlantic Ruling Class*, p.55

102. Lippmann, *U.S. Foreign Policy*, p.26

103. Roberta A. Dayer (1988) *Finance and Empire: Sir Charles Addis, 1861–1945* London: Macmillan, p.113. In a review of the book, P.J. Cain writes that Dayer's work reveals 'the intensity and global sweep of the rivalry between the United States and Britain'. Untitled review, *Economic History Review*, New Series, 42: 4 (November 1989), pp.609–10

104. See Peter Alter's (1994[1989]) typology of nationalisms in *Nationalism* London: Arnold

105. Polanyi, *The Great Transformation*, p.4

106. Antonio Gramsci (1998) in Quintin Hoare and Goffrey Nowell Smith (eds) (1998) *Selections from the Prison Notebooks* London: Lawrence and Wishart Ltd. See Arrighi, *The Long Twentieth Century*, for a discussion of the notion of world hegemony

CHAPTER 4

1. Cited in Donald W. White (1989) 'History and American Internationalism: The Formulation from the Past After World War II', *Pacific Historical Review*, 58: 2 (May), p.151
2. Moses I. Finley (1985) *Ancient History, Evidence and Models* London: Chatto and Windus, p.79
3. Walter Lippmann (1939) *The American Destiny* New York: Life Magazine. See also James L. Baughman (2001) *Henry R. Luce and the Rise of the American Century* Baltimore: Johns Hopkins University Press, p.132; Ronald Steel (1980) *Walter Lippmann and the American Century* Boston: Littlebrown and Co., p.363
4. Speech before the annual convention of the Investment Bankers Association, December 10, 1940, cited in James J. Martin (1971) *Revisionist Viewpoints: Essays in a Dissident Historical Tradition* Colorado Springs: Ralph Myles Publisher, Inc., p.25
5. Henry R. Luce (1999[1941]) 'The American Century', *Life Magazine*, February 17, 1941. Republished in *Diplomatic History*, 23: 2 (Spring)
6. Walter Lippmann (1944) *U.S. War Aims* New York: Overseas Publishers Inc., pp.251–2
7. A 1942 State Department memorandum reporting on a meeting of the Senate Foreign Relations Committee noted 'an unusual manifestation of submerged opposition to England [that] was not confined to any category or group of members of the Committee'. See 'Memorandum by the Assistant Secretary of State (Long) to the Under Secretary of State (Welles)', February 25, 1942, in *FRUS diplomatic papers, 1942. General; the British Commonweath; the Far East:* Vol. 1 (1942) (University of Wisconsin Digital Collections, available at http://digital.library.wisc.edu/1711.dl/FRUS
8. 'Joint Chiefs of Staff Minutes of a Meeting at the White House', January 7, 1943, in *FRUS, The Conferences at Washington, 1941–1942, and Casablanca, 1943* (1941–1943), p.514, (University of Wisconsin Digital Collections, available at http://digital.library.wisc.edu/1711.dl/FRUS
9. Gabriel Kolko (1990[1968]) *The Politics of War, The World and United States Foreign Policy, 1943–1945* New York: Pantheon Books, p.266
10. Dean Acheson (1987) *Present at the Creation: My Years in the State Department* New York: W.W. Norton, p.9
11. Going into the second Quebec conference in 1944, and prior to new talks with Britain over the extension of Lend-Lease after the war, Harry Hopkins suggested to Roosevelt that he 'should tell the Prime Minister how strongly you feel about knocking down some of the trade barriers...I think it is essential to our bargaining with Great Britain that you disabuse the Prime Minister's mind...I rather think that he thinks that the genius of this program in America lies with Secretary Hull, while the truth of the matter is that it is a program that, from the beginning, has been pushed by you'. Cited in Robert E. Sherwood (1948) *Roosevelt and Hopkins: An Intimate History* New York: Harper and Brothers, p.817
12. Melvyn P. Leffler (1994) *The Specter of Communism: The United States and the Origins of the Cold War, 1917–1953* New York: Hill and Wang, p.47

13. Randall Bennett Woods (1990) *A Changing of the Guard: Anglo-American Relations, 1941–1946* Chapel Hill, N.C.: The University of North Carolina Press, p.10

14. Christopher D. O'Sullivan (2007) *Sumner Welles, Postwar Planning and the Quest for a New World Order*, in the Gutenberg-e program, New York: Columbia University Press, p.45, available at www.gutenberg-e.org/osc01/frames/fosc03.html

15. Secretary of State Cordell Hull cited in Kolko, *The Politics of War*, p.276. This is confirmed by O'Sullivan who cites the resolution of senior post-war planners in 1943 not to 'seek to destroy any existing empire or to dictate to other countries concerning colonial administration', O'Sullivan, *Sumner Welles*, p.105

16. Laurence E. Salisbury (1944) 'The Pacific Front, Colonial Asia', *Far Eastern Review*, 13: 25 (December), p.237. Salisbury's view was shared by other State Department officials. See for instance 'Memorandum by the Chief of the Division of Near Eastern Affairs (Ailing) 79', *FRUS diplomatic papers*, 1943, The Near East and Africa, Vol. IV (1943), p.239. The Memorandum of 1943 argued that the US should not align their intelligence operations with those of the British since this would lead to the identification '[by] the Burmese and all of the colonial Asiatics with British imperialism'. On the colonial policies of the Roosevelt administration see: Robert J. McMahon (1999) *The Limits of Empire: The United States and Southeast Asia Since World War II* New York: Columbia University Press; Robert J. McMahon (1981) *Colonialism and Cold War: The United States and the Struggle for Indonesian Independence, 1945–49* Ithaca, NY: Cornell University Press; Frances Gouda and Thijs B. Zaalberg (2002) *American Visions of the Netherlands East Indies/Indonesia: U.S. Foreign Policy and Indonesian Nationalism, 1920–1949* Amsterdam: Amsterdam University Press; Foster Rhea Dulles and Gerald E. Ridinger (1955) 'The Anticolonial Policies of Franklin D. Roosevelt', *Political Science Quarterly*, 70: 1 (March), pp.1–18; John J. Sebrega (1986) 'The Anticolonial Policies of Franklin D. Roosevelt: A Reappraisal', *Political Science Quarterly*, 101: 1, pp.65–84; Gary Hess (1972) 'Franklin Roosevelt and Indochina', *The Journal of American History*, 59: 2 (September), pp.353–68

17. Woods, *A Changing of the Guard*, p.7. See also Gabriel Kolko, *The Politics of War*; Roberta Allbert Dayer, *Finance and Empire*. Alan Dobson writes that 'Lend-Lease helped Britain resist Germany, Italy and later Japan, but it made Britain vulnerable to economic demands and interference in her economy by her closest ally which compromised her sovereignty'. See Alan P. Dobson (1986) *US Wartime Aid to Britain, 1940–1946* London: Taylor and Francis, p.226

18. Cited in Robert Skidelsky (2003) *John Maynard Keynes, 1883–1946: Economist, Philosopher, Statesman* London: Penguin Books, p.756

19. Melvyn Leffler (1984) 'The American Conception of National Security and the Beginning of the Cold War', *American Historical Review*, 89: 2 (April), p.349. Leffler writes that Roosevelt endorsed the bases plan in 1944. Kolko cites Secretary of War Henry Stimson in 1944: 'After this war's over the sentiment of the people will be in favor of having what the government thinks will be enough to maintain our power in the Pacific'. Kolko, *The Politics of War*, p.465

20. Lippmann, *U.S. Foreign Policy*, p.61

21. Harry Truman cited in White, 'History and American Internationalism'
22. Susan Strange (1982) 'Cave! Hic Dragones: A Critique of Regime Analysis', *International Organization*, 33: 2, International Regimes (Spring), p.482
23. See FRUS, National security affairs; foreign economic policy, Volume I (1950), United States national security policy: estimates of threats to the national security; the extension of military assistance to foreign nations; the preparation of NSC 68, 'United States Objectives and Programs for National Security', pp.126–492, available at http://digital.library.wisc.edu/1711.dl/FRUS
24. Setting a pattern of threat inflation that persisted throughout the Cold War, NSC 68, the 1950 foundational policy document of the Cold War, maintained that the Soviet Union was aiming to 'impose its absolute authority over the rest of the world' and advocated a total and sustained mobilisation of US resources to achieve 'superior overall [American] power'. This was followed, in the aftermath of Stalin's death and the end of the Korean War, by the 'bomber gap' uproar in the mid 1950s, the 1957 Gaither Committee report and the 'missile gap' debate of the late 1950s, the Team-B exercise in the mid 1970s which was part of a concerted effort by radical cold warriors to 'bury *détente*'. Ronald Reagan campaigned during the 1980 presidential election on the theme that 'this nation has become number two in a world where it is dangerous, if not fatal to be second best'. On Team B, see Anne Hessing Cahn (1998) *Killing Détente: The Right Attacks the CIA* University Park, PA: Pennsylvania State University Press. For a comprehensive account of Cold War militarist groupings, see Sanders, *Peddlers of Crisis*. For the CIA's own assessment see Raymond Garthoff (2003) 'Estimating Soviet Military Intentions and Capabilities', in Gerald K. Haines and Robert E. Leggett (eds) (2003) *Watching the Bear: Essays on CIA's Analysis of the Soviet Union* Washington, D.C.: Central Intelligence Agency, Center for the Study of Intelligence. Garthoff writes that the Soviet strategic threat was 'generally overstated throughout the Cold War', available at www.cia.gov/library/center-for-the-study-of-intel-ligence/index.html
25. Interview with Seymour Melman conducted in New York, March 9, 2001. Melman (1985[1975]) discusses this in detail in *The Permanent War Economy* New York: Simon and Schuster
26. Richard Perle (1997) 'Interview With Richard Perle – 30.3.1997', *National Security Archive Cold War Project* Washington, D.C.: March 13), available at www.gwu.edu/~nsarchiv/coldwar/interviews/episode-19/perle1.html
27. Zbigniew Brzezinski (1974–75) 'Recognizing the Crisis', *Foreign Policy*, 17 (Winter), pp.63–74
28. John G. Ruggie (1982) 'International Regimes, Transactions, and Change: Embedded Liberalism in the Postwar Economic Order', in 'International Regimes', *International Organization*, 36: 2 (Spring), p.393
29. Calleo, *Beyond American Hegemony*, p.15
30. Bruce Cumings (1984) 'The Origins and Development of the Northeast Asian Political Economy: Industrial Sectors, Product Cycles, and Political Consequences', *International Organization*, 38: 1 (Winter), p.6
31. Cox, *Production, Power*, p.215
32. Jean-Baptiste Duroselle (1978) *Histoire diplomatique de 1919 à nos jours* Paris: Dalloz, p.735
33. Henry Magdoff (1969) *The Age of Imperialism, the Economics of U.S. Foreign Policy* Monthly Review Press, New York, p.59

34. US companies accounted, for instance, for over 40 per cent of sales of refined petroleum products, computers, cars, refrigerators, tractors and agricultural machinery, etc. in Great Britain in 1964. Magdoff, *The Age of Imperialism*, p.61

35. Melman, *The Permanent War Economy*, p.144

36. In the early 1950s, the United States obtained military facilities and rights in Morocco and Tunisia that the French 'protector', heavily dependent on US post-war aid and support in Indochina, could hardly refuse. The US, as Annie Lacroix-Riz has documented, worked methodically during the Second World War to establish themselves in Tunisia and Morocco at France's expense, and 'felt at home' in both countries. Annie Lacroix-Riz (1988) *Les protectorats d'Afrique du Nord entre la France et Washington* Paris: L'Harmattan, pp.234–44

37. The United States voted on November 7, 1956 in favour of UN Resolution 1001 (ES-1) that called on the United Kingdom and France and Israel 'immediately to withdraw their forces from Egyptian territory'

38. See Jonathan Kirshner (1997) *Currency and Coercion: the Political Economy of International Monetary Power* Princeton, N.J.: Princeton University Press. Kirshner emphasises that 'the magnitude of the selling clearly revealed the act to be one of predatory currency manipulation' and concludes that 'monetary diplomacy was exercised costlessly, privately, quickly and with great success' (p.81)

39. William Roger Louis and Ronald E. Robinson (1994) 'The Imperialism of Decolonization', *Journal of Imperial and Commonwealth History*, 22: 3, p.478

40. See Erwin M. Wall (2001) *France, the United States, and the Algerian War* Berkeley, CA: University of California Press

41. Dulles and Ridinger, 'The Anti-Colonial Policies of Franklin D. Roosevelt'

42. Cited in William R. Louis (1985) 'American Anti-Colonialism and the Dissolution of the British Empire', *International Affairs*, Royal Institute of International Affairs, 61: 3 (Summer), p.414

43. Ibid., p.412

44. In a note drafted after a trip to Washington by French Prime Minister Pierre Mendes France, Eisenhower wrote: 'He is completely Victorian in this regard, even though he is absolutely right in his contention that a number of these peoples who are screaming for independence are not yet equipped to support it, and that by now laying down British responsibility in this regard, he would be merely contributing to further unrest and possibly the spread of Communism in the world. My own belief is that colonialism should be militantly condemned by the colonial powers, especially Britain and France. The attempt should be made to transform a necessity into a virtue, so each should insist upon the independence of all these peoples and announce in glowing language a great program of preparing these people to support independence'. See 'The Papers of Dwight David Eisenhower', (electronic edition), published in print form by the Johns Hopkins University Press, Baltimore and London, parts of which are accessible on the website of the Eisenhower Memorial Commission in Washington D.C., 'To Alfred Maximilian Gruenther', Document #1173 (November 30, 1954), available at www.eisenhowermemorial.org/presidential-papers/first-term/documents/1173.cfm

45. *Eisenhower Papers*, 'To Robert Anthony Eden', Document #1972 (September 2, 1956), available at www.eisenhowermemorial.org/presidential-papers/ first-term/documents/1972.cfm
46. 'Colonialism and the U.S.: The Conflict of Ideal v. Reality', *Time Magazine*, March 24, 1958
47. The US worked to shape the domestic politics of allied nations, funding trade unions, sponsoring political parties and intellectuals. In some countries this went very far, for instance in Italy where the US set up deep covert networks to counter the 'Soviet threat' (these networks, such as Gladio, an underground militarised network set up by US intelligence, later became a threat to Italian democracy)
48. Kennan, 'Memorandum', p.524
49. Christopher Hemmer and Peter Katzenstein (2002) 'Why Is There No NATO in Asia? Collective Identity, Regionalism, and the Origins of Multilateralism', *International Organization*, 56: 3 (Summer), p.575
50. Cited in Jerald A. Combs (1991) 'The Compromise That Never Was: George Kennan, Paul Nitze, and the Issue of Conventional Deterrence in Europe', *Diplomatic History*, 15: 3 (Summer), pp.367–8
51. Cited in Kolko, *The Politics of War*, p.546
52. Michael Schaller (1982) 'Securing the Great Crescent: Occupied Japan and the Origins of the Cold War in Asia', *Journal of American History*, 69: 2 (September) p.395
53. Ibid., p.396
54. Meredith Woo-Cumings (1993) 'East Asia's America Problem' in Meredith Woo-Cumings and Michael Loriaux (1993) *Past as Prelude, the Makings of a New World Order* Boulder, Co.: Westview
55. Bruce Cumings (1999) *Parallax Visions, Making Sense of American-East Asian Relations at the End of the Century* Durham, N.C.: Duke University Press
56. Schaller, 'Securing the Great Crescent', p.398
57. Robert Wade (1990) *Governing the Market* Princeton, N.J.: Princeton University Press, p.34
58. Woo-Cumings, 'East Asia's America Problem', p.149
59. Declassified US government documents available at the *National Security Archive* of George Washington University show US acquiescence and involvement in General Suharto's coup d'état, American intelligence involvement in the identification of left-leaning figures who were then liquidated, and support for the invasion of East Timor. See The National Security Archive, 'East Timor Revisited: Ford, Kissinger and the Indonesian Invasion, 1975–76', in William Burr and Michael L. Evans (eds) (2001) *National Security Archive Electronic Briefing Book No. 62* Washington, D.C.: The George Washington University, December 6, available at www.gwu.edu/~nsarchiv/NSAEBB/ NSAEBB62. As far as the Khmer Rouge are concerned, Secretary of State Henry Kissinger characterised them as 'murderous thugs' but asked Thai leaders to convey to them 'that we will be friends with them'. The Nixon administration saw Cambodia as a useful 'counterweight', especially if aligned with China, to the real adversary, North Vietnam. Thus, 'our strategy is to get the Chinese into Laos and Cambodia as a barrier to the Vietnamese'. See Memorandum of Conversation, 'Secretary's Meeting with Foreign Minister Chatchai of Thailand', November 26, 1975, State Department, in William Burr (ed.) (2001) *The National Security Archive Electronic Briefing Book* No. 192,

Document 17, available at www.gwu.edu/~nsarchiv/NSAEBB/ NSAEBB193/ index.htm

60. Walter Russell Mead (2001) *Special Providence, American Foreign Policy and how it Changed the World* New York: Alfred A. Knopf, p.219

61. Aaron Forsberg (2000) *America and the Japanese Miracle: The Cold War Context of Japan's Postwar Economic Revival, 1950–1960* Chapel Hill, N.C.: University of North Carolina Press

62. The factors accounting for the rapid break-out from the periphery by east Asian developmental states have been widely debated. Neo-Weberian accounts of modernisation emphasising cultural factors (the 'Protestant analogue'), as well as neo-classical and neo-liberal economic explanations, have been challenged by comparative research focusing on the role of the state. For the neo-Weberian thesis see Robert Bellah (1985[1957]) *Tokugawa Religion, The Cultural Roots of Modern Japan* New York: Free Press. For syntheses on the debate over the developmental state see Meredith Woo-Cumings (ed.) (1999) *The Developmental State* Ithaca, NY: Cornell University Press; Wade, *Governing the Market*. On the role of war, see Richard Stubbs (1999) 'War and Economic Development: Export Oriented Industrialization in East and Southeast Asia', *Comparative Politics*, Vol. 31 (April), pp.337–55

63. Grimmett, 'Instances of Use'

64. For a synthesis, see Philip S. Golub (2004) 'Le golfe arabo-persique, laboratoire de la révolution stratégique américaine', *Cahiers de l'Orient*, 73, pp.51–8

65. George Liska (1967) *Imperial America: The International Politics of Primacy* Baltimore, Md.: Johns Hopkins University Press

66. Ibid., p.4. Liska adds: 'The commitment to uphold the bases of international order is apparently more sweeping than the commitment to contain the spearheads of international communism' (p.99)

67. Hunt, *Ideology and U.S Foreign Policy,* p.164

68. Ibid., p.164

69. Seeley, *The Expansion of England*, p.141

70. See Alexander Wendt and Michael Barnett (1993) 'Dependent State Formation and Third World Militarization', *Review of International Studies*, 19: 4, pp.321–47

71. Ernst Badian (1971[1968]) *Roman Imperialism in the Late Republic* Ithaca, NY: Cornell University Press, pp.7–11

72. See James Onley (2005) 'Britain's Informal Empire in the Gulf, 1820–1971', *Journal of Social Affairs*, 22: 87 (Fall), pp.29–45. See also Peter Sluglett (1999) 'Formal and Informal Empire in the Middle East,' in Robin W. Winks (ed.) (1999) *OHBE*, Vol. 5: *Historiography* Oxford: Oxford University Press

CHAPTER 5

1. Helms, 'Entering the Pacific Century'

2. I am borrowing the expression from Franz Schurmann. See Schurmann (1974) *The Logic of World Power: An Enquiry into the Origins, Currents and Contradictions of World Politics* New York: Pantheon Books. See also Johnson, *The Sorrows of Empire*. For a sociological perspective on the domestic dimensions of the security structure, see Bacevich, *The New American Militarism*

3. These statistics and Figure 5.1 are derived from data provided by US Department of Defense's historical series *Active Duty Military Personnel Strengths by Regional Area and by Country* Washington D.C.: Department of Defense. The 2007 figure includes navy personnel ashore and afloat and National Guard forces deployed in the two conflict areas. It does not include the tens of thousands of private contractors involved in the wars, available at http://siadapp.dmdc.osd.mil/personnel/ MILITARY/history/hst0712.pdf

4. Thomas P.M. Barnett (2004) *The Pentagon's New Map: War and Peace in the Twenty-First Century* New York: G.P. Putnam's Sons. Barnett was a senior adviser to Defense Secretary Donald Rumsfeld in the early years of the George W. Bush administration

5. The People's Republic of China (PRC) and Russia, the only states outside the US security system with large defence outlays, together account for just over 7 per cent of world defence expenditure ($84.2 billion, out of a world total of $1,158 billion, in constant 2005 dollars). Source: SIPRI Yearbook, 2008, available at http://yearbook2007.sipri.org/chap8/

6. Alberto R. Coll (1992) 'America as the Grand Facilitator', *Foreign Policy*, 87 (Summer), pp.47–65

7. Ronald Steel remarks, appositely, that 'American political strategists have all along been concerned not only with containing communism, but with creating an integrated global system, resting on a political and economic base, orchestrated from Washington. The end of the Cold War has loosened the cement holding that system together, but not its underlying rationale'. Ronald Steel (1995) *Temptations of a Superpower* Cambridge, Mass.: Harvard University Press, p.55

8. Australia, Colombia, Egypt, India, Indonesia, Iraq, Israel, Japan, Jordan, Republic of Korea, Kuwait, Mexico, Morocco, New Zealand, Pakistan, the Philippines, Saudi Arabia, Singapore, Taiwan, Thailand, Tunisia. This list is not exhaustive but includes the major friendly states

9. Reliable statistics are not available for North Korea and Sudan. The *CIA Factbook* estimates Cuban defence spending at 3.8 per cent of GDP in 2006, or $1.73 billion. According to SIPRI, Syrian ($5.703 billion) and Iranian ($6.592 billion) defence expenditures in constant 2005 dollars accounted for 1 per cent of world defence spending. See www.cia.gov/library/publications/the-world-factbook/

10. Because of its affinities with official views I focus my remarks on the first variant of declinism, rather than Marxist or neo-Marxist declinist arguments. Neo-realism, as Robert W. Cox, Richard K. Ashley and others have argued, is a problem-solving paradigm normatively geared to the preservation of American power. This is most clearly expressed in hegemonic stability theory (HST). First formulated by Charles Kindleberger to account for the breakdown of the nineteenth-century world system, and later incorporated in most neo-realist writing, HST postulates that the international system requires a hegemonic stabiliser, or 'benevolent despot', to establish and maintain international order. In circumstances of hegemonic decay, the system tends towards entropy and, in one variant of the theory, systemic breakdown and war. The corollaries of this postulate are that systemic transformation is threat-laden and that hegemony is itself an international public good. See Isabelle Grunberg (1990) 'Exploring the "Myth" of Hegemonic Stability', *International Organization*, 44: 4 (Autumn), pp.431–77

11. While defeat in Vietnam demonstrated the limits of military power it did not alter the balance of forces in East Asia, notably because of the rapprochement between the United States and the People's Republic of China (PRC). The loss of Iran, the 'land bridge between Europe and Asia, often the hinge of world history' in Henry Kissinger's words, severely weakened the US position in the Gulf and still threatens it today. Henry Kissinger (1979) *The White House Years* London: Weidenfeld and Nicolson, p.1262

12. Prefigured in the Program of Action of the Fourth Summit of the Non Aligned in Algiers in 1973, United Nations General Assembly resolution 3201 (S VI), May 1, 1974, *Declaration on the Establishment of a New International Economic Order*, called for a fundamental restructuring of the international order based on 'sovereign equality', cooperation to 'banish disparities', equal participation in multilateral institutions in 'solving world economic problems', the right of nations to 'adopt the economic and social systems deemed most appropriate', compensation for 'colonial exploitation' and resource depletion, technology transfer and 'full sovereignty over natural resources' and the right to expropriate or transfer ownership of the foreign property of multinational firms, with compensation arbitrated by national courts. Though non-binding, the resolution represented a sharp and coherent challenge to the foundations of the post-war order. For the full declaration see www.un-documents.net/s6r3201.htm

13. Philip Zelikow's expression in 'The Statesman in Winter: Kissinger on the Ford Years', *Foreign Affairs*, New York, 78: 3 (May–June 1999)

14. Felix Rohatyn (1984) *The Twenty Year Century: Essays on Economics and Public Finance* New York: Random House

15. Robert Gilpin (1981) *War and Change in World Politics* New York: Cambridge University Press, pp.242–3

16. According to the CIA's *Center for the Study of Intelligence*, the United States appears early on to have been cognisant of structural Soviet economic problems and of a marked 'slowdown of Soviet industrial production' after 1975. A series of estimates were written in the 1970s and 1980s describing a 'slow and steady decline in the rate of economic growth, a lack of improvement in the quality of life in Soviet society, and finally growing indications of political destabilization that ultimately resulted in the break-up of the Soviet Union'. In 1983, in the midst of the Reagan military build-up, a CIA estimate entitled 'The Slowdown in Soviet Industry, 1976–1982' concluded that the Soviet Union was facing major infrastructural constraints and that cuts in 'new fixed investment and output' transformed a 'planned temporary retreat into a rout'. As Soviet growth slowed, so did military expenditure, which only grew at an annual rate of 1.3 per cent between 1975 and 1985 despite the invasion and occupation of Afghanistan (1979–1988). See James Noren, 'Assessing Soviet Economic Performance', in *CIA's Analysis of the Soviet Union, 1947–1991* Washington, D.C.: Center for the Study of Intelligence, Central Intelligence Agency. *CIA's Analysis* resulted from a conference at Princeton University March 9–10, 2001, sponsored by the Princeton Center of International Studies and the CIA's Center for the Study of Intelligence. See: www.cia.gov/library/center-for-the-study-of-intelligence/csi-publications/books-and-monographs/watching-the-bear-essays-on-cias-analysis-of-the-soviet-union/intro.htm

17. Paul Kennedy (1987) *The Rise and Fall of the Great Powers* New York: Vintage Books, p.533

18. John G. Ikenberry (1989) 'Rethinking the Origins of American Hegemony', *Political Science Quarterly*, 104: 3 (Autumn), p.375

19. National Research Council, Board on Science, Technology and Economic Policy (1999) *Securing America's Industrial Strength* Washington, D.C.: National Academy Press

20. MIT Commission on Industrial Productivity (1990) *Made in America: Regaining the Productive Edge* New York: Touchstone, 1990. The Commission began its work in 1986 and published the report in 1990

21. Ethan B. Kapstein (2000) 'Hegemony Wired: American Politics and the New Economy', *Les Notes de l'IFRI* Paris: Institut français de relations internationales, p.18

22. The cultural subtexts of discourses on Japan during the period have been scrutinised by Meredith Woo-Cumings. Deconstructing the 'new orientalism', she writes: 'The East Asian countries are perceived to be in but not of the world, free-riding on defense, and predatory in economics...the contemporary rancor of representatives of this view indicates a frustration about Asians getting off the reservation and doing their own thing, so to speak'. See Woo-Cumings, *East Asia's America Problem*, p.139

23. Cited by Richard Katz (1999) *Japan: The System that Soured* New York: M.E. Sharpe, p.9

24. American critics include Bruce Russett (1985) 'The Mysterious Case of Vanishing Hegemony; or, Is Mark Twain Really Dead?', *International Organization*, 39: 2 (Spring), pp.207–31. See also Joseph Nye Jr (1990) *Bound To Lead: The Changing Nature Of American Power* New York: Basic Books, in which the author argued that 'the United States remains the largest and richest power with the greatest capacity to shape the future'

25. Fernand Braudel (1977) *Afterthoughts on Material Civilization and Capitalism* Baltimore, Md: Johns Hopkins University Press

26. Strange, 'Cave! Hic Dragones', p.482

27. Ibid.

28. Strange, 'Towards a Theory of Transnational Empire', p.169

29. Gill, *American Hegemony,* p.64

30. Studies of British declinism usefully highlight its uses as political narrative, in particular a narrative of empire. David Edgerton writes: 'Declinism is beginning to appear as one of the last vestiges of imperial grandeur: for declinism holds, implicitly but clearly, that if Britain had done better it would have remained a much larger player on the world stage'. See David Edgerton (1997) 'The Decline of Declinism', *The Business History Review*, 71: 2 (Summer), p.202. There has been far less study of American declinism, but some American intellectuals have noted the use of declinism as a mobilisation narrative. Samuel Huntington, for instance, commented in 1989 that declinism 'performs a useful historical function. It provides a warning and a goad to action in order to head off and reverse the decline that it says is taking place. It serves that purpose now as it did in its earlier manifestations in the 1950s, 1960s, and 1970s'. Samuel Huntington (1989) 'No Exit: The Errors of Endism', *The National Interest*, No. 17 (Fall)

31. Walter Laqueur, cited by Sanders, *Peddlers of Crisis,* p.299

32. John Braithwaite and Peter Drahos (2000) *Global Business Regulation* New York: Cambridge University Press, p.99. See also Kirshner, *Currency and*

Coercion. Kirshner writes that the United States was 'in some ways more powerful' in the monetary sphere after 1971 than before

33. George Ball (1976) *Diplomacy in a Crowded World: An American Foreign Policy* Boston: Little, Brown and Company, p.9

34. See Donald E. Spiro (1999) *Petrodollar Recycling and International Markets: The Hidden Hand of American Hegemony* Ithaca, NY: Cornell University Press. Spiro provides a detailed account of how the US' hegemonic position in the world political economy produced 'outcomes favourable to the United States'

35. Declassified documents of the British Joint Intelligence Committee (JIC) from the period indicate that the British government expected to be called upon to participate in operations. The JIC document, 'Middle East – Possible Use of Force by the United States' (December 12, 1973), cites Secretary of Defense James Schlesinger saying that the US would not tolerate challenges from 'underdeveloped countries'. The not quite so explicit but unmistakable public warnings of Henry Kissinger ('It is clear that if pressures continue unreasonably and indefinitely, then the United States will have to consider what countermeasures it may have to take') could not have been lost on the Saudis. The JIC memo was widely reported in the American and British media in 2004. See for instance Glenn Frankel (2004) 'U.S. Mulled Seizing Oil Fields in 73', *The Washington Post* (January 1). The JIC document is available at the UK National Archives, CAB 190/56, 'Intelligence Co-ordinator's Working Party on Oil: papers 1–4', available at www.nationalarchives. gov.uk

36. Brzezinski, 'Recognizing the Crisis', p.74

37. Ball, *Diplomacy*, p.9. One of the very few liberal-internationalist establishment figures in the Johnson administration to oppose the Vietnam War, Ball was very critical of the unilateralism of the Nixon administration and its way of dealing with Europe. He wrote that Nixon and Kissinger were transforming the American 'Delian League' into an empire and, rather than factoring in the views of allies, was expecting them 'to follow our lead without grumbling while we measured their value to us by the degree to which they uncritically supported our action' (ibid., p.9)

38. Interview with Paul A. Volcker, *Public Broadcasting System* (PBS), conducted September 26, 2000, available at www.pbs.org/wgbh/commandingheights/shared/minitextlo/int_paulvolcker.html

39. Giovanni Arrighi (2003) 'The Social and Political Economy of Global Turbulence', *New Left Review* (March–April), p.54

40. Interview with Richard Falk, July 12, 2008

41. See Theotonio Dos Santos (1970) 'The Structure of Dependence', *American Economic Review*, 60: 2, pp.231–6; Andre Gunder Frank (1969) *Capitalism and Underdevelopment in Latin America* New York: Monthly Review Press; Immanuel Wallerstein (1983) *Historical Capitalism* New York: Schocken

42. Alfred O. Hirschman (1981[1945]) *National Power and the Structure of Foreign Trade: The Politics of the International Economy* Berkeley, CA: University of California Press

43. Latin American countries moved during the 1980s from developmentalist to neo-liberal models. See Paul W. Drake (2006) 'The Hegemony of U.S. Economic Doctrines in Latin America', in Eric Hershberg and Fred Rosen (eds) (2006) *Latin America After Neoliberalism: Turning the Tide in the 21st*

Century? The New Press and North American Congress on Latin America [NACLA], pp.26–48

44. See Philip S. Golub (1998) 'When East Asia Falters', *Le Monde diplomatique* (English edition, London) (July); Eddy Lee (1998) *The Asian Financial Crisis: The Challenge for Social Policy* Geneva: International Labour Organization

45. Stephen Peter Rosen (2003) 'An Empire, If You Can Keep It', *The National Interest*, 71 (Spring), p.57

46. President de Gaulle began to convert France's dollar holdings into gold in 1965, an exit from the monetary structure that was followed the year later by a partial exit from NATO. For a typical contemporary American reaction see 'De Gaulle v. the Dollar', *Time Magazine* editorial (February 12, 1965): 'Perhaps never before had a chief of state launched such an open assault on the monetary power of a friendly nation'. For a discussion of the various dimensions of French Atlantic policy, see Kies Van der Pijl (2006) *Global Rivalry, From the Cold War to Iraq* London: Pluto Press. For de Gaulle's own views, see Charles de Gaulle (2000) *Mémoires* Paris: Gallimard, Bibliothèque de la Pléiade

47. Marina v. N. Whitman (1975) 'Leadership Without Hegemony: Our Role in the World Economy', *Foreign Policy*, 20 (Autumn), p.140

48. In May 1971, Connally said: 'the persistent underlying balance-of-payments deficit which causes such concern is more than covered, year in and year out, by our net military expenditures abroad, over and above amounts received from foreign military purchases'. Cited in Calleo and Rowland, *America and the World Political Economy*, p.99

49. Richard M. Nixon (1971) Address to the Nation outlining a New Economic Policy: 'The Challenge of Peace' (August 15), in *The American Presidency Project* [online], Santa Barbara, CA: University of California, available at www.presidency.ucsb.edu/ ws/?pid=3115

50. See World Trade Organization (WTO), International Trade Statistics, 2001, 'Long term trends', available at www.wto.org/english/res_e/statis_e/its2001_e/its01_longterm_e.htm

51. François Godement (1998) *Dragon de feu, Dragon de papier: l'Asie a-t-elle un avenir?* Paris: Flammarion, p.93

52. Henry Kissinger (1994) *Diplomacy* New York: Simon and Schuster, p.23

53. Democratic transitions throughout east Asia were synchronous with the waning and the end of the Cold War. In northeast Asia, Taiwan's transition began in 1986 with the partial opening of the political system, leading in 1996 to the first general election in the island's history; South Korea's began in 1987, leading to regular and competitive general elections and to President Kim Dae Jung's policy of engagement with North Korea (the 'Sunshine' policy). In southeast Asia, the Marcos regime was overthrown by popular revolt in 1986 and the Thai democratic transition began in 1992

54. Katzenstein, *The Culture of National Security*, p.536

55. See Philip S. Golub (2001) 'America's Imperial Longings', *Le Monde diplomatique* (English edition, London) (July); and Golub (2004) 'Imperial Politics, Imperial Will and the Crisis of U.S. Hegemony', *Review of International Political Economy*, 11: 4 (October), pp.763–86

56. The typology has significant points of convergence with the one proposed by Richard Falk in the mid 1970s. See Falk, 'Beyond Internationalism', pp.65–113. Falk distinguishes between 'isolationalists', 'imperialists',

'managers' and 'transformers'. He wrote off the first group as irrelevant because of the US' 'unavoidable participation in the world', a judgment that remains valid today. Transformers advocated a new democratised world order to deal with 'planetary dangers'. While not irrelevant, Falk noted that this group could not mobilise 'widespread support' for an agenda of progressive post-Westphalian transformation

57. For a synthesis of the argument, see C. Fred Bergsten (1992) 'The Primacy of Economics', *Foreign Policy*, 87 (Summer), pp.3–24

58. See, for instance, the speech at the Johns Hopkins University School of Advanced International Studies of President Clinton's first National Security Adviser, Anthony Lake, 'From Containment to Enlargement', Washington, D.C.: September 21, 1993, available at www.state.gov/www/publications/dispatch/index.html

59. David Hendrickson and Robert W. Tucker (1992) *The Imperial Temptation: The New World Order and America's Purpose* New York: Council on Foreign Relations

60. Henry Kissinger offers a good example of realist thinking in the aftermath of the Cold War. See, Kissinger, *Diplomacy*

61. Helms, 'Entering the Pacific Century'

62. Charles Krauthammer, 'The Unipolar Moment', *Foreign Affairs*, 70: 1 (Winter 1990–91), pp.23–33

63. For a synthesis of the arguments of the sovereignists see Jeremy Rabkin (1999) 'International Law Versus Our Constitution', *The National Interest*, 55 (Spring), pp.30–41. For critiques see Patrick Stewart (2001) 'Don't Fence Me In: The Perils of Going It Alone', *World Policy Journal* (Fall) and Peter J. Spiro (2000) 'The New Sovereignists: American Exceptionalism and its False Prophets', *Foreign Affairs* 79: 6 (November–December)

64. Alter, *Nationalism*, p.26

65. Ibid., p.30

66. Samuel P. Huntington (1999) 'Robust Nationalism', *The National Interest* Washington, D.C. Huntington writes: 'American wealth and power are at their peak. The national unity, economic equity and cultural integrity of America are not. In the broadest sense, American national identity is under challenge from a multiculturalism that subverts it from below and a cosmopolitanism that erodes it from above. Patriotism is *passé* among large sectors of American elites. Conceivably, in the future serious external threats to America could arise from China, Russia, Islam or some combination of hostile states. At present, however, the principal threats to American unity, culture and power are closer to home. The appropriate response of both classic conservatives and neoconservatives is to come together in support of a robust nationalism that reaffirms some basic truths. America is a religious country. Patriotism is a virtue. Universalism is not Americanism. Nationalism is not isolationism... Robust nationalism could have substantial public appeal and could also serve as an alternative to more narrow isolationist measures that might also win public support. Robust nationalism is an alternative to divisive multiculturalism, xenophobic isolationism and wimpy universalism. It is a foundation on which conservatives could unite to promote American national interests abroad and national unity at home.'

67. George H.W. Bush and Brent Scowcroft (1999) *A World Transformed* New York: Vintage Books, p.433

68. See Bruce Cumings (2002) 'The United States and Korean Reunification', *Working Paper* Chicago, Ill.: The Center for International Policy Asia Program and The Center for East Asian Studies, University of Chicago, December 5, available at www.ciponline.org/asia/reports/task_force/Cumings.htm

69. Coll, 'America as Grand Facilitator', p.54

70. Cited by Michael T. Klare (2001) *Resources Wars, The New Landscape of Global Conflict* New York: Metropolitan Books, p.8

71. Bergsten, 'The Primacy of Economics', p.4

72. J. Bradford DeLong and Barry Eichengreen (2001) 'Between Meltdown and Moral Hazard: The International Monetary and Financial Policies of the Clinton Administration', National Bureau of Economic Research (NBER) *Working Paper*, No. 8443 (August)

73. In 1991, Clinton met with leading Wall Street figures, including Roger Altman of the Blackstone group and Robert Rubin, then head of Goldman Sachs and Company. The first was named Undersecretary of the Treasury in 1993, the second became the first head of the NEC and then Secretary of the Treasury in 1995. See Steven Greenhouse (1993) 'When Rubin Talks...', *The New York Times* (July 25)

74. Nicholas D. Kristof and David Sanger (1999) 'How the U.S. Wooed Asia To Let Cash Flow In', *New York Times* (February 16)

75. Ibid.

76. See Evan H. Potter (ed.) (1998) *Economic Intelligence and National Security* Kingston, Ont., Canada: McGill-Queen's Press, p.103. See also 'Indiana Jim and the Temple of Spooks', *The Economist*, March 20, 1993

77. Peter Ford (1999) 'Friction over "friendly" spying', *The Christian Science Monitor* (September 3). See also Stanley Kober (1996) 'Why Spy: The Uses and Misuses of Intelligence', *CATO Policy Analysis* No. 265, Washington, D.C.: CATO Institute

78. For a case study of US dominance of multilateral institutions, see Robert H. Wade (2002) 'U.S. Hegemony and the World Bank: the Fight over People and Ideas', *Review of International Political Economy*, 9: 2 (Summer), pp.215–43

79. Jean-Christophe Graz (2003) 'Qui gouverne? le Forum de Davos et le pouvoir informel des clubs d'élites transnationales', *A Contrario*, 1: 2

80. Rob Kroes (1999) 'American Empire and Cultural Imperialism, A View from the Receiving End', *Conference Papers on the Web* Washington, D.C.: German Historical Institute, March, available at www.ghi-dc.org

81. The Latin American leaders who led the neo-liberal transformation during the 1980s and 1990s, mostly trained in American universities and sharing the ethos and interests of US elites, are a very good example of just such a constituency. See Paul W. Drake (2006) 'The Hegemony of U.S. Economic Doctrines in Latin America', in Eric Hershberg and Fred Rosen (2006) *Latin America After Neoliberalism: Turning the Tide in the 21st Century?* New York: The New Press and North American Congress on Latin America (NACLA), pp.26–48

82. See Saskia Sassen (1996) *Losing Control. Sovereignty in the Age of Globalization* New York: Columbia University Press

83. Helen V. Milner and Robert Keohane (eds) (1996) *Internationalization and Domestic Politics* New York: Cambridge University Press, p.24

84. Robert Wade (2002) 'The American Empire and its Limits', *DESTIN Working Papers Series*, No. 02–22, London: London School of Economics

85. See Joseph E. Stiglitz (2003) *Globalization and its Discontents* W.W. Norton: New York
86. Bernard K. Gordon (2003) 'A High-Risk Trade Policy', *Foreign Affairs*, 82: 4 (July–August)
87. The author was working in east Asia at the time and was repeatedly told by regional officials that US behaviour was 'imperialist' in character. At popular level, the demonstrations against the IMF in Thailand, Indonesia and South Korea during the crisis, as well as the statements of Malaysian Prime Minister Mahathir Mohamad, had strong nationalist anti-western contents. See Philip S. Golub (1997) 'South East Asia Feels the Chill', *Le Monde diplomatique* (English edition, London) (December); Philip S. Golub (1998) 'When East Asia Falters', *Le Monde diplomatique* (English edition, London) (July); Gordon, 'A High-Risk'; Daniel Lian (2003) 'Mr Thaksin's Role in the East-West Dichotomy', *Morgan Stanley Economic Trends Reports* (July 25)
88. Statement made during a press conference on April 24, 1998 in Geneva, reported by the French daily *Le Monde*. Serge Marti (1998) *Le Monde économie* (May 12)
89. Donald K. Emmerson (1998) 'Americanizing Asia', *Foreign Affairs*, 7: 3 (May–June)
90. Alan Greenspan (1998) 'The Ascendance of Market Capitalism', remarks by Chairman Alan Greenspan before the *Annual Convention of the American Society of Newspaper Editors* Washington, D.C.: The Federal Reserve Board (April 2), available at www.federalreserve.gov/BoardDocs/Speeches/&988/19980402.htm. See Philip S. Golub (2003) 'World's Trade and Manufacturing Centres Shift East. China: the New Economic Giant', *Le Monde diplomatique* (English edition, London) (October)
91. Robert Reich (2008) *Supercapitalism: The Transformation of Business, Democracy and Everyday Life* New York: Vintage Books
92. See Kapstein, 'Hegemony Wired', p.22. Kapstein points out that the Clinton administration made a concerted effort to create favourable frameworks, promote innovation and investment and to 'promote the American model of a competitive but interconnected ICT infrastructure onto the world stage' (ibid.)
93. See Panitch, 'The New Imperial State'

CHAPTER 6

1. Cited by Ron Suskind (2004) 'Without a Doubt', *The New York Times* (October 17)
2. Madeleine Albright, NBC *Today Show* (February 19, 1998)
3. Zbigniew Brzezinski (1998) *The Grand Chessboard, American Primacy and its Geostrategic Objectives* New York: Basic Books, p.23
4. Ibid., p.40
5. Kissinger, *Does America Need a Foreign Policy*, p.19
6. Ibid., p.469
7. Joseph S. Nye (2002) *The Paradox of American Power: Why the World's Only Superpower Can't Go It Alone* New York: Oxford University Press, p.1
8. Brzezinski writes: 'The twin interests of the United States are the short term preservation of its unique global power and in the long run transformation of it into increasingly institutionalized global cooperation'. Brzezinski, *The*

Grand Chessboard, p.40. Kissinger cautioned against 'a deliberate quest for hegemony' and a 'road to empire' that would lead to 'domestic decay'. Instead he proposed to 'transform [American] power into moral consensus'. Kissinger, *Does America Need a Foreign Policy*, pp.468–9. Nye cautioned: 'American power is not eternal. If we squander our soft power through a combination of arrogance and indifference, we will increase our vulnerability, sell our values short, and hasten the erosion of our pre-eminence'. Nye, *The Paradox*, p.xvii. See also Richard N. Haass (1999) 'What to do with American Primacy', *Foreign Affairs*, 78: 5 (September–October), pp.37–49

9. Stephen M. Walt (2002) 'Keeping the World "Off-Balance": Self-Restraint and U.S. Foreign Policy', in John G. Ikenberry (ed.) (2002) *America Unrivaled: The Future of the Balance of Power* Ithica: Cornell University Press, pp.121–54

10. Eliot Cohen (1998) 'Calling Mr.X: The Pentagon's brain-dead two-war strategy', *The New Republic* (January 19). Cohen, on leave from the School of International and Advanced Studies (SIAS), Johns Hopkins University, was named Counselor of the State Department and Special Adviser of Secretary of State Condoleezza Rice, 'particularly with regard to matters of war and peace', on April 30, 2007

11. Ibid.

12. *Rebuilding America's Defenses: Strategy, Forces and Resources for a New Century*, A Report of the *Project for a New American Century* Washington, D.C.: September 2000, p.4. The authors of the report included four future senior officials of the Bush administration: Stephen Cambone, Eliot Cohen, I. Lewis Libby and Paul Wolfowitz

13. Charles Krauthammer (1999) 'A Second American Century', *Time Magazine* (December 27)

14. Mortimer B. Zuckerman (1998) 'A Second American Century', *Foreign Affairs*, 77: 3 (May–June), pp.18–31

15. Alter, *Nationalism*. Alter stresses that integral nationalism is not a phenomenon restricted to late industrialisers such as Germany and Japan or to the special cases of Italian fascism or German National Socialism. Likewise, Robert Paxton writes: 'At bottom [fascism] is passionate nationalism. Allied to it is a conspiratorial and Manichean view of history as a battle between the good and evil camps'. See Paxton, *Anatomy of Fascism*, p.41

16. Huntington, 'Robust Nationalism'

17. Rice, 'Promoting the National Interest'

18. Full text of NSC 68 available at Executive Department of the United States, National Security Council (NSC), available at www.fas.org/irp/offdocs/nsc-hst/nsc-68.htm

19. See Sanders, *Peddlers of Crisis*, which discusses the policy differences between proponents of military containment and the Trilateral Commission

20. Richard Perle, 'Interview 1997'. Henry Kissinger, the target of sharp criticism from Cold War militarists because of his *détente* policy, remarks that they sought a 'restoration of America's strategic superiority' and 'were promising significant changes in the Soviet system as a result of direct American pressure' rather than incremental change. Kissinger, *Diplomacy*, pp.751–5

21. According to a paper of the CIA's Center for the Study of Intelligence, US statements and behaviour during the first Reagan administration fostered Soviet fears that the US was preparing a nuclear first strike. Benjamin B. Fisher writes: 'The KGB in the early 1980s saw the international situation –

in Soviet terminology, the "correlation of world forces" – as turning against the USSR and increasing its vulnerability. These developments, along with the new US administration's tough stance toward the USSR, prompted Soviet officials and much of the populace to voice concern over the prospect of a US nuclear attack. New information suggests that Moscow also was reacting to US-led naval and air operations, including psychological warfare missions conducted close to the Soviet Union'. The author writes: 'war was very much on the minds of Soviet leaders. Moscow was in the midst of a war scare'. He reports that then KGB head Yuri Andropov warned in 1981 that 'the United States was making preparations for a surprise nuclear attack on the USSR'. See Benjamin B. Fischer (1997) 'A Cold War Conundrum', Washington, D.C.: Central Intelligence Agency, Center for the Study of Intelligence, available at www.cia.gov/library/center-for-the-study-of-intelligence/csi-publications/books-and monographs/a-cold-war-conundrum/source.htm

22. Daniel P. Moynihan cited by Jacob Heilbrunn in 'Who Won the Cold War', *The American Prospect* (September 1, 1996)

23. For a synthetic critique of triumphalist American assessments of the end of the Cold War see Vladislav M. Zubok (2000) 'Why did the Cold War End in 1989? Explanations of the Turn', in Odd Arne Westad (ed) (2000) *Reviewing the Cold War: Approaches, Interpretations, Theory* London: Frank Cass, pp.343–61

24. Cited in Hendrickson and Tucker, *The Imperial Temptation*, p.36

25. Ibid., pp.4–16

26. Cumings, 'The End of the Seventy Years' Crisis', p.29

27. The Nuclear Vault, 'Prevent the Reemergence of a New Rival': The Making of the Cheney Regional Defense Strategy, 1991–1992. The National Security Archive, Washington, D.C.: George Washington University, available at www.gwu.edu/~nsarchiv/nukevault/ebb245/index.htm

28. All the citations are from excerpts published by the *New York Times* in 1992, many of which were curiously deleted in the declassified document provided to the National Security Archive. See Patrick Tyler (1992) 'U.S. Strategy Plan Calls for Insuring No Rivals Develop', *The New York Times* (March 8)

29. Steel, *Temptations*, p.56

30. Large parts of the *Guidance* were leaked to the *New York Times* by officials concerned with and opposed to the thrust of the document. The publication of excerpts provoked strong domestic reactions. Senator Joseph Biden, for instance, criticised the *Guidance* for trying to make the US into the 'world policeman' and to establish *Pax Americana*, a global security system where threats to stability are suppressed or destroyed by US military power. Instead, he suggested working out a strategy of 'collective power through the United Nations'. See Patrick Tyler (1992) 'Lone Superpower Plan: Ammunition for Critics', *The New York Times* (March 10). Nonetheless, Defense Secretary Cheney never disavowed the main contents of the *Guidance*

31. Zalmay Khalilzad (1995) *From Containment to Global Leadership: America and the World After the Cold War*, Rand Corporation Project Air Force, Santa Monica, CA, p.21. The declassified report was made public in 1995 and summarised in 'Losing the Moment? The U.S. and the World after the Cold War', *The Washington Quarterly*, 18: 2 (Spring, 1995). Khalilzad was a senior official in the Department of Defense under Dick Cheney

32. Ibid., p.33

33. Jesse Helms (1996) 'Entering the Pacific Century', Heritage Lecture #562, Washington, D.C.: Heritage Foundation

34. Available at www.whitehouse.gov/omb/budget/fy2009/pdf/hist.pdf

35. Interview with Steven Clemons, New America Foundation, Washington, D.C.: April 19, 2001

36. Stanley Hoffmann (2002) 'U.S. and International Organizations', in Robert J. Lieber (ed.) (2002) *Eagle Rules, Foreign Policy and American Primacy in the 21st Century* Upper Saddle River, N.J.: Prentice Hall

37. Arthur Schlesinger Jr (2000) 'Unilateralism in Historic Perspective', in Gwyn Prins (ed.) (2000) *Understanding Unilateralism in American Foreign Relations* London: Royal Institute of International Relations

38. Cited in Arthur Schlesinger Jr (1995) 'Back to the Womb? Isolationism's Renewed Threat', *Foreign Affairs*, 74: 4 (July–August), p.6

39. Newt Gingrich and Dick Arney (1994) *The Contract With America* New York: Times Books–Random House, p.101. Clinton was in fact quite assertive about asserting US control over the UN, notably by campaigning to remove Secretary General Boutros Boutros-Ghali. See for instance Eric Rouleau (1996) 'The U.S. and World Hegemony: Why Washington Wants Rid of Mr. Boutros-Ghali', *Le Monde diplomatique* (English edition, London) (November)

40. See Glenn Kessler and Colum Lynch (2005) 'Critic of U.N. Named Envoy', *The Washington Post* (March 8)

41. Rice, 'Promoting the National Interest'

42. Strobe Talbott (2007) 'Anatomy of a Disaster', *The International Herald Tribune* (February 22)

43. The author has filed a Freedom of Information Act (FOIA) request for disclosure of the document and the debate surrounding it. See Dana Priest (2003) *The Mission, Waging War and Keeping Peace With America's Military* New York: W.W. Norton, p.30

44. See Ron Suskind (2004) *The Price of Loyalty: George Bush, the White House and the Education of Paul O'Neill* New York: Simon and Schuster. O'Neill's account, related by Suskind, differs from the more widespread idea that Iraq came up in White House discussion in the immediate aftermath of September 11. See for instance the account of former official Richard A. Clarke (2004) *Against All Enemies: Inside America's War on Terror* New York: Simon and Schuster

45. Morgenthau, 'We are Deluding Ourselves'

46. See 'War With Iraq is not in America's National Interest', petition signed by 33 scholars of international relations, *New York Times*, September 26, 2002. The signatories argued: 'As scholars of international security affairs, we recognize that war is sometimes necessary to ensure our national security or other vital interests. We also recognize that Saddam Hussein is a tyrant and that Iraq has defied a number of U.N. resolutions. But military force should be used only when it advances U.S. national interests.' In 2004, realist scholars regrouped in *The Coalition for a Realistic Foreign Policy*, 'a group of scholars, policy-makers and concerned citizens united by our opposition to an American empire', circulated a petition calling 'urgently for a change of course in American foreign and national security policy'. They added: 'We judge that the current American policy centered around the war in Iraq is the most misguided one since the Vietnam period', available at www.realisticforeignpolicy.org

47. Waltz, 'Neorealism Reappraised', p.4
48. Jervis, 'Understanding the Bush Doctrine', p.383
49. Ibid., p.376
50. Ibid., p.380
51. Mearsheimer and Walt, *The Israeli Lobby*
52. Shimshon Bichler and Jonathan Nitzan (2004) 'Differential Accumulation and Middle East Wars – Beyond Neo-Liberalism', in Kees Van der Pijl, Libby Assassi and Duncan Wigan (eds) (2004) *Global Regulation: Managing Crises After the Imperial Turn* New York: Palgrave Macmillan, pp.57–8
53. Ibid.
54. Gérard Duménil and Dominique Lévy (2003) 'Néolibéralisme–Néomilitarisme', *Actuel Marx*, 33: 1 (March), pp.77–99
55. US external oil dependence rose from 35 per cent in 1973 to 54.3 per cent in 2001 and is expected to reach 67 per cent in 2020
56. Klare, *Resource Wars*, p.10
57. Alan Greenspan (2007) *The Age of Turbulence: Adventures in a New World* New York: Penguin Press, p.463
58. See David E. Sanger (2003) 'Viewing the War as a Lesson to the World', *The New York Times* (April 6). Based on interviews with administration officials, Sanger writes that Iraq is 'something of a demonstration conflict'
59. *NSS* 2002
60. See Philip S. Golub (2001) 'America's Imperial Longings', *Le Monde diplomatique* (English Edition, London) (July). The title of the original French text published in the French edition of the journal was 'Rêves d'empire de l'administration américaine' (Dreams of Empire of the American Administration)
61. Donald Rumsfeld, interview with Thom Shanker, *The New York Times* (October 12, 2001), transcript at Department of Defense, available at www.defenselink.mil/transcripts/transcript.aspx?transcriptid=2097
62. Cited by Nicholas Lemann (2002) 'The Next World Order: The Bush Administration may have a brand-new doctrine of power', *The New Yorker* (April 1)
63. 'Remarks by the Vice President to the Los Angeles World Affairs Council, Followed by Brief Question and Answer Session', Office of the Vice President, Washington, D.C.: January 14, 2004. See www.whitehouse.gov/news/releases/2004/01/20040114-7.html
64. Charles Krauthammer (2002) 'The Unipolar Moment Revisited', *The National Interest*, 70 (Winter), pp.5–17
65. Stephen Peter Rosen (2002) 'The Future of War and the American Military', *Harvard Review*, 104: 5 (May–June). A former senior Department of Defense official in the Reagan and George H.W. Bush administrations, Stephen Peter Rosen is the Beton Michael Kaneb Professor of National Security and Military Affairs in the Department of Government at Harvard University
66. Stephen Peter Rosen (2003) 'An Empire if You Can Keep It', *The National Interest*, 71 (Spring), pp.51–61
67. Carr, *The Twenty Years' Crisis*, p.13
68. Interview in Cambridge, Mass. (February 20, 2003)
69. Hoffmann, 'America Goes Backward'
70. Some leading American constitutional scholars have described the way in which George W. Bush came to power in 2000 as a 'constitutional coup'. See Jack Balkin and Sanford Levinson (2001) 'Understanding the Constitutional

Revolution', *Virginia Law Review*, Charlottesville, 87: 6 (October); Bruce Ackerman (2001) 'Anatomy of a Constitutional Coup', *The London Review of Books*, 23: 3 (February 8)

71. See Jess Bravin (2004) 'Pentagon Report Set Framework For Use of Torture: Security or Legal Factors Could Trump Restrictions, Memo to Rumsfeld Argued', *The Wall Street Journal* (June 7). Bravin cites a military lawyer saying 'political appointees sought to assign to the president virtually unlimited authority on matters of torture'. The constitutional and political import of the infamous 'torture memos' of the White House Office of Legal Cousel (OLC) and its insistence on the undivided authority of the 'unitary executive branch', a rather obscure and previously marginal juridical philosophy affirming the absolute primacy of the executive branch, have been exhaustively examined by jurists. See for instance David Cole (2008) 'Justice at War: The Men and Ideas that Shaped America's War on Terror', *New York Review of Books* (June 24); Jack L. Goldsmith (2007) *The Terror Presidency: Law and Judgment Inside the Bush Administration* New York, W.W. Norton; Sanford Levinson (ed.) (2004) *Torture: A Collection* New York: Oxford University Press. See also David J. Barron and Martin S. Lederman (2008) 'The Commander in Chief at the Lowest Ebb – Framing the Problem: Doctrine and Original Understanding', *Harvard Law Review*, 121: 4 (February), pp.944–93

72. David Cole (2005) 'What Bush Wants to Hear', *The New York Review of Books*, 52: 18 (November 17)

73. *NSS* 2002, p.31

74. US Department of Defense (2006) *Quadrennial Defense Review Report* Washington, D.C., available at www.defenselink.mil/qdr/

75. Josh White and Ann Scott Tyson (2006) 'Rumsfeld Offers Strategies for Current War, Pentagon to Release 20-Year Plan Today', *The Washington Post* (February 3)

76. Judith Butler (2004) *Precarious Life. The Powers of Mourning and Violence* London: Verso, pp.64–5. Butler writes that the 'prospect of an exercise [of lawless] state power structures the future indefinitely. The future becomes a lawless future, not anarchical, but given over to the discretionary decisions of a set of designated sovereigns'. On the authoritarian implications of permanent war see Philip S. Golub (2006) 'The Will to Undemocratic Power', *Le Monde diplomatique* (English Edition, London) (September)

77. Christopher S. Kelley (2005) 'Rethinking Presidential Power: the Unitary Executive and the George W. Bush Presidency', paper presented at the Annual Meeting of the Midwest Political Science Association, April 7, Chicago, Ill.: Palmer House Hilton, available at www.allacademic.com/meta/p85947_index.html

78. Jack M. Balkin (2006) 'Rights against Torture – Without Remedies', *Balkinization* (October 17), available at http://balkin.blogspot.com

79. Carl Schmitt (2005[1922]) *Political Theology: Four Chapters on the Concept of Sovereignty* London: The University of Chicago Press. See also Giorgio Agamben (2005) *State of Exception* London: The University of Chicago Press; Oren Gross (2000) 'The normless and exceptionless exception: Carl Schmitt's theory of emergency powers and the "norm-exception" dichotomy', *Cardozo Law Review*, 21

80. See, for instance, George W. Bush's remarks at the 20th Anniversary of the National Endowment for Democracy, 'President Bush Discusses Freedom in

Iraq and Middle East', United States Chamber of Commerce, Washington, D.C.: November 6, 2003, available at www.whitehouse.gov/news/releases/2003/11/20031106-2.html

81. Said, in the 2003 preface to *Orientalism*, p.xxi
82. Interview with the author, Cambridge, Mass., April 18, 2001. Joseph Nye was referring to neo-conservatives such as Paul Wolfowitz. He pointed out that Wolfowitz and he had worked together in East Asia in the late 1990s when Nye was Assistant Secretary of Defense for International Security Affairs and Wolfowitz was Ambassador to Indonesia. The major cleavage, he said, was between ultra nationalists, such as Jesse Helms, characterised as 'kooks', and internationalists
83. Michael Ignatieff (2002) 'Barbarians at the Gate', *The New York Review of Books*, 49: 3 (February 28)
84. Paul Kennedy (2002) 'The Eagle Has Landed', *Financial Times* (February 2). See also Kennedy (2002) 'The Greatest Superpower Ever', *New Perspectives Quarterly*, 19 (Winter)
85. Ignatieff, 'The Burden'
86. John G. Ikenberry (2003) 'Strategic Reactions to American Preeminence: Great Power Politics in the Age of Unipolarity', *Discussion Paper*, National Intelligence Council (July 28), available at www.dni.gov/nic/PDF_GIF_2020_Support/2003_11_24_papers/ikenberry_StrategicReactions.pdf
87. Ikenberry's normative aim in suggesting a liberal world hegemonic strategy was to make American power 'more legitimate, expansive and durable'
88. Ignatieff, 'Barbarians'
89. Sebastian Mallaby, 'The Reluctant Imperialist', pp.2–7. In 2004, as evidence of 'the botched postwar effort in Iraq' emerged, Mallaby expressed 'regret' for 'playing a small part in stoking that talk of imperialism'. He however maintained the main thrust of his argument: 'What I don't regret is the argument behind my label.' See Sebastian Mallaby (2004) 'Liberal Imperialism: R.I.P.', *Foreign Affairs*, 83: 3 (May–June)
90. Max Boot (2001) 'The Case for American Empire: The most realistic response to terrorism is for America to embrace its imperial role', *Weekly Standard*, 7: 5 (October 15)
91. Jeffrey Garten (2003) 'Memo to the President: The U.S. Needs to Create a Colonial Service', *Foreign Policy*, 138 (September–October), pp.63–7. Garten expected areas of intervention to include sub-Saharan Africa, central Asia, south Asia and central and South America
92. Robert Cooper (2002) 'The New Liberal Imperialism', *The Observer* (April 7). Cooper is now Director-General for External and Political-Military Affairs, the Council of the EU
93. Benedict Brogan, 'It's time to celebrate the Empire, says Brown', *The Daily Mail*, January 15, 2005. These semi-official and official pronouncements did not occur in a void. There was a flow of conservative academic and journalistic commentary in the UK extolling empire and colonisation. In 2001, Paul Johnson penned a piece for *The New York Times* in which he compared the need to 'occupy and administer terrorist states' today to the way in which international imperial forces were deployed to suppress the Boxer Rebellion in China in 1900. See Paul Johnson (1993) 'Colonialism is back, and not a moment too soon', *The New York Times Sunday Magazine* (April 18). Better

known is Niall Ferguson's prolific writings in defence of 'liberal imperialism'. See Ferguson, *Colossus*

94. Richard J. Barnet, cited in John C. Donovan (1974) *The Cold Warriors: A Policy-Making Elite* Lexington, Mass.: D.C. Heath and Company

CHAPTER 7

1. Walt Rostow, cited by Hannah Arendt, *Crises of the Republic: Lying in Politics; Civil Disobedience; On Violence; Thoughts on Politics and Revolution* Fort Washington, PA: Harvest Books, 1972, p.17
2. Bairoch and Kozul-Wright, 'Globalization Myths', p.7
3. Polanyi, *The Great Transformation*, p.12
4. See Suzanne Berger (2003) *Notre première mondialisation: leçons d'un echec oublié* Paris: Le Seuil
5. Harvey, *The New Imperialism*, p.29
6. See for instance Panitch, 'The New Imperial State'
7. Anatol Lieven (2002) 'The Push for War', *London Review of Books*, 24: 19 (October 3)
8. Hobsbawm, 'Preface' to Kiernan, p.xiii
9. See Bernard K. Gordon, 'A High Risk'
10. 'ILO and the global job crisis', Geneva: International Labour Organization, January 22, 2009, available at www.ilo.org/global/Themes/lang--en/WCMS_101130/index.htm
11. See US Department of Labor (DOL), Bureau of Labor Statistics, available at www.bls.gov/cps. DOL statistics do not include unregistered unemployed or the working poor and therefore understate real levels of unemployment and underemployment. On the state of work in the United States today see Steven Greenhouse (2008) *The Big Squeeze: Tough Times for the American Worker* New York: Alfred A. Knopf. See also Frances Fox Piven and Richard A. Cloward (1993) *Regulating the Poor: The Functions of Public Welfare* New York: Vintage
12. The London financial daily, *The Financial Times* (*FT*), has been a good barometer of this. The *FT* was cautiously but consistently critical of US policy leading up to war in Iraq as well as afterwards. See, for instance, Martin Wolf's comment 'Bush must commit to winning the peace as much as the war', *The Financial Times* (February 5, 2003). For a lucid early commentary by a senior Wall Street banker on the unsustainable character of US expansionism see Stephen Roach (2002) 'Worldthink, Disequilibrium, and the Dollar', *Morgan Stanley Global Economic Forum* New York: May 7. Roach argued that 'a savings-short U.S. economy' could not 'continue to finance an ever-widening expansion of [US] military superiority…The confluence of history, geopolitics, and economics leaves me more convinced than ever that a U.S.-centric world is on an unsustainable path'.
13. Turner and Peel, 'Is the Post-1945 World Order Falling Apart?'
14. See for instance Stephen G. Brooks and William C. Wohlforth (2002) 'American Primacy in Perspective', *Foreign Affairs*, 81: 4 (July–August); and William Wohlforth (1999) 'The Stability of a Unipolar World', *International Security*, 24: 1 (Summer)

15. Nicolas Checa, John Maguire, and Jonathan Barney (2004) 'The New World Disorder', in *Harvard Business Review on Leadership in a Changed World*, Harvard Business School, Boston, pp.47–69

16. Martin Shaw (2003) 'The State of Globalization: Towards a Theory of State Transformation', in Neil Brenner, Bob Jessop, Martin Jones, Gordon MacLeod (eds) (2003) *State Space: A Reader* London: Blackwell

17. See, for instance, Anthony H. Cordesman (2006) 'Options for Iraq: The Almost Good, the Bad, the Ugly', Washington, D.C.: Centre for Strategic and International Studies, October 11, available at www.csis.org/media/csis/pubs/061011_iraqoptions.pdf

18. Senior American military commanders warned as early as 2004 that 'the United States is already on the road to defeat', statement of an unnamed general officer cited by *The Washington Post* in early May, 2004. The *Washington Post* also cites Major General Charles H. Swannack Jr, the Commander of the 82nd Airborne Division that spearheaded the campaign in Iraq, saying that while the US was winning every battle, it was on the verge of losing the war. 'The American people may not stand for it – and they should not.' See Thomas E. Ricks (2004) 'Dissension Grows In Senior Ranks On War Strategy', *The Washington Post* (May 9)

19. Author interview with Edward Luttwak, Washington, D.C., March 1, 2007

20. See David Ignatius (2007) 'Rice's Strategic Reset', *The Washington Post*, January 26. The support given to formerly insurgent Sunni tribal groups ('awakening councils') was part of the new 'realignment' policy later officialised by Condoleezza Rice in 'Rethinking the National Interest: American Realism for a New World', *Foreign Affairs*, 87: 4 (July–August 2008). The policy coincided with an intensification of clandestine operations within Iran and widespread public discussion of a possible US strike against Iranian nuclear and military installations. See Seymour M. Hersh (2008) 'Preparing the Battlefield: The Bush Administration steps up its secret moves against Iran', *The New Yorker* (July 7). See also, 'The Iran Plans: Would President Bush go to war to stop Tehran from getting the bomb?', *The New Yorker* (April 17, 2006) and 'Watching Lebanon: Washington's Interests in Israel's War', *The New Yorker* (August 21, 2006), both by Seymour M. Hersh

21. Juan Cole (2008) 'Iraq's Three Civil Wars', Massachusetts Institute of Technology, MIT Center for International Studies, available at http://web.mit.edu/cis/pdf/Audit_01_08_Cole.pdf

22. In addition to an estimated 4 million refugees, including internally displaced people, composite surveys of the human cost of the war estimate total 'excess deaths' since the US invasion at 600,000 to 700,000. See Gilbert Burnham, Shannon Doocy, Elizabeth Dzeng, Riyadh Lafta and Les Roberts (2006) 'The Human Cost of the War in Iraq: a Mortality Study', *The Lancet* (October 11). Republished by The MIT Center for International Studies, available at http://mit.edu/humancostiraq/reports/human-cost-war-101106.pdf

23. See Barnett R. Rubin and Ahmed Rashid (2008) 'From Great Game to Grand Bargain: Ending Chaos in Afghanistan and Pakistan', *Foreign Affairs*, 87: 6 (November–December)

24. Arendt, *Crises of the Republic*, p.17

25. Ibid.

26. John McNaughton cited in Stanley Karnow (1986) *Vietnam: a History* New York: Penguin Books, p.508. McNaughton was a senior Defense Department

official during the war and a key adviser of Defense Secretary Robert McNamara.

27. See Donovan, *The Cold Warriors*
28. Author interview with Charles Kupchan, Senior Fellow, Council on Foreign Relations, Washington, D.C., February 27, 2007
29. Author interview with Steve Clemons, New America Foundation, Washington, D.C., February 28, 2007
30. The fracture in the national security establishment surfaced soon after the invasion and grew in intensity thereafter, leading to unusually strong expressions of dissent at senior levels, notably within the US Army, the State Department and the CIA. The depth of acrimony is made plain by the bitter attack launched by supporters of the White House against dissenters within the CIA: the administration, wrote *The Wall Street Journal* in 2004, 'has two insurgencies to defeat: the one that the CIA is struggling to help put down in Iraq, and the other inside Langley against the Bush administration'. See 'The CIA's Insurgency: The Agency's Political Disinformation Campaign', *The Wall Street Journal* editorial (September 29, 2004). For an expression of CIA dissent, see Paul R. Pillar (2006) 'Intelligence, Policy, and the War in Iraq', *Foreign Affairs*, 85: 2 (March–April), pp.15–28. Pillar, former National Intelligence Officer for the Near East and south Asia from 2000 to 2005 writes: 'In the wake of the Iraq war, it has become clear that official intelligence analysis was not relied on in making even the most significant national security decisions, that intelligence was misused publicly to justify decisions already made, that damaging ill will developed between policymakers and intelligence officers, and that the intelligence community's own work was politicized'. For an early critique emerging from circles close to the armed forces see Jeffrey Record (2004) *Bounding the Global War on Terrorism* Honolulu, Hawaii: University Press of the Pacific. For a sample of other early dissent, see Golub, 'Imperial Politics, Imperial Will'. See also Golub, 'The Sun Sets Early'
31. Zbigniew Brzezinski (2007) 'Testimony before the Senate Foreign Relations Committee' (February 1). See Golub, 'The Sun Sets Early'
32. Author interview with Senator Chuck Hagel, Washington, D.C., March 2, 2004
33. John Kenneth Galbraith, 'The Plain Lessons of a Bad Decade', *Foreign Policy*, 1 (Winter 1970–71), p.35
34. Strange, 'Towards a Theory of Transnational Empire', pp.162–76
35. See Philip S. Golub and Jean-Paul Maréchal (2004) 'Hyperpuissance americaine et biens publics internationaux', *Géoéconomie*, 30 (Summer)
36. In an interview with the BBC World Service, September 16, 2004, Kofi Annan, the then Secretary General of the United Nations, characterised the war as illegal: 'Q: It was illegal? A: Yes, if you wish. Q: It was illegal? A: Yes, I have indicated it is not in conformity with the UN Charter, from our point of view and from the Charter point of view it was illegal', available at http://news.bbc.co.uk/2/hi/middle_east/3661640.stm
37. December 11, 2008, the Senate Arms Services Committee published a declassified Executive Summary and conclusions of a report on the 'Treatment of Detainees in U.S. Custody' which for the first time officially points to the direct personal responsibility of President Bush and of former Defense Secretary Donald Rumsfeld in authorising detainee abuse. See http://levin.senate.gov/newsroom/supporting/2008/Detainees.121108.pdf

38. Heraldo Muñoz (2008) *A Solitary War: a Diplomat's Chronicle of the Iraq War and its Lessons* Denver, Co.: Fulcrum Publishing, p.32

39. Statement of Secretary of State Colin Powell reported by the French daily *Le Monde*. Daniel Rondeau, 'Villepin Pile et Face', *Le Monde* (October 4, 2005)

40. Statement attributed to then National Security Adviser Condoleezza Rice, who is said to have instructed the American bureaucracy to think out appropriate responses. Some prominent US commentators, such as William Safire, went so far as to describe the French and German positions as a plot to break up the Atlantic Alliance and to assert control of Europe: '[Germany] made France an offer it could not refuse to permanently assert French German dominance over the 23 other nations of Continental Europe...France then had to repay Schröder by double-crossing the United States at the United Nations...The German design is apparently to saw off the Atlantic part of the Atlantic Alliance, separating Britain and the United States dominated by Germany and France.' William Safire (2003) 'Breaking up the Alliance', *The New York Times* (January 24)

41. Rondeau, 'Villepin'

42. Published in the Spanish daily *El Pais* on September 26, 2007, the transcript of the February 22, 2003 conversation between President Bush and then Spanish Prime Minister José María Aznar has Bush telling Aznar that the US would sanction the non-permanent members of the Security Council such as Mexico, Chile and Angola if they failed to rally the US position on Iraq. See 'The Crawford Transcript', *The New York Review of Books*, 54: 17 (November 8, 2007). Chile's Ambassador to the United Nations, who was involved in the crisis, confirms that the Bush administration threatened trade and other reprisals against friendly countries that refused to endorse the war. See Heraldo Muñoz, *A Solitary War*

43. Mark Danner's expression. Mark Danner, 'The Moment Has Come to Get Rid of Saddam', *The New York Review of Books*, 54: 17 (November 8, 2007).

44. William Wohlforth and Stephen Brooks' expression. In 2002, the authors argued that American unipolarity meant that 'no country, or group of countries, wants to maneuver itself into a situation in which it will have to contend with the focused enmity of the United States'. Wohlforth and Brooks, 'American Primacy in Perspective'

45. 'Statement of President Thabo Mbeki on the Possible War on Iraq', Permanent Mission of South Africa to the United Nations, January 24, 2003, available at www.southafrica-newyork.net/pmun/view_press_release.php?release=6653841

46. The terms of the agreement with North Korea, worked out in a multilateral context, mirror the 1994 framework agreement under the Clinton administration. See Bruce Cumings (2007) 'North Korea. Neutral instead of nuclear: Kim Jong Il confronts Bush – and wins', *Le Monde diplomatique* (English edition, London) (October)

47. Charles Gore (2000) 'The Rise and Fall of the Washington Consensus as a Paradigm for Developing Countries', *World Development*, 28: 5 (May), pp.789–804

48. Tony Judt (2003) 'America and the World', *New York Review of Books*, 50: 6 (April 10)

49. See for instance Pedro Sainz (2006) 'Equity in Latin American since the 1990s', *DESA Working Paper N°22*, (ST/ESA/2006/DWP/22), United Nations Department of Economic and Social Affairs, New York

50. Mercosur was founded in 1991. The four original member states were Brazil, Paraguay, Uruguay and Argentina

51. Marc Weisbrot (2007) 'Ten Years After: The Lasting Impact of the Asian Financial Crisis', in Bhumika Muchhala (ed.) (2007) *Ten Years After: Revisiting the Asian Financial Crisis* Washington, D.C.: Woodrow Wilson International Center for Scholars

52. For US reactions see Kerry Dumbaugh and Mark P. Sullivan (2005) 'China's Growing Interest in Latin America', *CRS Report for Congress* Washington, D.C., Congressional Research Service, April 2; Peter Hakim (2006) 'Is Washington Losing Latin America?', *Foreign Affairs*, 85: 1 (January–February), pp.39–53

53. Muñoz, *A Solitary War*, p.170

54. IBSA's official website describes the relationship in the following way: 'IBSA is a trilateral, developmental initiative between India, Brazil and South Africa to promote South–South cooperation and exchange', available at www.ibsa-trilateral.org

55. Statement made in Brasilia on September 19, 2008 and reported by the world media.

56. Speech to the US–Brazil CEO Forum in Sao Paulo, Friday, October 10, 2008. See Conn Hallinan (2008) 'Latin America's New Consensus', *Foreign Policy in Focus*, October 29, available at www.fpif.org/fpiftxt/5631

57. See http://aric.adb.org/indicator.php . Statistics vary from one international institution to another. The IMF gives lower estimates (51.9 per cent) but highlights the same general phenomenon. See International Monetary Fund (2007) *Regional Economic Outlook Asia Pacific* Washington, D.C. Although a significant share of regional trade is in intermediate goods for final destination export to the most developed countries, it is having developmental effects in the region, allowing for technology transfers and stimulating endogenous growth factors in east Asia. See Claude Pottier (2003) *Les multinationales et la mise en concurrence des salariés* Paris: L'Harmattan, p.118

58. Heribert Dieter and Richard Higgott (2002) 'Exploring alternative theories of economic regionalism: From trade to finance in Asian co-operation', *CSGR Working Paper* No. 89/02, Centre for the Study of Globalisation and Regionalisation, University of Warwick

59. UN Statistics Division, available at unstats.un.org/unsd/default.htm and Economist Intelligence Unit (2006) *Foresight 2020* London

60. Pottier, *Les multinationales*, p.118. See also T.J. Pempel (1999) 'Regional Ups, Regional Downs' in T.J. Pempel (ed.) (1999) *The Politics of the Asian Crisis* Ithaca, NY: Cornell University Press, pp.62–78

61. Pottier, *Les multinationales*, p.118

62. Cumings, *Parallax Visions*, p.213

63. Richard Katz (1999) *Japan, The System that Soured* New York: M.E. Sharpe. See also Chalmers Johnson (2000) *Blowback: The Costs and Consequences of American Empire* New York: Metropolitan Books

64. Lian, 'Mr Thaksin's role'

65. Immanuel Wallerstein (2003) 'America and the World: The Twin Towers as Metaphor', in I. Wallerstein (2003) *The Decline of American Power: The U.S. in a Chaotic World* New York: W.W. Norton, pp.193–218

66. See Stiglitz, *Globalisation and its Discontents*

67. Dieter and Higgott, 'Exploring alternative theories', p.10

68. See the partial transcript of *The Future of Asia* conference held in Tokyo in June 2003 and reported by *Nikkei Weekly*. During the conference, there was a broad convergence over general objectives. The then Thai Prime Minister Thaksin Shinawatra said that the aim of the ABF was to move progressively from a dollar-based fund to an Asian basket of currencies: 'Funds held by Asian countries, which account for about half of the world's foreign currency reserves, used to be invested mainly in the U.S. and Europe. Now funds should head toward Asia thanks to the birth of an Asian Bond Market... Although the Asia Bond Fund will start out in U.S. dollars, we hope to shift to Asian currencies in the future'. At the same conference, Mohamad Mahatir added: 'We will all benefit from the Asia Bond Market because it is Asian and is in our own interest, not a device for somebody else somewhere and imposed on us. Initially, the bonds should be denominated in the U.S. dollar but we should move away from the U.S. dollar in the future'. The former Japanese Prime Minister Ryutaro Hashimoto said: 'The lessons learned from the Asian currency crisis are producing good results'. See 'The Future of Asia 2003', *Nikkei Weekly* (June 21, 2003), available at www.nni.nikkei.co.jp/FR/ NIKKEI/inasia/future/2003/2003weekly005.html

69. See Anand Giridharadas (2006) 'Asian Finance Ministers Seek Common Currency', *New York Times* (May 5). The author reports that the US opposed the proposal: 'The Asian Development Bank has been pushing the idea of an Asian currency unit, or A.C.U., over the past year. The unit's value would be set by an index of participating currencies. The idea has gained popularity among several Asian finance ministers as a step toward harmonising regional monetary policies. The development bank's Japanese president, Haruhiko Kuroda, a supporter of an Asian monetary union, had pledged to propose the creation of an A.C.U. at the meeting in Hyderabad, but reportedly held back in light of opposition from Washington.'

70. See 'East Asian Countries to Create $80 billion Currency Fund', *International Herald Tribune* (Paris: May 4, 2008)

71. Barry Naughton, 'China: Domestic Restructuring and a New Role in Asia' in Pempel, *The Politics of the Asian Crisis*, p.209

72. Gordon, 'A High Risk Trade Policy'

73. Li Cui (2007) 'China's Growing External Dependence', *Finance and Development*, 44: 3, Washington, D.C.: IMF, September

74. 'Further reciprocal cooperation to build a harmonious East Asia', speech by Vice Minister of Commerce Yi Xiaozhun, May 26, 2008, reported by the *People's Daily*, available at www.english.peopledaily.com.cn/ 90002/93687/93689/6418402.html

75. The Royal Institute for International Relations hosted a conference in London in late January 2007 on 'The Changing Dynamics of Global Financial Power' in which participants were asked to respond to the question of whether 'global financial power has shifted to surplus states'. In its January 2008 report on global capital markets, McKinsey and Company noted 'shifting power in the world financial order' with 'financial power spreading beyond to the United States as other markets mature'. See 'Mapping Global Capital Markets: Fourth Annual Report', New York: McKinsey and Company, January 2008, available at www.mckinsey.com/mgi/publications/Mapping_Global/index.asp

76. Out of a world total of $5,549 billion, Japanese foreign reserve assets stood at $895 billion in 2006, China's at $1,073 billion and the rest of east Asia at

$1,028 billion. The Gulf Cooperation Council Countries (GCC) held reserves estimated at $2.2 trillion. 'Mapping Global Capital Markets', p.71

77. Available at www.ustreas.gov/tic/mfh.txt
78. See Mark Landler (2008) 'Chinese Savings Helped Inflate American Bubble', *The New York Times* (December 25)
79. Lawrence H. Summers (2004) 'The United States and the Global Adjustment Process', Speech at the Third Annual Stavros S. Niarchos Lecture, Washington, D.C., Institute for International Economics, March 23, 2004, available at www.petersoninstitute.org/publications/papers/paper.cfm?ResearchID=200
80. Ibid.
81. Chinese economic growth since 1980 has been marked by sharp spatial and social disparities. These led in 1989 to the mass protests that were severely repressed by Deng Xiao Ping and to a subsequent slowing of economic liberalisation. In 1992, liberalisation was accelerated again. See Wang Hui (2003) *China's New Order, Society, Politics, and Economy in Transition* Cambridge, Mass.: Harvard University Press
82. Mr Liao Min of the China Banking Regulatory Commission (CBRC), cited by Edward Wong (2008) 'Booming, China Faults U.S. Policy on the Economy', *New York Times* (June 17). Wong also cites Joseph Stiglitz: 'U.S. credibility and the credibility of U.S. financial markets is zero everywhere in the world'. See also the speech of the Chairman of the CBRC, Liu Minkang, at the British Museum on April 26, 2008, in which he warned that 'globalisation, if mismanaged, can be disruptive and even disastrous to the course of civilization', available at www.chinese-embassy.org.uk/eng/zyxw/t450000.htm
83. Hu Angang (2007) 'Five Major Scale Effects of China's Rise on the World', *Discussion Paper* 19, China Policy Institute, University of Nottingham, available at www.chinapolicyinstitute.org
84. In off-the-record discussions in Shanghai in 2000, senior figures of the Chinese Academy of Sciences told this author that China had a structural policy of restraint since it needed at least a quarter of a century of stable external relations with the United States to ensure the sustainability of the economic transition. The PRC's voting record at the UNSC evidences this conflict avoidance policy. See Yitzhak Shichor (2007) 'China's Voting Behavior in the U.N. Security Council', *China Brief*, 6: 18, Jamestown Foundation, May 9, 2007, available at www.jamestown.org/programs/chinabrief/. From 1971 to 2006, PRC has only used its veto power as a permanent member of the Council twice, whereas the US cast vetoes 76 times, the UK 24 times, France 14 times and the Soviet Union and the later Russian Federation 13 times. China voted for 11 UNSC resolutions on Iraq after 1990 but abstained from voting Resolution 678 authorising the use of force. On July 31, 2006, the PRC voted for UNSC Resolution 1696 that provides for sanctions against Iran if it does not suspend the enrichment and reprocessing of uranium
85. Hu Angang, 'Five Major Scale Effects'

CHAPTER 8

1. J.M. Coetzee (1982) *The Coming of the Barbarians* New York: Penguin Books, p.133
2. Stephen J. Whitfield (2000) 'The Imperial Self in American Life', *Columbia Journal of American Studies*, 4:1

3. Brooks Adams cited by Mallan, 'Roosevelt, Brooks Adams and Lea'
4. Liska, *Imperial America*, p.10
5. Ball, *Diplomacy*, p.9
6. Liska, *Imperial America*, p.10
7. Ibid.
8. Samuel P. Huntington (1993) 'Why International Primacy Matters', *International Security*, 17: 4 (Spring), pp.68–83
9. Kagan, 'Benevolent Empire', pp.24–35
10. Kindleberger, *World Economic Primacy*, p.227
11. Ikenberry, *After Victory*, p.4
12. Walt, *Taming American Power*, p.26
13. Ibid., p.243
14. Statement of an Athenian envoy to Sparta, cited by Thucydides in *History of the Peloponnesian War*, I.76, (New York: Prometheus Books, 1998). For an argument in favour of the thesis of empire by invitation, see Geir Lundestad (1986) 'Empire by Invitation? The United States and Western Europe, 1945–1952', *Journal of Peace Research*, 23: 3, pp.263–77
15. Pierre Bourdieu (2000) 'Participant Objectivation', Huxley Memorial Lecture, London, Royal Anthropolitical Institute, December 6
16. Carr, *The Twenty Years' Crisis*, p.5
17. Besides the academics who have held cabinet or sub-cabinet level positions (Zbigniew Brzezinski, Henry Kissinger, Joseph Nye, Condoleezza Rice, Paul Wolfowitz, etc.), there is a broad interpenetration of government and those parts of the academy specialised in foreign affairs or security. The Kennedy School of Government of Harvard University is a prominent case in point: 14 out of 21 members of its faculty working in security-related fields have held senior positions in government at one time or another. All of the scholars cited in this chapter have held advisory positions in government: John Ikenberry worked in the Policy Planning Staff of the State Department in the early 1990s and was a member of an advisory group at the State Department in 2003–2004; Stephen Walt served as a consultant for the Institute of Defense Analyses, the Center for Naval Analyses and the National Defense University; Charles Kindleberger worked at the Department of State in the immediate post-war. On the relationship between the academy and government see Bruce Cumings (1997) 'Boundary Displacement: Area Studies and International Studies during and after the Cold War', *Bulletin of Concerned Asian Scholars*, Vol. 29; David Halberstam (1993) *The Best and the Brightest* New York: Ballantine Books
18. John M. Keynes (1965) *General Theory of Employment, Interest, and Money* London: Harcourt, p.383
19. John Lewis Gaddis (1998) *We Now Know: Rethinking Cold War History* New York: Oxford University Press, p.167
20. Hendrickson and Tucker, *The Imperial Temptation*, p.68. The authors, both realists, write that the US 'set a trap' for Saddam Hussein by making voluntary withdrawal from Kuwait less attractive than war. They also argue that the US could have obtained the withdrawal of Iraqi forces from Kuwait short of war through punitive containment, but the 'president had war in his heart but peace on his lips' (p.91)
21. See Klare, *Resource Wars* and Golub, 'Le Golfe arabo-persique'

22. Remarks of President Barack Obama to Joint Session of Congress, White House, Washington, D.C., February 24, 2009, available at www.whitehouse. gov/the_press_office/remarks-of-president-barack-obama-address-to-joint-session-of-congress/

23. Michael Cox, 'The Empire's Back in Town', p.4

24. Steel, *Temptations*, p.43

25. Monroe, *Britain's Moment*, p.142

26. Jerry W. Sanders, *Peddlers of Crisis*, p.172

27. Falk, 'Beyond Internationalism', p.85. Mark Berger makes a similar point: 'In the "Third World", Trilateralism advocated and sought accommodation rather than confrontation. It sought to encourage a limited amount of reform in order to maintain long-term stability.' Mark Berger (1994) 'The End of the Third World?', *Third World Quarterly*, 15: 2

28. Ball, *Diplomacy*, p.9

29. Falk, 'Beyond Internationalism'. The 1977 Trilateral Commission's policy document *Towards a Renovated International System*, written by Richard Cooper, Karl Kaiser and Masataka Kosada, gives a good idea of this approach. Published the same year, Robert Keohane's and Joseph Nye's book (2000[1977]) *Power and Interdependence* New York: Longman, reflects similar concerns

30. Jerry Sanders, *Peddlers of Crisis*, p.173

31. Brzezinski, 'Recognizing the Crisis', p.66

32. Jimmy Carter, 'Address at Commencement Exercises at the University of Notre Dame', May 22, 1977, in John T. Woolley and Gerhard Peters (eds) (ongoing) *The American Presidency Project*, available at www.presidency. ucsb.edu/ws/?pid=7552

33. Jeane Kirkpatrick (1999) Interview, *National Security Archives, Cold War Project*, Episode 19, February 28, available at www.gwu.edu/~nsarchiv/coldwar/interviews/episode-19/kirkpatrick1.html

34. Perle, 'Interview 1997'

35. Jeane Kirkpatrick (1979) 'Dictatorships and Double Standards', *Commentary*, 68: 5 (November)

36. Robert M. Gates (1997) *From the Shadows: The Ultimate Insider's Story of Five Presidents and How They Won the Cold War* New York: Simon and Schuster, p.111. On clandestine operations in Afghanistan, decided long before the Soviet invasion, see pp.144–50

37. Klare, *Resource Wars*, p.6

38. Cox, 'Social Forces', p.144

39. Gilpin, *War and Change*, pp.209–10

40. Ibid., p.210

41. Fred Halliday makes an important point when he writes that accounting for this hierarchy represents 'the greatest analytic and *normative* challenge facing social science today'. Fred Halliday, 'For an International Sociology', in Hobden and Hobson, *Historical Sociology*, p.256

42. Abu-Lughod, *Before European Hegemony*, pp.370–1

43. Ibid.

44. Kissinger, *Diplomacy*, p.822

45. See John J. Mearsheimer (199) 'Back to the Future: Instability in Europe After the Cold War', *International Security*, 15: 1 (Summer), pp.5–56

46. Author interview with Assistant Secretary for Arms Control, Ms. Avis Bohlen (Washington, D.C., April 11, 2001)
47. Kissinger, *Diplomacy*, p.813
48. Ibid., pp.813–22
49. Cain and Hopkins, *British Imperialism*, p.656
50. Monroe, *Britain's Moment*, p.131
51. Ibid., p.396
52. Ibid., p.657
53. Michael Blackwell (1993) *Clinging to Grandeur, British Attitudes and Foreign Policy in the Aftermath of the Second World War* London: Greenwood Press, p.5
54. Christopher Mayhew, cited in Blackwell, *Clinging to Grandeur,* p.148
55. Wayne S. Smith (2000) 'The Trend Towards Unilateralism in U.S. Foreign Policy', in Gwyn Prins (ed.) (2000) *Understanding Unilateralism in American Foreign Relations* London: Royal Institute for International Relations
56. Mireille Delmas-Marty (2004) *Le relatif et l'universel, les forces imaginaries du droit* Paris: Le Seuil, p.406
57. Ibid., p.414

Select Bibliography

(All websites accessed between 2001 and 2009.)

Abu-Lughod, Janet L. (1991) *Before European Hegemony: The World System A.D. 1250–1350* New York: Oxford University Press
Ackerman, Bruce (2001) 'Anatomy of a Constitutional Coup', *The London Review of Books*, 23: 3
Adams, Brooks (1900) *America's Economic Supremacy* New York and London: The Macmillan Company
Agamben, Giorgio (2005) *State of Exception* London: The University of Chicago Press
Alter, Peter (1994[1989]) *Nationalism* London: Arnold
American Academy of Political and Social Science (1899) 'The Foreign Policy of the United States: Political and Commercial', Annual Conference, *Annals of the Academy of Political and Social Science*, 13: 12 Supplement
American Historical Association (1899) 'The New Haven Meeting of the American Historical Association', *The American Historical Review*, 4: 3, pp.409–22
Andrews, Charles M. (1900) 'The Boston Meeting of the American Historical Association', *The American Historical Review*, 5: 3, pp.423–39
Angang, Hu (2007) 'Five Major Scale Effects of China's Rise on the World', Discussion Paper 19 (April), China Policy Institute, University of Nottingham, UK
Anghie, Anthony (2005) *Imperialism, Sovereignty and the Making of International Law* Cambridge, UK: Cambridge University Press
Arendt, Hannah (1972) *Crises of the Republic: Lying in Politics; Civil Disobedience; On Violence; Thoughts on Politics and Revolution* Fort Washington, PA: Harvest Books
— (1994[1950]) *The Origins of Totalitarianism* New York: Harcourt
Arrighi, Giovanni (1994) *The Long Twentieth Century: Money, Power and the Origins of Our Times* London: Verso
— (1996) 'Capitalism and the Modern World-System: Rethinking the Non-Debates of the 1970s', paper presented at the American Sociological Association Meetings (New York, August 16–20)
— (2005) 'Hegemony Unravelling', *New Left Review*, 32 (March–April), pp.50–80
Bacevich, Andrew (2005) *The New American Militarism* New York: Oxford University Press
— (2008) *The Limits of Power: the End of American Exceptionalism* New York: Metropolitan Books
Badian, Ernst (1971[1968]) *Roman Imperialism in the Late Republic* Ithaca, NY: Cornell University Press
Bairoch, Paul (1997) *Victoires et déboires. Histoire économique et sociale du monde du XVIᵉ siècle jusqu'à nos jours* (3 vols) Paris: Gallimard
— (1982) 'International Industrialisation Levels from 1750 to 1980', *The Journal of European Economic History*, 11: 2, pp.269–333

Bairoch, Paul and Kozul-Wright, Richard (1996) 'Globalization Myths: Some Historical Reflections on Integration, Industrialization and Growth in the World Economy', *UNCTAD Discussion Paper* No. 113, Geneva, pp.1–32

Balkin, Jack and Levinson, Sanford (2001) 'Understanding the Constitutional Revolution', *Virginia Law Review*, 87: 6 (October), pp.1045–1104

Ball, George (1976) *Diplomacy in a Crowded World: An American Foreign Policy* Boston: Little, Brown and Company

Barron, David J. and Lederman, Martin S. (2008) 'The Commander in Chief at the Lowest Ebb: Framing the Problem, Doctrine and Original Understanding', *Harvard Law Review*, 121: 4 (February), pp. 944–93

Baughman, James L. (2001) *Henry R. Luce and the Rise of the American Century* Baltimore: Johns Hopkins University Press

Bayly, Christopher A. (2004) *The Birth of the Modern World, 1780–1914: Global Connections and Comparisons* London: Blackwell

Beale, Howard K. (1989[1956]) *Theodore Roosevelt and the Rise of America to World Power* Baltimore: Johns Hopkins University Press

Bellah, Robert (1985[1957]) *Tokugawa Religion, the Cultural Roots of Modern Japan* New York: Free Press

Berger, Mark (1994) 'The End of the Third World?', *Third World Quarterly*, 15: 2, pp.257–75

Berger, Suzanne (2003) *Notre première mondialisation: leçons d'un échec oublié* Paris: Le Seuil

Bergsten, C. Fred. (1992) 'The Primacy of Economics', *Foreign Policy*, 87 (Summer), pp.3–24

Blackwell, Michael (1993) *Clinging to Grandeur, British Attitudes and Foreign Policy in the Aftermath of the Second World War* London: Greenwood Press

Bourdieu, Pierre (2000) 'Participant Objectivation', Huxley Memorial Lecture, December 6, London: Royal Anthropological Institute

Braithwaite, John and Drahos, Peter (2000) *Global Business Regulation* New York: Cambridge University Press

Braudel, Fernand (1977) *Afterthoughts on Material Civilization and Capitalism* Baltimore: Johns Hopkins University Press

— (1985) *La dynamique du capitalisme* Paris: Arthaud

— (1986) *Civilisation matérielle, économie et capitalisme. XV–XVIIIᵉ siècle* Paris: Armand Colin

Brewer, Anthony (1990) *Marxist Theories of Imperialism, A Critical Survey* London: Routledge

Brooks, Stephen G. and Wohlforth, William C. (2002) 'American Primacy in Perspective', *Foreign Affairs*, 81: 4 (July–August)

Brzezinski, Zbigniew (1974–1975) 'Recognizing the Crisis', *Foreign Policy*, No. 17 (Winter), pp.63–74

— (1998) *The Grand Chessboard, American Primacy and its Geostrategic Objective* New York: Basic Books

Bull, Hedley (1995) *The Anarchical Society* New York: Columbia University Press

Burk, Kathleen (1992) 'Money and Power: the Shift from Great Britain to the United States', in Joussef Cassis (ed.) *Finance and Financiers in European History, 1880–1960* New York: Cambridge University Press, pp.359–69

Butler, Judith (2004) *Precarious Life: The Powers of Mourning and Violence* London: Verso

Buzzanco, Robert (1999) 'What Happened to the New Left: Toward a Radical Reading of American Foreign Relations', Bernath Lecture, *Diplomatic History*, 23: 4 (Fall), pp.575–607

Cain, Peter. J. (1989) Untitled Review of Roberta A. Dayer's *Finance and Empire* (1988), *The Economic History Review*, New Series, 42: 4 (November), pp.609–10

Cain, Peter J. and Hopkins, Anthony G. (2002) *British Imperialism, 1688–2000* London: Longman-Peason

Calleo, David (1987) *Beyond American Hegemony, the Future of the Western Alliance* New York: Basic Books

Calleo, David P. and Rowland, Benjamin M. (1972) *America and the World Political Economy: Atlantic Dreams and National Realities* Bloomington, Ind.: Indiana University Press

Carr, Edward H. (2001[1939]) *The Twenty Years' Crisis, 1919–1939: An Introduction to the Study of International Relations* New York: Palgrave

Chaudhuri, Kirti N. (1991) *Asia Before Europe: Economy and Civilization of the Indian Ocean From the Rise of Islam to 1750* New York: Cambridge University Press

Chilcote, Ronald H. (2000) *Theories of Comparative Political Economy* Boulder, Co.: Westview Press

Coclanis, Peter A. (1990) 'The Wealth of British America on the Eve of the Revolution', *Journal of Interdisciplinary History*, 21: 2 (Autumn), pp.245–60

— (1991) *The Shadow of a Dream: Economic Life and Death in the South Carolina Low Country, 1670–1920* New York: Oxford University Press

Cole, David (2008) *Justice at War: The Men and Ideas that Shaped America's War on Terror* New York Review of Books Collections: New York

Cole, Juan (2008) *Iraq's Three Civil Wars* Massachusetts Institute of Technology (MIT), Center for International Studies (January)

Combs, Jerald A. (1991) 'The Compromise That Never Was: George Kennan, Paul Nitze, and the Issue of Conventional Deterrence in Europe', *Diplomatic History*, 15: 3 (Summer), pp.361–86

Cooper, Richard N., Kaiser, Karl and Kosada, Masataka (1997) *Towards a Renovated International System*, Task Force Report No.14, The Trilateral Commission: New York

Cooper, Robert (2002) 'The New Liberal Imperialism', *The Observer*, April 7, London

Cox, Michael (2003) 'The Empire's Back in Town: Or America's Imperial Temptation – Again', *Millennium: Journal of International Studies*, 32: 1, pp.1–27

Cox, Robert W. (1981) 'Social Forces, States and World Orders: Beyond International Relations Theory', *Millennium: Journal of International Studies*, 10: 2, pp.127–55

— (1986) 'Social Forces, States and World Orders: Beyond International Relations Theory', in Robert O. Keohane (ed.) (1986) *Neo-Realism and its Critics* New York: Columbia University Press, pp.204–54

— (1987) *Production, Power, and World Order: Social Forces in the Making of History* New York: Columbia University Press

Cumings, Bruce (1984) 'The Origins and Development of the Northeast Asian Political Economy: Industrial Sectors, Product Cycles, and Political Consequences', *International Organization*, 38: 1 (Winter), pp.1–40

— (1993) 'The End of the Seventy Years' Crisis: Trilateralism and the New World Order', in Meredith Woo-Cumings and Michael Loriaux (eds) (1993) *Past as*

Prelude: History in the Making of a New World Order Boulder, Co.: Westview Press, 1993, pp.9–32

— (1997) 'Boundary Displacement: Area Studies and International Studies during and after the Cold War', *Bulletin of Concerned Asian Scholars*, 29

— (1999) *Parallax Visions, Making Sense of American-East Asian Relations at the End of the Century* Durham, N.C.: Duke University Press

Cummings, James W. (2008) *Towards Modern Public Finance: The American War with Mexico, 1846–1848* London: Pickering and Chatto

Czempiel, Ernst-Otto and Rosenau, James N. (eds) (1987) *Global Changes and Theoretical Challenges, Approaches to World Politics for the 1990s* Lanham, Md.: Lexington Books

Davies, John P. (1977) 'Two Hundred Years of American Foreign Policy: The U.S. and East Asia', *Foreign Affairs*, 55: 2 (January)

Davis, Lance E. and Cull, Robert J. (1994) *International Capital Markets and American Economic Growth 1820–1914* New York: Cambridge University Press

Dayer, Roberta A. (1988) *Finance and Empire: Sir Charles Addis, 1861–1945* London: Macmillan

De Vries, Jan (1994) 'The Industrious Revolution and the Industrial Revolution', *Journal of Economic History*, 54, pp.249–70

Deane, Phyllis (1979) *The First Industrial Revolution* Cambridge, UK: Cambridge University Press

Delmas-Marty, Mireille (2004) *Le relatif et l'universel, les forces imaginaries du droit* Paris: Le Seuil

DeLong, J. Bradford and Eichengreen, Barry (2001) 'Between Meltdown and Moral Hazard: The International Monetary and Financial Policies of the Clinton Administration', *NBER Working Paper*, No. 8443, August

Dieter, Heribert and Higgott, Richard (2002) 'Exploring alternative theories of economic regionalism: From trade to finance in Asian co-operation', *CSGR Working Paper No. 89/02*, Centre for the Study of Globalisation and Regionalisation, Warwick University

Dobson, Alan P. (1986) *U.S. Wartime Aid to Britain, 1940–1946* London: Taylor and Francis

Donovan, John C. (1974) *The Cold Warriors: A Policy-Making Elite* Lexington, Mass.: D.C. Heath & Co.

Dos Santos, Theotonio (1970) 'The Structure of Dependence', *American Economic Review*, 60: 2, pp.231–6

Doyle, Michael W. (1997) *Ways of War and Peace: Realism, Liberalism, and Socialism* New York: W.W. Norton

Drake, Paul W. (2006) 'The Hegemony of U.S. Economic Doctrines in Latin America', in Eric Hershberg and Fred Rosen (eds) *Latin America After Neoliberalism: Turning the Tide in the 21st Century?* The New Press and North American Congress on Latin America (NACLA): New York, pp.26–48

Dulles, Foster R. and Ridinger, Gerald E. (1955) 'The Anticolonial Policies of Franklin D. Roosevelt', *Political Science Quarterly*, 70: 1 (March), pp.1–18

Duroselle, Jean-Baptiste (1978) *Histoire diplomatique de 1919 à nos jours* Paris: Dalloz

Edgerton, David (1997) 'The Decline of Declinism', *The Business History Review*, 71: 2 (Summer), pp.201–6

Edmonston, Barry and Passel, Jeffrey (eds) (1994) *Immigration and Ethnicity: The Integration of America's Newest Arrivals* Washington, D.C.: Urban Institute Press

Elkins, Caroline (2005) *Imperial Reckoning: The Untold Story of Britain's Gulag in Kenya* New York: Owl Books

Emmerson, Donald K. (1998) 'Americanizing Asia', *Foreign Affairs*, 77.3 (May–June)

Falk, Richard A. (1976) 'Beyond Internationalism', *Foreign Policy*, 24 (Autumn), pp.65–113

— (2004) *The Declining World Order, America's Imperial Geopolitics* New York: Routledge

Feis, Herbert (1973[1930]) *Europe: The World's Banker, 1870–1914* Clifton, N.J.: Augustus M. Kelley Publishers

Ferguson, Niall (2004) *Colossus, the Price of America's Empire* New York: The Penguin Press

Finkleman, Paul (2001) *Slavery and the Founders, Race and Liberty in the Age of Jefferson* New York: M.E. Sharpe

Finley, Moses I. (1985) *Ancient History, Evidence and Models* London: Chatto and Windus

Floud, Roderick C. (1974) 'The Adolescence of American Engineering Competition, 1860–1900', *The Economic History Review*, New Series, 27: 1 (February), pp.57–71

Forsberg, Aaron (2000) *America and the Japanese Miracle: The Cold War Context of Japan's Postwar Economic Revival, 1950–1960* Chapel Hill, N.C.: University of North Carolina Press

Gaddis, John L. (1998) *We Now Know: Rethinking Cold War History* New York: Oxford University Press

Galbraith, John Kenneth (1970) 'The Plain Lessons of a Bad Decade', *Foreign Policy*, 1 (Winter 1970–71), pp.31–45

Gallagher, John and Robinson, Ronald (1953) 'The Imperialism of Free Trade', *The Economic History Review*, New Series, 6: 1, pp.1–15

Garten, Jeffrey (2003) 'Memo to the President: The U.S. Needs to Create a Colonial Service', *Foreign Policy*, No. 138 (September–October)

Garthoff, Raymond (2007) 'Estimating Soviet Military Intentions and Capabilities', in *CIA's Analysis of the Soviet Union, 1947–1991* Center for the Study of Intelligence, Central Intelligence Agency, Washington, D.C.

Gates, Robert M. (1997) *From the Shadows: The Ultimate Insider's Story of Five Presidents and How They Won the Cold War* New York: Simon and Schuster

Gill, Stephen (1990) *American Hegemony and the Trilateral Commission* London: Cambridge University Press

— (1993) 'Neo-Liberalism and the Shift Towards a US-Centred Transnational Hegemony', in Henk Overbeek (ed.) (1993) *Restructuring Hegemony in the Global Political Economy* London: Routledge, pp.246–82

Gilpin, Robert (1981) *War and Change in World Politics* New York: Cambridge University Press

— (1987) *The Political Economy of International Relations* Princeton, N.J.: Princeton University Press

Godement, François (1998) *Dragon de feu, Dragon de papier. L'Asie a-t-elle un avenir?* Paris: Flammarion

Golub, Philip S. (1997) 'South East Asia Feels the Chill', *Le Monde diplomatique* (English edition, London) (December)

— (2001) 'America's Imperial Longings', *Le Monde diplomatique* (English edition, London) (July)

— (2003) 'World's Trade and Manufacturing Centres Shift East. China: the New Economic Giant', *Le Monde diplomatique* (English edition, London) (October)

— (2004a) 'Imperial Politics, Imperial Will and the Crisis of US Hegemony', *Review of International Political Economy*, 11: 4 (October), pp.763–86

— (2004b) 'Le golfe arabo-persique, laboratoire de la révolution stratégique américaine', *Cahiers de l'Orient*, Paris, No. 73, pp.51–8

— (2007a) 'Cosmopolitisme et impérialisme', *Revue internationale et stratégique*, No. 67, pp.105–12

— (2007b) 'The Sun Sets Early on the American Century', *Le Monde diplomatique* (English edition, London) (October)

Golub, Philip S. and Maréchal, Jean-Paul (2004) 'Hyperpuissance et biens publics internationaux', *Géoéconomie*, 30 (Summer)

Goody, Jack (1996) *The East in the West* New York: Cambridge University Press

Gore, Charles (2000) 'The Rise and Fall of the Washington Consensus as a Paradigm for Developing Countries', *World Development*, 28: 5 (May)

Gouda, Frances and Zaalberg, Thijs B. (2002) *American Visions of the Netherlands East Indies/Indonesia: U.S. Foreign Policy and Indonesian Nationalism, 1920–1949* Amsterdam: Amsterdam University Press

Gowan, Peter (2002) 'The American Campaign for Global Sovereignty', in Leo Panitch and Colin Leys (2002) *The Socialist Register 2003: Fighting Identities: Race, Religion and Ethno-Nationalism* London: The Merlin Press

Gramsci, Antonio (1998) *Selections from the Prison Notebooks* London: Lawrence and Wishart

Graz, Jean-Christophe (2003) 'Qui gouverne? le Forum de Davos et le pouvoir informel des clubs d'élites transnationales', *A Contrario*, 1: 2

— (2007) *La gouvernance de la mondialisation* Paris: La Découverte

Greenspan, Alan (2007) *The Age of Turbulence: Adventures in a New World* New York: Penguin Press

Grimmett, Richard F. (2008) 'Instances of Use of United States Armed Forces Abroad, 1798–2007', *CRS Report for Congress*, January 14, Washington, D.C.: Congressional Research Service

Gross, Oren (2000) 'The Normless and Exceptionless Exception: Carl Schmitt's Theory of Emergency Powers and the "Norm-Exception" Dichotomy', *Cardozo Law Review*, 21, pp.1825–67

Grunberg, Isabelle (1990) 'Exploring the "Myth" of Hegemonic Stability', *International Organization*, 44: 4 (Autumn), pp.431–77

Gunder Frank, Andre (1969) *Capitalism and Underdevelopment in Latin America* New York: Monthly Review Press

— (2001) *Re-Orient: Global Economy in the Asian Age* Berkeley, CA: University of California Press

Haass, Richard (1999) 'What to do with American Primacy', *Foreign Affairs* (September–October), pp.37–49

Halberstam, David (1993) *The Best and the Brightest* New York: Ballantine Books

Halliday, Fred (2002) 'For an International Sociology', in Stephen Hobden and John M. Hobson (eds) (2002) *Historical Sociology of International Relations* Cambridge, UK: Cambridge University Press, pp.244–64

Harootunian, Harry (2004) *The Empire's New Clothes, Paradigm Lost, Paradigm Regained* Chicago, Ill.: Prickly Paradigm Press

Hartz, Louis (1991[1956]) *The Liberal Tradition in America* Fort Washington, PA: Harvest Books

Harvey, David (2003) *The New Imperialism* New York: Oxford University Press

Healy, David (1970) *US Expansionism, The Imperialist Urge of the 1890s* Madison, Wis.: University of Wisconsin Press

Hemmer, Christopher and Katzenstein, Peter (2002) 'Why Is There No NATO in Asia? Collective Identity, Regionalism, and the Origins of Multilateralism', *International Organization*, 56: 3 (Summer), pp.575–607

Hendrickson, David C. and Tucker, Robert W. (1992) *The Imperial Temptation: The New World Order and America's Purpose* New York: Council on Foreign Relations Press

Hess, Gary (1972) 'Franklin Roosevelt and Indochina', *The Journal of American History*, 59: 2 (September), pp.353–68

Hessing Cahn, Anne (1998) *Killing Detente: The Right Attacks the CIA* University Park, PA: Pennsylvania State University Press

Hirschman, Alfred O. (1981[1945]) *National Power and the Structure of Foreign Trade: The Politics of the International Economy* Berkeley, CA: University of California Press

Hirschman, Charles (2005) 'Immigration and the American Century', *Demography*, 42: 4 (November), pp.595–620

Hobden, Stephen and Hobson, John M. (eds) (2002) *Historical Sociology of International Relations* Cambridge, UK: Cambridge University Press

Hobsbawm, Eric J. (1990[1968]) *Industry and Empire: From 1750 to the Present Day* London: Penguin Books

— (2005[1978]) 'Preface' to V. G. Kiernan (2005[1978]) *America: The New Imperialism: From White Settlement to World Hegemony* London: Verso, pp.vii–xiii

Hochschild, Adam (2006) *King Leopold's Ghost: A Story of Greed, Terror and Heroism in Colonial Africa* London: Pan Books

Hoffmann, Stanley (1987) 'An American Social Science: International Relations', in Stanley Hoffmann (ed.) (1987) *Janus and Minerva: Essays in the Theory and Practice of International Politics* Boulder, Co.: Westview Press

— (2002) 'U.S. and International Organizations', in Robert J. Lieber (ed.) (2002) *Eagle Rules, Foreign Policy and American Primacy in the 21st Century* Upper Saddle River, N.J.: Prentice Hall

— (2003) 'America Goes Backward', *The New York Review of Books*, 50: 10 (June 12)

Holland, Robert (1999) 'The British Empire and the Great War, 1914–1918', in Judith. M. Brown and William Roger Louis (eds) (1999) *The Oxford History of the British Empire: Vol. 4: The Twentieth Century* New York: Oxford University Press, pp.114–37

Horsman, Reginald (1981) *Race and Manifest Destiny: The Origins of American Racial Anglo-Saxonism* Cambridge, Mass.: Harvard University Press

Howe, Stephen (2003) 'American Empire: The History and Future of an Idea', available at www.opendemocracy.net/conflict-americanpower/article_1279.js

Huffcut, E. W. (1899) 'Constitutional Aspects of the Government of Dependencies', in 'The Foreign Policy of the United States: Political and Commercial', Proceedings of the Annual Meeting of the American Academy of Political and Social Science, April 7–8, *Annals of the Academy of Political and Social Science*, Vol. 13, Supplement 12 (May 1899), pp.19–45

Hui, Wang (2003) *China's New Order, Society, Politics, and Economy in Transition* Cambridge, Mass.: Harvard University Press

Hunt, Michael H. (1987) *Ideology and U.S Foreign Policy* New Haven, Conn.:
Yale University Press
Huntington, Samuel P. (1989) 'No Exit', *The National Interest*, 17 (Fall)
— (1993) 'Why International Primacy Matters', *International Security*, 17: 4
(Spring), pp.68–83
— (1999) 'Robust Nationalism', *The National Interest* (January 20)
Ignatieff, Michael (2002) 'Barbarians at the Gate', *The New York Review of Books*,
49: 3 (February 28)
— (2003) 'The Burden', *The New York Times Magazine* (January 5)
Ikenberry, John G. (1989) 'Rethinking the Origins of American Hegemony', *Political
Science Quarterly*, 104: 3 (Autumn), pp.375–400
— (2000) *After Victory* Princeton, N.J.: Princeton University Press
— (2003) 'Strategic Reactions to American Preeminence: Great Power Politics in the
Age of Unipolarity', Discussion Paper, National Intelligence Council, (July 28),
available at www.dni.gov/nic/PDF_GIF_2020_Support/2003_11_24_papers/
ikenberry_StrategicReactions.pdf
Inikori, Joseph E. (2002) *Africans and the Industrial Revolution in England: A
Study in International Trade and Economic Development* New York: Cambridge
University Press
Iriye, Akira (1995[1993]) *The Cambridge History of American Foreign Relations,
Vol. 3: The Globalizing of America 1913–1945* London: Cambridge University
Press
Jervis, Robert (2003) 'Understanding the Bush Doctrine', *Political Science Quarterly*,
118: 3 (Fall), pp.365–88
Johnson, Chalmers (2004) *The Sorrows of Empire: Militarism, Secrecy, and the End
of the Republic* New York: Metropolitan Books
Joxe, Alain (2003) *L'empire du chaos* Paris: La Découverte
Judt, Tony (2003) 'America and the World', *The New York Review of Books*, 50: 6
(April 10)
Kagan, Robert (1998) 'The Benevolent Empire', *Foreign Policy*, 111 (Summer),
pp.24–35
Kaplan, Amy (2002) *The Anarchy of Empire in the Making of U.S. Culture*
Cambridge, Mass.: Harvard University Press
Kaplan, Amy and Paese, Donald E. (eds) (1993) *Cultures of United States Imperialism*
Durham, N.C.: Duke University Press
Kapstein, Ethan B. (2000) 'Hegemony Wired: American Politics and the New
Economy', *Les Notes de l'IFRI*, Paris: Institut Français de Relations Interna-
tionales
Karnow, Stanley (1986) *Vietnam: A History* New York: Penguin Books
Katz, Richard (1999) *Japan: The System that Soured* New York: M.E. Sharpe
Katzenstein, Peter J. (ed.) (1996) *The Culture of National Security: Norms and
Identity in World Politics* New York: Columbia University Press
Katznelson, Ira and Shefter, Martin (eds) (2002) *Shaped by War and Trade,
International Influences on American Political Development* Princeton, N.J.:
Princeton University Press
Keasbey, Lindley M. (1896) 'The Nicaraguan Canal and the Monroe Doctrine',
Annals of the American Academy of Political and Social Science, January, pp.1–31
Kennan, George F. (1951) *American Diplomacy, 1900–1950* Chicago, Ill.: University
of Chicago Press

Kennedy, Paul (1987) *The Rise and Fall of the Great Powers* New York: Vintage Books

— (2002) 'The Greatest Superpower Ever', *New Perspectives Quarterly*, 19 (Winter)

Keohane, Robert O. (1986) 'Realism, Neorealism and the Study of World Politics', in Robert O. Keohane (ed.) (1986) *Neorealism and its Critics* New York: Columbia University Press

Keohane, Robert O. and Nye Joseph S. (2000[1977]) *Power and Interdependence* New York: Longman

Keynes, John M. (1965) *General Theory of Employment, Interest, and Money* London: Harcourt

Khalidi, Rashid (2004) *Resurrecting Empire: Western Footprints and America's Perilous Path in the Middle East* New York: Beacon Press

Khalilzad, Zalmay (1995) *From Containment to Global Leadership: America and the World After the Cold War* Rand Corporation Project Air Force: Santa Monica, CA

Kiernan, Victor G. (2005[1978]) *America: The New Imperialism – From White Settlement to World Hegemony* London: Verso

Kindleberger, Charles (1977) 'Two Hundred Years of American Foreign Policy: U.S. Foreign Economic Policy, 1776–1976', *Foreign Affairs*, 55: 2 (January), pp.395–417

— (1996) *World Economic Primacy: 1500–1990* New York: Oxford University Press

Kirshner, Jonathan (1995) *Currency and Coercion: The Political Economy of International Monetary Power* Princeton, N.J.: Princeton University Press

Kissinger, Henry (1979) *The White House Years* London: Weidenfeld and Nicolson

— (1994) *Diplomacy* New York: Simon and Schuster

— (2001) *Does America Need a Foreign Policy?: Toward a Diplomacy for the 21st Century* New York: Simon and Schuster

Klare, Michael T. (2001) *Resource Wars: the New Landscape of Global Conflict* New York: Metropolitan Books

— (2006) *Blood and Oil, the Dangers and Consequences of America's Growing Oil Dependency* New York: Metropolitan Books

Kolko, Gabriel (1990[1968]) *The Politics of War, The World and United States Foreign Policy 1943–1945* New York: Pantheon Books

— (1969) *The Roots of American Foreign Policy* Boston: Beacon Press

Kramer, Paul A. (2002) 'Empires, Exceptions, and Anglo-Saxons: Race and Rule Between the British and United States Empires, 1880–1910', *The Journal of American History*, 88: 4 (March), pp.1313–53

— (2008) 'The Water Cure: Debating Torture and Counterinsurgency – A Century Ago', *The New Yorker* (February 25)

Kroes, Rob (1999) 'American Empire and Cultural Imperialism, A View from the Receiving End', German Historical Institute, Conference Papers on the Web, Washington, D.C., available at www.ghi-dc.org

Lacroix-Riz, Annie (1988) *Les protectorats d'Afrique du Nord entre la France et Washington* Paris: L'Harmattan

LaFeber, Walter (1998[1968]) *The New Empire: An Interpretation of American Expansion, 1860–1898* Ithaca, NY: Cornell University Press

Lawrence, Lowell A. (1899) 'The Government of Dependencies', in *The Annals of the American Academy of Political and Social Science*, 13: 12 Supplement (May), pp.46–59

Le Cour Grandmaison, Olivier (2005) *Coloniser, exterminer. Sur la guerre et l'Etat Colonial* Paris: Fayard

Lederman, Marty (2007) 'The Anti-Torture Memos: Balkinization Posts on Torture, Interrogation, Detention, War Powers, Executive Authority, DOJ and OLC', *Balkinization*, available at http://balkin.blogspot.com/2005/09/anti-torture-memos-balkinization-posts.html

Leffler, Melvyn P. (1984) 'The American Conception of National Security and the Beginning of the Cold War', *American Historical Review*, 89: 2 (April), pp.346–81

— (1994) *The Specter of Communism: The United States and the Origins of the Cold War, 1917–1953* New York: Hill and Wang

Lemann, Nicholas (2002) 'The Next World Order: The Bush Administration may have a brand new doctrine of power', *The New Yorker* (April 1)

Levinson, Sanford (ed.) (2004) *Torture: A Collection* New York: Oxford University Press

— (2006) *Our Undemocratic Constitution* New York: Oxford University Press

Lippmann, Walter (1943) *U.S. Foreign Policy* New York: Overseas Publishers

— (1944) *U.S. War Aims* New York: Overseas Publishers

Liska, George (1967) *Imperial America: The International Politics of Primacy* Baltimore, Md.: Johns Hopkins University Press

Louis, William Roger (1985) 'American Anti-Colonialism and the Dissolution of the British Empire', *International Affairs*, 61: 3 (Summer), pp.395–420

Louis, William Roger and Robinson, Ronald E. (1994) 'The Imperialism of Decolonization', *Journal of Imperial and Commonwealth History*, 22: 3, pp.462–511

Lowell, A. Lawrence (1900) *Colonial Civil Service: The Selection and Training of Colonial Officials in England, Holland and France* New York: The Macmillan Company

Luce, Henry R. (1941) 'The American Century', *Life Magazine*, February 17, 1941, republished in *Diplomatic History*, 23: 2 (Spring 1999), pp.159–71

Lundestad, Geir (1986) 'Empire by Invitation? The United States and Western Europe, 1945–1952', *Journal of Peace Research*, 23: 3, pp.263–77

Magdoff, Henry (1969) *The Age of Imperialism, the Economics of U.S. Foreign Policy* New York: Monthly Review Press

Maier, Charles (2006) *Among Empires: American Ascendancy and Its Predecessors* Cambridge, Mass.: Harvard University Press

Manela, Erez (2007) *The Wilsonian Moment: Self-Determination and the International Origins of Anticolonial Nationalism* Oxford: Oxford University Press

Mann, Michael (2003) *Incoherent Empire* London: Verso

Marshall, Thurgood (1987) 'Reflections on the Bicentennial of the United States Constitution', *Harvard Law Review*, 101: 1 (November)

Marx, Karl (1853) 'Revolution in China and in Europe', *The New York Daily Tribune* (June 14)

Marx, Karl and Engels, Friedrich (1988[1848]) *The Communist Manifesto* New York: Norton (originally published in London)

McMahon, Robert J. (1981) *Colonialism and Cold War: The United States and the Struggle for Indonesian Independence, 1945–49* Ithaca, NY: Cornell University Press

— (1994) *The Cold War on the Periphery* New York: Columbia University Press

— (1999) *The Limits of Empire: The United States and Southeast Asia since World War II* New York: Columbia University Press

McMillin, James A. (2004) *The Final Victims: Foreign Slave Trade to North America, 1783–1810 (The Carolina Low Country and the Atlantic World)* Columbia, S.C.: University of South Carolina Press

Mead, Walter R. (2001) *Special Providence, American Foreign Policy and How it Changed the World* New York: Alfred A. Knopf

Mearsheimer, John J. (1990) 'Back to the Future: Instability in Europe After the Cold War', *International Security*, 15: 1 (Summer), pp.5–56

— (2001) *The Tragedy of Great Power Politics* New York: W.W. Norton

Mearsheimer, John J. and Walt, Stephen M. (2007) *The Israeli Lobby and US Foreign Policy* New York: Farrar, Straus and Giroux

Melman, Seymour (1985[1974]) *The Permanent War Economy* New York: Simon and Schuster

Mill, John Stuart (1984[1859]) 'A Few Words on Non-Intervention', in *The Collected Works of John Stuart Mill*, Vol. 21, Toronto: University of Toronto Press (originally published in London)

Mills, Charles Wright (2000[1956]) *The Power Elite* New York: Oxford University Press

Milner, Helen V. and Keohane, Robert (eds) (1996) *Internationalization and Domestic Politics* New York: Cambridge University Press

Mommsen, Wolfgang J. (1982) *Theories of Imperialism* Chicago, Ill.: University of Chicago Press

Monroe, Elizabeth (1963) *Britain's Moment in the Middle East, 1914–1956* London: Chatto and Windus

Morgenthau, Hans (1965) 'We Are Deluding Ourselves in Vietnam', *The New York Times Magazine* (April 18)

— (1992) *Politics Among Nations* New York: McGraw-Hill

Moses, A. Dirk (ed.) (2005) *Genocide and Settler Society: Frontier Violence and Stolen Indigenous Children in Australian History* New York: Berghahn

Muñoz, Heraldo (2008) *A Solitary War: a Diplomat's Chronicle of the Iraq War and its Lessons* Denver, Co.: Fulcrum Publishing

Naughton, Barry (1999) 'China: Domestic Restructuring and a New Role in Asia', in T. J. Pempel (ed.) (1999) *The Politics of the Asian Crisis* Ithaca, NY: Cornell University Press, pp.203–23

Newfield, Christopher (2006) 'The Culture of Force', *The South Atlantic Quarterly*, 105: 1 (Winter) pp.241–63

Noren, James (2007) 'Assessing Soviet Economic Performance', in *CIA's Analysis of the Soviet Union, 1947–1991* Washington, D.C.: Center for the Study of Intelligence, Central Intelligence Agency

Nugent, Walter T. K. (1995) *Crossings: The Great Transatlantic Migrations, 1870–1914* Bloomington, Ind.: Indiana University Press

Nye Jr, Joseph S. (1990) *Bound to Lead* New York: Basic Books

— (2002) *The Paradox of American Power: Why the World's Only Superpower Can't Go It Alone* New York: Oxford University Press

O'Sullivan, Christopher D. (2007) *Sumner Welles: Postwar Policy and the Quest for a New World Order* The Gutenberg-e program, New York: Columbia University Press, available at www.gutenberg-e.org/osc01/frames/fosc03.html

Onley, James (2005) 'Britain's Informal Empire in the Gulf, 1820–1971', *Journal of Social Affairs*, 22: 87 (Fall), pp.29–45

Overbeek, Henk (ed.) (1993) *Restructuring Hegemony in the Global Political Economy: The Rise of Transnational Neo-liberalism in the 1980s* London: Routledge

— (2000) 'Transnational Historical Materialism: Theories of Transnational Class Formation and World Order', in Ronan P. Palan (ed.) (2000) *Global Political Economy: Contemporary Theories* London: Routledge–RIPE, pp.168–83

Palan, Ronan P. (2000) 'Constructivist Underpinnings of the New International Political Economy', in Ronan P. Palan (ed.) (2000) *Global Political Economy: Contemporary Theories* London: Routledge–RIPE, pp.215–28

Palan, Ronen P. and Blair, Brook (1993) 'On the Idealist Origins of the Realist Theory of International Relations', *Review of International Studies*, 19: 4, pp.385–99

Panitch, Leo (2000) 'The New Imperial State', *New Left Review*, 2 (March–April)

Patterson, James T. (1976) 'The Rise of Presidential Power before World War II', in 'Presidential Power: Part 1', *Law and Contemporary Problems*, 40: 2 (Spring), pp.39–57

Paxton, Robert O. (2004) *The Anatomy of Fascism* New York: Alfred A. Knopf

Pempel, T.J. (1999) 'Regional Ups, Regional Downs', in T.J. Pempel (ed.) (1999) *The Politics of the Asian Crisis* Ithaca, NY: Cornell University Press, pp.62–78

Pérez, Louis A. (1990) *Cuba and the United States: Ties of Singular Intimacy* Athens, Ga.: University of Georgia Press

Perkins, Bradford (2002[1993]) *The Creation of a Republican Empire, 1776–1865* The Cambridge History of American Foreign Relations, Vol. 1, New York: Cambridge University Press

Perroux, François (1994[1973]) *Pouvoir et économie généralisée* Grenoble: Presses universitaires de Grenoble

Pieterse, Jan N. (2001) *Development Theory: Deconstructions/Reconstructions* London: Sage

Pitts, Jennifer (2005) *A Turn to Empire, The Rise of Imperial Liberalism in Britain and France* Princeton, N.J.: Princeton University Press

Polanyi, Karl (1972[1944]) *The Great Transformation* Boston: Beacon Press

Pomeranz, Kenneth (2000) *The Great Divergence* Princeton, N.J.: Princeton University Press

Pomeroy, Earl S. (1944) 'The American Colonial Office', *The Mississippi Valley Historical Review*, 30: 4 (March), pp.521–32

Potter, Evan H. (ed.) (1998) *Economic Intelligence and National Security* Kingston, Ontario, Canada: McGill-Queen's University Press

Pottier, Claude (2003) *Les multinationales et la mise en concurrence des salariés* Paris: L'Harmattan

Powers, H.H. (1898) 'The War as a Suggestion of Manifest Destiny', *Annals of the Academy of Political and Social Science*, Vol. 12 (September), pp.1–20

Pratt, Julius W. (1927) 'The Origins of Manifest Destiny', *American Historical Review*, 32: 4 (July)

Priest, Dana (2003) *The Mission, Waging War and Keeping Peace with America's Military* New York: W.W. Norton & Company

Quijano, Anibal (2000) 'Coloniality of Power and Eurocentrism in Latin America', *International Sociology*, 15: 2, pp.215–32

Reich, Robert (2008) *Supercapitalism: The Transformation of Business, Democracy and Everyday Life* New York: Vintage Books

Renan, Ernest (1990[1871]) *La réforme intellectuelle et morale de la France* Brussels: Complexe

Rice, Condoleezza (2000) 'Promoting the National Interest', *Foreign Affairs*, 79: 1 (January–February)

— (2008) 'Rethinking the National Interest: American Realism for a New World', *Foreign Affairs*, 87: 4 (July–August)

Richardson, David (1987) 'The Slave Trade, Sugar, and British Economic Growth, 1748–1776', *Journal of Interdisciplinary History*, 17: 4 (Spring)

Rosen, Steven P. (2002) 'The Future of War and the American Military', *Harvard Review*, 104: 5 (May–June)

— (2003) 'An Empire, If You Can Keep It', *The National Interest*, 71 (Spring), pp.51–61

Rosenau, James N. (1987) 'Global Changes and Theoretical Challenges: Toward a Postinternational Politics in the 1990s', in Ernst-Otto Czempiel and James N. Rosenau (eds) (1987) *Global Changes and Theoretical Challenges, Approaches to World Politics for the 1990s* Lanham, Md.: Lexington Books, pp.1–20

Rothman, Adam (2005) *Slave Country: American Expansion and the Origins of the Deep South* Cambridge, Mass.: Harvard University Press

Rothstein, Morton (1970) 'The Cotton Frontier of the Antebellum South: A Methodological Battleground', *Agricultural History*, 44: 1 (January)

Ruggie, John G. (1982) 'International Regimes, Transactions, and Change: Embedded Liberalism in the Postwar Economic Order', in 'International Regimes', *International Organization*, 36: 2 (Spring), pp.379–415

Russett, Bruce (1985) 'The Mysterious Case of Vanishing Hegemony; or, is Mark Twain Really Dead?', *International Organization*, 39: 2 (Spring)

Said, Edward (2003[1979]) *Orientalism* New York: Vintage Books

Sainz, Pedro (2006) 'Equity in Latin America since the 1990s', *DESA Working Paper No.22*, (ST/ESA/2006/DWP/22), New York: United Nations Department of Economic and Social Affairs, June

Salisbury, Laurence E. (1944) 'The Pacific Front, Colonial Asia', *Far Eastern Review*, 13: 25 (December 13), pp.235–7

Sanders, Jerry W. (1983) *Peddlers of Crisis and the Politics of Containment* Boston: South End Press

Sassen, Saskia (1996) *Losing Control. Sovereignty in the Age of Globalization* New York: Columbia University Press

Saunders, Christopher and Smith, Iain R. (2001) 'Southern Africa, 1795–1910', in Andrew Porter (ed.) *The Oxford History of the British Empire*, Vol. 3: *The Nineteenth Century* New York: Oxford University Press, pp.597–623

Schaller, Michael (1982) 'Securing the Great Crescent: Occupied Japan and the Origins of the Cold War in Asia', *Journal of American History*, 69: 2 (September), pp.392–414

Schlesinger Jnr, Arthur (1963) 'Liberalism in America: A note to Europeans', in Arthur Schlesinger Jnr (1963) *The Politics of Hope* Boston: Houghton Mifflin, pp.63–71

— (1995) 'Back to the Womb? Isolationism's Renewed Threat', *Foreign Affairs*, 74: 4 (July–August), pp.2–8

— (2000) 'Unilateralism in Historic Perspective', in Gwyn Prins (ed.) (2000) *Understanding Unilateralism in American Foreign Relations* London: Royal Institute of International Relations, pp.18–29

Schmitt, Carl (2005[1922]) *Political Theology: Four Chapters on the Concept of Sovereignty* London: The University of Chicago Press

Scholnick, Robert J. (2005) 'Extermination and Democracy: O'Sullivan, the *Democratic Review*, and Empire, 1837–1840', *American Periodicals*, 15: 2, pp.123–41

Schumacher, Franz (2002) 'The American Way of Empire: National Tradition and Transatlantic Adaptation in America's Search for Imperial Identity, 1898–1910', Washington, D.C.: German Historical Institute, *GHI Bulletin*, No. 31 (Fall), pp.35–50

Schumpeter, Joseph A. (1966) *Imperialism and Social Classes: Two Essays by Joseph Schumpeter* New York: Meridian Books

Schurmann, Franz (1974) *The Logic of World Power: An Enquiry into the Origins, Currents and Contradictions of World Politics* New York: Pantheon Books

Seager II, Robert (1997) *Alfred Thayer Mahan: The Man and His Letters* Annapolis, Md.: Naval Institute Press

Sebrega, John J. (1986) 'The Anticolonial Policies of Franklin D. Roosevelt: A Reappraisal', *Political Science Quarterly*, 101: 1 (Spring), pp.65–84

Seeley, John R. (1971[1883]) *The Expansion of England* Chicago, Ill.: University of Chicago Press

Semmel, Bernard (1960) *Imperialism and Social Reform: English Social-Imperial Thought, 1895–1914* London: George Allen and Unwin

Shaw, Martin (2003) 'The State of Globalization: Towards a Theory of State Transformation', in Neil Brenner, Bob Jessop, Martin Jones, Gordon MacLeod (eds) (2003) *State Space: A Reader* London: Blackwell, pp.117–30

Shefter, Martin (2002) 'War, Trade and U.S. Party Politics', in Ira Katznelson and Martin Shefter (eds) (2002) *Shaped by War and Trade* Princeton, N.J.: Princeton University Press, pp.113–33

Sherwood, Robert E. (1948) *Roosevelt and Hopkins: An Intimate History* New York: Harper and Brothers

Shklar, Judith N. (1998) *Redeeming American Political Thought*, Stanley Hoffmann and Dennis F. Thompson (eds), New York: The University of Chicago Press

Skidelsky, Robert (2003) *John Maynard Keynes, 1883–1946: Economist, Philosopher, Statesman* London: Penguin Books

Skocpol, Theda (ed.) (1984) *Vision and Method in Historical Sociology* Cambridge: Cambridge University Press, pp.1–21

Sluglett, Peter (1999) 'Formal and Informal Empire in the Middle East', in Robin W. Winks (ed.) (1999) *The Oxford History of the British Empire*, Vol. 5: *Historiography* Oxford: Oxford University Press, pp.416–36

Smith, Adam (1991[1776]) *The Wealth of Nations* New York: Prometheus Books (originally published in London)

Spiro, Donald E. (1999) *Petrodollar Recycling and International Markets: The Hidden Hand of American Hegemony* Ithaca, NY: Cornell University Press

Spiro, Peter J. (2000) 'The New Sovereignists: American Exceptionalism and its False Prophets', *Foreign Affairs*, 79 (November–December)

Steel, Ronald (1995) *Temptations of a Superpower* Cambridge, Mass.: Harvard University Press

— (1980) *Walter Lippmann and the American Century* Boston: Little, Brown and Company, p.363

Stewart, Patrick (2001) 'Don't Fence Me In: The Perils of Going It Alone', *World Policy Journal*, 18: 3 (Fall)

Stiglitz, Joseph E. (2003) *Globalization and its Discontents* New York: W.W. Norton

Strange, Susan (1982) 'Cave! Hic Dragones: A Critique of Regime Analysis', in 'International Regimes', *International Organization*, 33: 2 (Spring)

— (1989) 'Towards a Theory of Transnational Empire', in Ernst-Otto Czempiel and James N. Rosenau (eds) (1989) *Global Changes and Theoretical Challenges: Approaches to World Politics for the 1990s* Lanham, Md.: Lexington Books, pp.161–76

— (1996) *The Retreat of the State: the Diffusion of Power in the World Economy* Cambridge, UK: Cambridge University Press

Stubbs, Richard (1999) 'War and Economic Development: Export Oriented Industrialization in East and Southeast Asia', *Comparative Politics*, 31 (April), pp.337–55

Summers, Lawrence H. (2004) 'The United States and the Global Adjustment Process', Third Annual Stavros S. Niarchos Lecture, Washington, D.C.: Institute for International Economics (March 23)

Suskind, Ron (2004a) 'Without a Doubt', *The New York Times Magazine* (October 17)

— (2004b) *The Price of Loyalty: George Bush, the White House and the Education of Paul O'Neill* New York: Simon and Schuster

Talbott, Strobe (2007) 'Anatomy of a Disaster', *The International Herald Tribune* (February 22)

The American Historical Review (1899) 'The New Haven Meeting of the American Historical Association', 4: 3 (April)

Trocki, Carl A. (1999) *Opium, Empire and the Global Political Economy: A Study of the Asian Opium Trade, 1750–1950* New York: Routledge

Turner, Mark and Peel, Quentin (2003) 'Is the Post-1945 World Order Falling Apart?', *The Financial Times* (March 10)

Tyler, Patrick (1992a) 'Lone Superpower Plan: Ammunition for Critics', *The New York Times* (March 10)

— (1992b) 'U.S. Strategy Plan Calls for Insuring No Rivals Develop', *The New York Times* (March 8)

Van der Pijl, Kees (1984) *The Making of an Atlantic Ruling Class* London: Verso

— (2006) *Global Rivalry, From the Cold War to Iraq* London: Pluto Press

Van der Pijl, Kees, Assassi, Libby and Wigan Duncan (eds) (2004) *Global Regulation: Managing Crises After the Imperial Turn* New York: Palgrave Macmillan

Wade, Robert (1990) *Governing the Market* Princeton, N.J.: Princeton University Press

— (2002a) 'US Hegemony and the World Bank: the Fight over People and Ideas', *Review of International Political Economy*, 9: 2 (Summer)

— (2002b) 'The American Empire and its Limits', *DESTIN Working Papers Series*, No. 02–22, London School of Economics

Wall, Erwin M. (2001) *France, the United States, and the Algerian War* Berkeley, CA: University of California Press

Wallerstein, Immanuel (1980) *The Modern World-System: Vol. 2: Mercantilism and the Consolidation of the European World-Economy, 1600–1750* New York: Academic Press

— (1989) *The Modern World-System: Vol. 3: The Second Era of Great Expansion of the Capitalist World-Economy, 1730–1840s* New York: Academic Press

— (2000) 'The Three Instances of Hegemony', in *The Essential Wallerstein* New York: The New Press

— (2003) *The Decline of American Power: The U.S. in a Chaotic World* New York: W.W. Norton

Walt, Stephen M. (2002) 'Keeping the World "Off-Balance": Self-Restraint and U.S. Foreign Policy', in Ikenberry, John G. (ed) (2002) *America Unrivaled: The Future of the Balance of Power* Ithica: Cornell University Press, pp.121–54

— (2006) *Taming American Power: The Global Response to U.S. Primacy* New York: W.W. Norton

Waltz, Kenneth (1979) *Theory of International Politics* New York: McGraw Hill

— (1993) 'Neorealism: Confusions and Criticisms', *Journal of Politics and Society*, 15: 1, pp.2–6

Weber, Max (1994[1919]) 'The Profession and Vocation of Politics', in Peter Lassman and Ronald Speirs (eds/trans.), *Political Writings* Cambridge, UK: Cambridge University Press

Weeks, William Earl (1994) 'American Nationalism, American Imperialism: An Interpretation of U.S. Political Economy, 1781–1861', *Journal of the Early Republic*, 14: 4 (Winter), pp.485–95

Weigley Russell, F. (1973) *The American Way of War: a History of United States Military Strategy and Policy* New York: Macmillan

Weiner, Jonathan M. (1989) 'Radical Historians and the Crisis of American History, 1959–1980', *The Journal of American History*, 76: 2 (September), pp.399–434

Weisbrot, Marc (2007) 'Ten Years After: The Lasting Impact of the Asian Financial Crisis', in Bhumika Muchhala (ed.) (2007) *Ten Years After: Revisiting the Asian Financial Crisis* Washington, D.C.: Woodrow Wilson International Center for Scholars

Wendt, Alexander and Barnett, Michael (1993) 'Dependent State Formation and Third World Militarization', *Review of International Studies*, 19: 4, pp.321–47

Wesseling, Hendrik L. (1997) *Imperialism and Colonialism, Essays on the History of European Expansion (Contributions in Comparative Colonial Studies)* Westport, Conn.: Greenwood Press

White, Donald W. (1989) 'History and American Internationalism: the Formulation from the Past After World War II', *Pacific Historical Review*, 58: 2 (May), pp.145–72

Whitfield, Stephen J. (2000) 'The Imperial Self in American Life', *Columbia Journal of American Studies*, 4: 1

Whitman, Marina V.N. (1975) 'Leadership Without Hegemony: Our Role in the World Economy', *Foreign Policy*, 20 (Autumn)

Williams, Walter L. (1980) 'United States Indian Policy and the Debate over Philippine Annexation: Implications for the Origins of American Imperialism', *The Journal of American History*, 66: 4 (March), pp.810–31

Williams, William Appleman (1952) 'Brooks Adams and American Expansion', *The New England Quarterly*, 25: 2 (June), pp.217–32

— (1962[1959]) *The Tragedy of American Diplomacy* New York: Delta Books

— (1982) *Empire as a Way of Life: An Essay on the Causes and Character of America's Present Predicament Along With a Few Thoughts About an Alternative* New York: Oxford University Press

Wilson, Keith (ed.) (2001) *The International Impact of the Boer War* London: Acumen

Wohlforth, William C. (1999) 'The Stability of a Unipolar World', *International Security* 24: 1 (Summer), pp.5–41

Woo-Cumings, Meredith (1993) 'East Asia's America Problem', in Meredith Woo-Cumings and Michael Loriaux (1993) *Past as Prelude, the Makings of a New World Order* Boulder, Co.: Westview Press, pp.137–5

— (ed.) (1999) *The Developmental State* Ithaca, NY: Cornell University Press

Woo-Cumings, Meredith and Loriaux, Michael (eds) (1993) *Past as Prelude: History in the Making of a New World Order* Boulder, Co.: Westview Press

Woods, Randall B. (1990) *A Changing of the Guard: Anglo-American Relations, 1941–1946* Chapel Hill, N.C.: University of North Carolina Press

Woolsey, Theodore S. (1899) 'The Government of Dependencies', *Annals of the Academy of Political and Social Science*, Vol. 13, Supplement 12 (May), pp.3–18

Young, Robert J.C. (2001) *Postcolonialism: An Historical Introduction* Oxford: Blackwell

Zimmerer, Jürgen (2005) 'Colonial Genocide and the Holocaust. Towards an Archaeology of Genocide', in A. Dirk Moses (ed.) (2005) *Genocide and Settler Society: Frontier Violence and Stolen Indigenous Children in Australian History* New York: Berghahn, pp.49–76

Zimmerman, Warren (2002) *First Great Triumph: How Five Americans made Their Country a World Power* New York: Farrar, Straus and Giroux

Zubok, Vladislav M. (2000) 'Why did the Cold War End in 1989? Explanations of the Turn', in Odd Arne Westad (ed.) *Reviewing the Cold War: Approaches, Interpretations, Theory* London: Frank Cass, pp.343–68

Index

Compiled by Sue Carlton